A Critical Synergy

ALI MEGHJI

A Critical Synergy

Race, Decoloniality, and World Crises

TEMPLE UNIVERSITY PRESS
Philadelphia • Rome • Tokyo

TEMPLE UNIVERSITY PRESS
Philadelphia, Pennsylvania 19122
tupress.temple.edu

Library of Congress Cataloging-in-Publication Data

Names: Meghji, Ali, author.
Title: A critical synergy : race, decoloniality, and world crises / Ali
Meghji.
Description: Philadelphia : Temple University Press, 2023. | Includes
bibliographical references and index. | Summary: "This book demonstrates
how decolonial theory and critical race theory can be used together to
better explain global social problems than either could alone. It
applies them in combination to theorize capital accumulation, the rise
of right-wing populist nationalism, the COVID pandemic, and the climate
crisis"— Provided by publisher.
Identifiers: LCCN 2023006409 (print) | LCCN 2023006410 (ebook) | ISBN
9781439922064 (cloth) | ISBN 9781439922071 (paperback) | ISBN
9781439922088 (pdf)
Subjects: LCSH: Social problems. | Postcolonialism. | Decolonization. |
Critical race theory.
Classification: LCC HN28 .M44 2023 (print) | LCC HN28 (ebook) | DDC
361.1—dc23/eng/20230616
LC record available at https://lccn.loc.gov/2023006409
LC ebook record available at https://lccn.loc.gov/2023006410

Printed in the United States of America

9 8 7 6 5 4 3 2 1

The world, with the many worlds that the world needs, continues.

Humanity, recognizing itself to be plural, different, inclusive,
tolerant of itself, full of hope, continues.

The human and the rebel voice, consulted on the five continents
in order to become a network of voices and resistances, continues.

—Subcomandante Marcos,

"Tomorrow Begins Today," August 3, 1996

Contents

Acknowledgments

In writing this book, I owe thanks to a range of people. Ryan Mulligan helped me develop my initial pitch into an effective book proposal and, eventually, into this monograph. His editorial vision and continued support were vital to me throughout the process of writing this book. At a proposal stage, two anonymous reviewers provided brilliant insights and constructive feedback on the book; another anonymous reviewer provided incredibly insightful feedback on the first draft. Each of the reviewers helped make this volume achieve its aims in a more precise fashion, and I thank each of them directly for sharing their thoughts and advice. Members of the Postcolonial Sociology "Work in Progress" group—specifically Rici Hammer, Meghan Tinsley, and Trish Ward—provided comments on early chapter drafts that helped clarify and deepen my writing, and I had the pleasure of sharing my thoughts on theoretical synergy across a variety of institutions in the 2021–2022 academic year. I am also privileged to have an incredible network of supportive colleagues who have helped develop my sociological imagination. You know who you are, and I thank you for your continuing support.

Finally, my thanks go to Emily, Maisie, and Brontë, each of whom delivers love and support in their own, unique way. This is the first book I've written since Emily and I got married, and she continues to be my constant inspiration and darling companion.

A Critical Synergy

Introduction

Star-Crossed Lovers?

Decolonial Thought and Critical Race Theory

n 2020, the murder of George Floyd at the hands of the police in
Minneapolis sparked anti-racist protests across the world. Demon-
strations in France connected Floyd's death with the county's own
state violence against postcolonial citizens; protestors in Kenya connected their problem with police brutality to the still extant Public
Order Act created by the British colonial government; Portuguese
protestors carried placards stating, "Racism Is Colonial Heritage";
Indigenous groups in New Zealand drew parallels between police
violence in the United States and police violence toward the Māori
and Pasifika; and in Belgium, South Africa, and Britain, statues of
colonial figures such as King Leopold II, Edward Colston, and Cecil
Rhodes were all brought crashing to the ground.

These protests raised a series of interesting sociological questions.
Why did an instance of systemic racism in the United States give
way to such global protests? How did people across the world draw
parallels between systemic racism and the racialized carceral system
in the United States and a wide range of phenomena, from settler
colonialism in New Zealand to the ongoing presence of colonial laws
in Kenya? To me, these waves of protests in the summer of 2020 demonstrate social processes that sit at the intersection of *national societal
arrangements* and *transnational systems of inequality*. People gathered

across the world to protest because they realized that, while Floyd's death was the outcome of specific national arrangements in the United States, it also connected with transnational processes of coloniality and racism that extend far beyond the United States' national borders.

This book focuses on contemporary cases in which we are required to balance the focus on local, national racial hierarchies with an appreciation of the more globally oriented logic of coloniality. Fruitful dialogue can be fostered between decolonial thought and critical race theory (CRT). In an example of "theoretical synergy," this dialogical approach between decolonial thought and CRT uses two theories in tandem, rather than attempting to hierarchize or synthesize them. Such a synergy between CRT and decolonial thought allows us to study social phenomena in a way that captures their global and historical roots while acknowledging their local and national particularities. Through focusing on the case studies of capitalism, the COVID-19 pandemic, the climate crisis, and twenty-first-century far-right populism, this book therefore investigates questions such as: "Why should decolonial thought and CRT be retained as discrete traditions of social thought?"; "Why synergize decolonial thought with CRT?"; "How do social processes shape both national racial hierarchies and the global system of coloniality?"; and "How do we study social processes in a way that is both attentive to their present, national particularities *and* their global, historical linkages?" To fail to answer, or even ask, such questions would be to limit our understanding of the interaction between the contextual and the transnational processes of racism. Of course, to tackle these questions, it is useful to have a guide to what is meant by the terms *decolonial thought* and *CRT* in the first place.

Between the Sociology of Race and Decolonial Thought

In calling for a dialogue between CRT and decolonial thought, this book acknowledges and develops the burgeoning interest in the differences between decolonial thought and the sociology of race more broadly. Assuming such a divide between the sociology of race and decolonial thought may first appear to be counterintuitive; after all, race was constructed in colonialism as a way to categorize and organize the world's populations.[1] Nevertheless, decolonial thought has particular epistemological, methodological, and empirical aims, and it would be imprudent to subsume this approach into a general sociology of race.

Of course, given that European colonialism began in the late fifteenth century, any precise definition of *decolonial thought* is bound to be reductive. For this reason, various scholars have found it useful to think of interconnected "clusters" or "waves" of decolonial thought. For instance, Melissa Weiner suggests we think of decolonial thought as having three moments of development.[2] First, she argues that anticolonial intellectuals in the early to mid-twentieth century demonstrated the importance of enslavement and colonialism to the making of the modern world and critiqued European colonialism while imagining how to remake the world in more equitable ways. Such a first wave included thinkers such as Aimé Césaire, W.E.B. Du Bois, Frantz Fanon, C.L.R. James, Kwame Nkrumah, and Eric Williams. Second, Weiner argues that thinkers in the second wave of decolonial thought—such as Enrique Dussel, Walter Mignolo, and Rosa María Rodríguez Magda—drew on the work of earlier anticolonial intellectuals to critique ongoing "hegemonic Eurocentric colonial narratives." Such second-wave work therefore focused on countering ideas that people from newly independent nations were "barbaric, uncivilized savages who should look to Europe for religion, work ethic, language, technology, and knowledge."[3] Finally, in the third wave, Weiner argues, decolonial thought centered on a critique of neoliberalism and the rise of Western-led corporate power across the global political economy; such a third wave is said to encompass a wide range of interdisciplinary scholars, including Gloria Anzaldúa, Ramón Grosfoguel, and Charles Mills.[4]

In an effort to get a handle on what decolonial thought has been and is, thinking of decolonial thought in terms of its different stages or waves is at once useful and limiting. It is useful to the extent that it allows us to pay attention to the historical specificity from which the various intellectuals articulated their arguments. For instance, there is surely a difference in the historical circumstances between the anticolonial intellectuals who were simultaneously writing critiques of European colonialism and literally partaking in warfare against colonial administrations (e.g., Amílcar Cabral leading guerrilla warfare against the Portuguese in Guinea) and those critiquing neoliberal corporations from their lecture theaters at elite educational institutions in the Global North.

However, even as it recognizes the variation in movements within the history of the approach, thinking of decolonial thought in terms of waves may also be limiting in the way it downplays the various continuities between its different articulations. For instance, Weiner is quite right that from the mid-twentieth century on, a cluster of decolonial thinkers were committed to critiquing "hegemonic Eurocentric colonial narratives," but there is no reason that this defining feature of second-wave thinkers could not equally be identified in who she construes as belonging to the first wave. Indeed, a large part of Fanon's work was focused on how European colonialists relied on an erasure of the colonized people's history to maintain their rule, as captured in his often quoted claim:

> Colonialism is not simply content to impose its rule upon the present and the future of a dominated country. Colonialism is not satisfied merely with holding a people in its grip and emptying the native's brain of all form and content. By a kind of perverted logic, it turns to the past of the oppressed people, and distorts, disfigures, and destroys it.[5]

Du Bois teases out a similar theme to Fanon's when he shows how the myth of racial difference was produced in European colonialism to contrast the superior civilizational and cultural values of the Western white Europeans with those of the "lesser races." As Du Bois summarized this racial hierarchy:

> We grant full citizenship in the World Commonwealth to the "Anglo-Saxon" (whatever that may mean), the Teuton and the Latin; then with just a shade of reluctance we extend it to the Celt and Slav. We half deny it to the yellow races of Asia, admit the brown Indians to an ante-room only on the strength of an undeniable past; but with the Negroes of Africa we come to a full stop, and in its heart the civilized world with one accord denies that these come within the pale of nineteenth-century Humanity.[6]

Du Bois developed this critique of what Weiner terms "Eurocentric colonial narratives" through texts such as *The World and Africa*.[7] There, he documents both the forms of African civilizations that preceded European colonialism—consequently countering the myth that the continent had no history or culture prior to its invasion—and the various anticolonial insurgencies, from 1500 in the Caribbean through 1895 with the war in Cuba, that Western accounts of colonialism overlook as they try to naturalize the view that the colonized consented to their own domination.

Indeed, through documenting such anticolonial insurgency, Du Bois points out another problem with the formerly mentioned framings of decolonial thought starting with twentieth-century anticolonial intellectuals—namely, why construe its beginnings in the twentieth century? Mignolo, for instance, brings attention to Felipe Guaman Poma de Ayala's *The First New Chronicle and Good Government*, written in Peru in the early 1600s and addressed to Spain's King Phillip III in 1616.[8] His work encompasses all three dimensions of Weiner's different typologies of decolonial thought. In *The First New Chronicle and Good Government*, Guaman Poma first critiques the Spanish Crown's violence toward Indigenous people (thus demonstrating the so-called first wave's focus on critiquing European colonialism); proposes a new form of governance that includes Indigenous leadership *because Indigenous people had ruled more fairly before the Spanish* (thus addressing the "Eurocentric colonial narratives" on which second-wave thinkers centered their critiques); and critiques the economic imposition of capitalism by the Spanish, which rendered Black and Indigenous lives disposable and degraded the natural world in the mission for capital accumulation (thus demonstrating a critique of Western hegemony in the global political economy that was central to putative third-wave decolonialists).

Focusing more explicitly on this critique of political economy, moreover, we see that even the third-wave critique of Western-led corporations—which we typically identify with neoliberalism—stretched across the supposedly different clusters of decolonial thought. Kwame Nkrumah, for instance, is supposedly characterized as a first-wave anticolonial thinker, yet his critique of neocolonialism and economic dependence, in texts such as *Class Struggle in Africa* and *Neo-colonialism: The Last Stage of Imperialism*, offers analyses of political economy that are extremely similar to what we see in the third-wave critique of neoliberalism offered by thinkers such as Dussel and Aníbal Quijano.[9] At the heart of Nkrumah's critique—an argument also developed by other anticolonial intellectuals who went on to hold positions of political power, such as Julius Nyerere in Tanzania, Michael Manley in Jamaica, and Nnamdi Azikiwe in Nigeria—was that on being granted independence, formerly colonized nations were still economically exploited by the West. The difference was that, rather than colonial states, private, Western-based corporations now took on the chief role of economic exploitation. Thus, as Nkrumah points out, on independence Nigeria became a rapidly growing exporter of petroleum throughout the 1960s, but the profits for such exports were mostly reaped by the British company Shell-BP; similar realities are captured across a wide range of examples in the postindependence era, from the British steel group Guest Keen and Nettlefolds controlling ore production in Swaziland to Western finance controlling the gold- and diamond-mining industry in South Africa.[10] It is this precise economic relationship identified by many first-wave intellectuals, characterized by the Global North (or "West") exploiting the Global South for cheap labor, produce, and markets, that is also expressed in critiques formed by the so-called third-wave intellectuals critiquing neoliberalism, as captured in Quijano's critique of neoliberalism:

> If we observe the main lines of exploitation and social domination on a global scale, the main lines of world power today, and the distribution of resources and work among the world population, it is very clear that the large majority of the exploited, the dominated, the discriminated against, are precisely the members of the "races," "ethnicities," or "nations" into which the colonized populations, were categorized in the formative process of that world power, from the conquest of America and onward.[11]

While it is important to retain a historical sensibility when thinking about the different conditions from which decolonial intellectuals were speaking, it is equally important to appreciate the long patterns of continuity that underlie decolonial thought's longevity.

Instead of thinking in terms of waves or stages, we ought to approach decolonial thought as a widely encompassing radical knowledge project that has the *foundational aim to delink societal arrangements from the colonial matrix of power*—that is, the network of power involving the West's epistemological, material, and ontological domination of the Global South.[12] Of course, the form that this delinking takes will be subject to the specific circumstances of the time. When Guaman Poma was writing in the 1600s, he was concerned with the Spanish Crown's sovereignty over Indigenous land in what is now labeled Peru. Three hundred years later, the Peruvian intellectual Jose Carlos Mariátegui was more concerned with the presence of U. S.-based corporations exploiting workers in mines and oil reserves on this same land.[13] While Guaman Poma and Mariátegui may have been writing about different instances of the West's exploitation of a specific geopolitical region, they shared the decolonial goal of delinking from (i.e., both a *disassociation* from and a *rejection* of) the colonial matrix of power. Thus, rather than trying to group together different decolonial thinkers into disparate groups, this book approaches decolonial thought as a multifaceted knowledge project that both rejects the colonial matrix of power and seeks to build a more equitable world after the colonial matrix of power has been dismantled. It is for this reason that it may be useful to think of decolonial thought as a sort of epistemological bulldozer.

Decolonial Thought as a Bulldozer: Epistemic Ruptures and Building Anew

As a bulldozer, decolonial thought is defined not simply in terms of what it is *against*, but also in terms of the social analyses that it produces and defends. In this regard, decolonial thought may vehemently reject the tenets of Eurocentric knowledge, but it simultaneously develops its own relational forms of social analyses that take seriously subalternized knowledge systems and practices.

At its foundation, decolonial thought seeks to move beyond understandings of the social universe that neglect the centrality of colonialism to the making of the modern world.[14] Within the social-science canon, for instance, authors such as Karl Marx and Max Weber have been critiqued for offering accounts of Western modernity and capitalist advancement that pay more attention to supposed *internal* factors of "the West" than to the processes of enslavement, exploitation, and expropriation forged through European empires.[15] When analyzing why modern capitalist development happened in the West, for instance, Weber focused on the specialization of labor and the Protestant work ethic.[16] Marx also largely understood Western modernity through the lens of Western exceptionalism, arguing that capitalist development derived from the particular European class structure.[17] Such sociological framings led to arguments that modernity *did not* happen in other geographical areas because of factors particular to those regions' culture, as is captured in Weber's dismissal of the spiritualism of Hinduism, Islam, and Confucianism, all of which were said to lack a valuation of labor and work, and in Marx's argument that the "Asiatic mode of production" lacked a class structure that could give rise to capitalist development.[18] Aside from the historical inaccuracies in these accounts, such framings occlude the symbiotic relationship between modernity and colonialism: that the latter was responsible for colonial powers not only "achieving" the former but also preventing the colonized from the same in the process.

Decolonial thought stresses that colonialism and modernity are two sides of the same coin and that to understand Western modernity, we need to appreciate its "darker side."[19] Decolonial theorists have thus used the concept of "modernity/coloniality" to highlight how Western modernity is "so deeply imbricated in the structures of European colonial domination over the rest of the world that it is impossible to separate the two."[20] Thus, Weber may have labeled China a stagnant society, but he occluded how Spain's colonization of the Americas enabled the Spanish to accrue enough silver and gold to make the Chinese economy plummet.[21] Marx may have labeled India economically immature, but he overlooked that more than £9 billion worth of capital was channeled from India into the British economy between 1765 and 1938.[22] The concept of modernity/coloniality, therefore, signals an epistemic break in the way that it rearticulates the history of Western development. In this rearticulated history, decolonial scholars therefore have shown that without colonialism, enslavement, and

European empires, modernity in the West—as we know it—would not have taken shape. As Fanon aptly summarizes: "Europe is literally the creation of the Third World. The wealth which smothers her is that which was stolen from the underdeveloped peoples."[23]

Through rearticulating history through the lens of modernity/coloniality, decolonial thought shows how the "age of (European) empires" created a global interconnectedness that still shapes the present day. In this regard, decolonial thought calls for a conceptual move beyond Eurocentric analyses that bifurcate the study of "the West" from its global relations.[24] The problem with this bifurcation is twofold. First, studying the West outside of its global connections runs the risk of historical inaccuracy—this was the problem Marx and Weber encountered in theorizing modernity through supposed *internal* factors of "Western" and "Asiatic" cultures more so than the material relations forged through empires. Second, the practice of bifurcating the West from its relations with "the rest" espouses an assumption of Western universalism: the assumption that one can produce universally true social theories if they work in the Western context. It is this epistemic centering of the West that allows social scientists such as Michael Mann to claim they are offering a "history of power in human societies" while analyzing only Western Europe and the United States (outside of their imperial relations) or sociologists such as Ulrich Beck and Anthony Giddens to claim they are offering a theory of globalization while only discussing how globalization is economically and culturally affecting societies in the Global North.[25] Within such sociological imaginaries, the West is an epistemological stand-in for the world. Indeed, many anticolonial revolutionaries grappled with this assumption of Western universalism throughout the twentieth century. Cabral, for instance, exposed what he saw as the false universalism of Western Marxism when he commented in *The Weapon of Theory*:

> Those who affirm . . . that the motive force of history is the class struggle would certainly agree to a revision of this affirmation to make it more precise and give it an even wider field of application if they had a better knowledge of the essential characteristics of certain colonized peoples, that is to say peoples dominated by imperialism.[26]

Cabral's argument, put succinctly, was that a Marxism that equated the revolutionary class struggle solely with industrial workers in Western nations would not be able to understand the logic of anticolonial revolutions, which were based not only on economic exploitation but also on issues that Western workers were not necessarily facing, such as liberation from foreign invasion and the expropriation and seizure of their land. A similar critique of universalism was developed by Césaire when he dismissed the ability of French Marxists to adequately offer pathways for anticolonial dissent:

> Our colonialism, the struggle of colonial people against racism, is much more complex, indeed, it is of a totally different nature than the struggle of the French workers against French capitalism, and cannot in any case be considered a part, as a fragment, of that struggle.[27]

In contrast to Eurocentric bifurcations that lean toward historical inaccuracy or false universalisms, decolonial thought consequently espouses a practice of "relationology."[28] This involves forging *temporal* and *transnational* links between social processes and events. Temporally, decolonial thought connects the past events of colonialism, enslavement, and empires with contemporary material and epistemic inequalities. For instance, we can connect contemporary Western Islamophobia—characterized by fears of an ongoing Muslim invasion of Europe and ideas about countries such as Britain and the United States having areas under control by Sharia law—with Orientalist ideas set in motion during colonialism that Islam is premodern, antithetical to progress, and inherently at tension with progressive Western civilizational values.[29] In terms of transnational links, decolonial thought connects happenings in the Global South with events in the Global North (or "the West"), and vice versa. For instance, much in the way that Nkrumah's critique of political economy played out, we can connect Western demand for particular consumer goods—from cheap clothing to quinoa and avocados—to the exploitation of workers and destruction of local food sources in the Global South.[30] Decolonial analysis therefore pushes us away from a "substantialism" that prioritizes the analysis of isolated "things" and instead makes *relations* the primary analytical focus.

In its conceptual shift toward relationology and its epistemic and empirical decentering of the West, decolonial thought also fuels the political mission to value the subjectivities of those from the Global South. Decolonial thought thus criticizes the tradition of Orientalism, which frames those from the Global South as being civilizationally inverse to those in the West.[31] Indeed, European empires constructed and used this hierarchal binary between "the West and the rest" to justify their colonization; such empires understood themselves as bringing civilization and modernity to the undeveloped world, therein making empires appear to be benevolent institutions.[32] As thinkers such as Grosfoguel have shown, moreover, this West-rest, civilized-uncivilized binary is not just a colonial relic; it is fundamental to many twentieth- and twenty-first-century economic and political global realities, from Western military and political intervention across supposedly "undemocratic" states (such as French intervention in Rwanda in the 1990s, the "Iraq war" in 2003, and the Organization of American States' alleged coup that brought about the resignation of Bolivian President Evo Morales in 2019) to the imposition of "free trade" economic policies and "structural adjustment" loans in the Global South via institutions such as the International Monetary Fund (IMF) and World Bank.[33] Such Western interventions are examples of a Western universalism (*our* way of doing economics and politics is the *only* way) coupled with the desire to instigate Western practices across the "backward" world, contextualizing the past half-century against a larger historical background:

We went from "convert to Christianity or I'll kill you" in the 16th century, to "civilize or I'll kill you" in the 18th and 19th centuries, to "develop or I'll kill you" in the 20th century, and more recently, the "democratize or I'll kill you" at the beginning of the 21st century.[34]

Decolonial thought directly opposes this devaluation of those from the Global South. At the heart of this decolonial critique, moreover, is the idea that the devaluation of those in the Global South, beyond the economic, is inherently *epistemological*. As Boaventura de Sousa Santos argues, the exploitation of the South, since colonialism, has never been just material; it also involves an *epistemicide*—an erasure of "other" ways and forms of knowing and knowledge that differ from those of the supposedly superior West.[35] Through this Western epistemicide, the religious, political, and cultural beliefs and practices of those in the Global South—including theories of humanism, sexuality, gender, and political rights—are recast as merely superstition, "magic," tradition, or premodern rather than as legitimate knowledge systems. The assumption and practice of Western universalism—the idea that the Western knowledge system is *the* knowledge system—is thus itself "an epistemology that devalues certain human beings" in virtue of dismissing their epistemological worlds.[36]

Indeed, this link between epistemology and ontology has always been evident in the colonial matrix of power. Take, for instance, the League of Nations, created in 1920, in the aftermath of World War I, as a means of maintaining international peace. One of the leading principles of this institution was the right to self-determination: the right of one's country to freely choose its sovereignty. Despite its commitment to self-determination, the League of Nations was happy to let colonialism continue. European leaders did not think that colonized people were sufficiently developed to be capable of self-governance; thus, there was an "ontological" supposition (colonized people are inferior to Europeans) connected to an epistemological argument (colonized people's potential forms of governance are not the "right way" to do politics).[37] By contrast to this Eurocentrism, decolonial thought opposes the devaluation of the Global South and calls for *epistemic equality*, arguing that "there is no global social justice without global cognitive justice."[38] To foster this cognitive justice, decolonial thought calls for a global respect and recognition of different ways of producing knowledge such that, for example, we do not automatically value an argument developed through a Western university press manuscript more than an argument developed through an Indigenous oral tradition. In this regard, decolonial thought at once critiques dominant epistemologies while also opening up new possibilities for equitable knowledge production on a global scale.

A Decolonial Sociology of Race?

Having specified its broad aims, it is clear how decolonial thought calls for something more than a general "sociology of race." Nevertheless, some readers may be wondering about those scholars in the sociology of race *who have also endorsed the principles of decolonial thought.*

Du Bois is a perfect example of a sociologist of race who also maintained a decolonial ethic. His analysis of racism in the United States, for example, was often attentive to global social processes. Du Bois regularly drew parallels between racism in the United States and European colonialism, viewing the two as interconnected components of the same racialized global structure. Du Bois, for instance, raised a comparison between colonized people in India and Black people in the United States, who were fighting

> the same terrible battle of the color bar. . . . We stretch out, therefore, hands of fellowship and understanding across the world and ask for sympathy in our difficulties just as you in your strife for a new country and a new freedom have the good wishes of every Negro in America.[39]

Moreover, Du Bois forged links between racism in the United States and the structure of global capitalism, describing the exploitation of Black Americans' labor as "the foundation stone . . . of the English factory system, of European commerce, of buying and selling on a worldwide scale."[40] Indeed, while Du Bois emphasized the centrality of Black exploitation in the United States to the global political economy, he also saw the necessary relation between this Western-led capitalism and the subjugation of the Global South. This is captured in his description of global capitalism as a "new phase of colonial imperialism" characterized by "control of the labor of Asia and Africa and the islands of the Pacific by the ruling classes in Western Europe and North America."[41] For Du Bois, the "myth" of race was the glue that stuck together this capitalist world order, as ideas of white, Western superiority over the "lesser" races were used to justify the economic exploitation and control of these subdominant people. As Du Bois clarifies when describing this global racial order: "Everything great, good, efficient, fair and honorable is 'white.' Everything mean, bad, blundering, cheating and dishonorable is 'yellow,' brown and black."[42] Du Bois was firmly committed to tackling what he saw as the "Negro Question" in the United States; his sociology of race was therefore also concerned with investigating temporal and transnational links between the situation of Black Americans and the processes of global capitalism, imperialism, and neocolonialism.

Nevertheless, the fact that a "decolonial sociology of race" exists does not mean that all decolonial thought can be reduced to the sociology of race. This is so because, simply put, not all sociological scholarship on race has followed the decolonial ethic of "delinking" from the colonial matrix of power. This is not to devalue such race scholarship; it is merely to highlight that this work has different aims to decolonial thought. In fact, as highlighted by Zine Magubane, particularly in the postwar United States, race scholarship shifted from being global in its focus toward being much more state-centered.[43] After World War II, U.S. sociology turned away from globalism toward an isolated focus on the nation-state. Within this period, many sociologists of race thus turned to micro-oriented ethnographic research, with notable examples being St. Clair Drake and Horace Cayton's *Black Metropolis* and E. Franklin Frazier's *Black Bourgeoisie*.[44] Indeed, even Du Bois—despite instigating a decolonial sociology of race—had produced copious amounts of research that was much more state-centered. Du Bois's work in the late 1800s and early 1900s at the Atlanta Sociological Laboratory, for instance, centered on using sociology to understand and ameliorate the problems facing Black Americans in inner cities.[45] While this Atlanta School produced a critical sociology of race and generated anti-racist policies, it did not seek to develop the transnational and temporal connections that are essential to decolonial thought. This is a straightforward example of why retaining a difference between the development of decolonial thought and that of the sociology of race makes sense.

Moreover, looking at the current state of the field, we now have a plethora of theories within the sociology of race. Again, not all of these paradigms place a specific emphasis on decolonial temporal and transnational connections. For instance, through approaches such as Lawrence Bobo's racial prejudice theory, Mustafa Emirbayer and Matthew Desmond's theory of the "Racial Order," Joe Feagin's systemic racism theory, Tanya Golash-Boza's "Critical and Comprehensive Sociological Theory of Race and Racism," Michael Omi and Howard Winant's racial formation theory, and critical race theory, we have a set of frameworks that study racial inequality in U.S. society bifurcated from the country's past and present imperial and colonial relations.[46]

This does not mean that all of these "non-decolonial" theories of race have essential shortcomings and must be disregarded. Rather, this book takes a more collaborative, dialogical approach to social theorizing. In particular, this book focuses on one specific theory within the sociology of race—critical race theory—and shows how synergizing CRT with decolonial thought produces analytical understandings of social reality. Synergizing CRT and decolonial thought, nevertheless, is not something that is intuitively straightforward, given the significant methodological, empirical, and conceptual differences between the two traditions of thought. These divergences become more apparent as we discuss the genesis and contours of CRT.

Three Waves of CRT

While decolonial thought emerged from people across the world resisting European colonialism and imperialism, CRT emerged specifically in the United States. Academic scholarship developed CRT as a way to critique the particular racial apparatus of the United States and did not seek to engage in the transnational and temporally connected analysis advocated by decolonial thought.

Critical race theory first developed within critical legal studies as a means of exposing and transcending two contradictions born in the United States' post-civil rights era. It analyzed how in the 1980s, decades after the introduction of civil rights legislation, Black people measured worse in conditions such as family income, university enrollment, and percentage of men between twenty-two and fifty-five earning less than $5,000 a year.[47] In other words, CRT exposed the contradiction that *after* the introduction of civil rights legislation, Black folks in the United States actually faced *increasing* inequality. Through exposing this contradiction, CRT critiqued the Reaganist neoconservatism of the 1980s, which argued that activists were demanding equal *outcomes* rather than equal *opportunities*, and the duty of the state was only to offer the latter. Through this neoconservative frame, the existence of civil rights legislation was taken as evidence that the United States provided equal opportunities to everyone, and any resulting inequality was therefore the fault of the group. Critical race theory thus developed to take an institution that was supposedly race-neutral—the legal system—and to work against its structural racism. This ethos of racializing the supposedly race-neutral appealed to education scholars, who then joined the CRT bandwagon.

In 1995, two legal scholars, Richard Delgado and Jean Stefancic, helped spread the interest of CRT to other U.S. academics through their coedited book *Critical Race Theory: The Cutting Edge*.[48] In it, speaking particularly about the racial structure in the United States, they argued that CRT had three guiding principles. First, "racism is normal, not aberrant, in American society."[49] Second, the methodological point that CRT provides counternarratives to dominant racial discourse, analyzing "the myths, presuppositions, and received wisdoms that make up the common culture about race and that invariably render blacks and other minorities one-down."[50] And third, akin to Derrick Bell's concept of racial realism, Delgado and Stefancic claim that white elites make anti-racist concessions only if those concessions benefit the white elite.[51]

Through outlining these principles, CRT assimilated into American education studies. After Delgado and Stefancic's book in 1995, Laurence Parker and his colleagues coedited *Race Is . . . Race Isn't: Critical Race Theory and Qualitative Studies in Education* in 1999, featuring Gloria Ladson-Billings's popular essay "Just What Is Critical Race Theory, and What's It Doing in a Nice Field like Education?"[52] In it, she shows how Delgado and Stefancic's principles of CRT apply to the American educational system. For instance, Ladson-Billings points out that the main beneficiaries of affirmative action in education are white: white students gain the benefits of "diversity" while maintaining the resources and comforts of a predominately white environment. Further, she shows how the education system demonstrates the point that racism is "normal, not aberrant": while the U.S. education system was meant to be a public good, Black folks, through processes such as biased curricula, stigmatization from teachers, biased assessments, and unequal school funding, face a significant deficit in it. While many observers recast the resulting educational inequalities through the lens of cultural racism, arguing that Black people do not care about education, Ladson-Billings stresses the need for critical race–counter-storytelling—that is, unearthing the structural inequalities in the American education system to reject naturalized myths of Black inferiority.

Another wave of CRT was happening as these dialogues developed between legal and educational studies.[53] Within American sociology, thinkers were interested in the strength of CRT and augmenting its concepts and principles, although their work was not centered in the same way that Delgado and Stefancic's tenets were. This is particularly apt when we consider Eduardo Bonilla-Silva's racialized social system approach.[54] Bonilla-Silva published "Rethinking Racism: Toward a Structural Interpretation" in 1997, in which he argues that racism begins with racialization. Upon being racialized, a society develops a racialized social system "in which economic, political, social, and ideological levels are partially structured by the placement of actors in racial categories or races."[55] Not only is the racialized social system a *material* system of inequality, but the dominant group within this system maintains an interest in reproducing its position. According to Bonilla-Silva, the racialized social system approach revolves around the premise that

> the placement of people in racial categories involves some form of hierarchy that produces definite social relations between the races. The race placed in the superior position tends to receive greater economic remuneration and access to better occupations and/or prospects in the labor market, occupies a primary position in the political system, is granted higher social estimation (e.g., is viewed as "smarter" or "better looking"), often has the license to draw physical (segregation) as well as social (racial etiquette) boundaries between itself and other races, and receives . . . a "psychological wage."[56]

To analyze the reproduction of such racialized social systems, Bonilla-Silva introduces the following concepts to CRT's conceptual framework:[57]

1. *Racial interests*, referring to how "whites . . . develop a racial interest to preserve the racial status quo."[58] For instance,

this may involve realities described by Du Bois, where white workers sided with white capitalists rather than their Black counterparts, thus prioritizing the psychological benefit of being racialized as white.[59]

2. *Racial ideology*, described as "the racially based frameworks used by actors to explain and justify . . . the racial status quo."[60] For instance, in many countries, post-racial ideology—the belief that structural racism no longer exists—is used by the racially dominant to explain racial inequality away as being the result of nonracist events; this may involve "Black educational disadvantage [being] recast as Black students being 'unacademic' . . . and Black overrepresentation in the criminal justice system [being] reinterpreted as Black criminality."[61]

3. *Racial grammar*, which refers to "how we see or don't see race in social phenomena, [and] how we frame matters as racial or not race-related."[62] For instance, in the United States, we speak of historically Black colleges and universities (HBCUs), but not of historically white colleges and universities (the existence of which necessitated HBCUs), and we have notions of "Black music" and "Black TV," but we do not have white inverses.[63] Such a racial grammar, therefore, universalizes and invisibilizes whiteness in the racial structure, reproducing the situation whereby "Whiteness constitutes normality and acceptance without stipulating that to be White is to be normal and right."[64]

4. *Racialized emotions*, described as "the socially engendered emotions in racialized societies."[65] Such racialized emotions form the basis for generating a sense of group membership in the racial structure and act as vehicles for the formation and mobilization of racial interests. For instance, in the run up to Donald Trump's 2016 election to the U.S. presidency, many white voters shared emotions of devaluation and nonrecognition in the context of the United States moving to a "minority-majority" demographic.[66] Not only did this allow for white people to strengthen their group identity through the formation of a collective emotional bond, but this emotive bond allowed for the successful implemen-

tation of a whole political project—Trumpamerica—built on redistributing value and recognition to ordinary white families.[67]

Therefore, although *CRT* has become a buzz term often thrown around to refer to any scholarship on race, and while it has been lambasted as involving "a loose hodgepodge of analytic tools," I think there is great value in seeing CRT as a social theory.[68] Particularly through the racialized social-system approach, CRT provides a flexible conceptual armory with which we can conduct empirical research on the macro, meso, and micro dimensions of racism.

Nevertheless, we have to appreciate that CRT—like all other social theories—cannot make a claim to universality. Following Julian Go, it is useful to think of social theories as maps "of the world that capture some things but overlook others."[69] As Go clarifies:

Like maps, social theories ascertain only certain elements of the reality they purport to represent while necessarily occluding other components. No social theories can claim universality and pure objectivity—they are all inevitably perspectival and hence partial—yet they can nonetheless be valid or "true."[70]

In this spirit of thought, I want to highlight some components of social reality that CRT occludes through its presentism and methodological nationalism. However, rather than using these occlusions to dismiss the value of CRT, this book puts CRT into conversation with decolonial thought to show the strength of a "synergy approach." Importantly, this synergizing does not involve just using decolonial thought to supplement CRT's limitations. Rather, just as decolonial thought addresses the transnational, temporal linkages overlooked by CRT, so, too, does CRT allow for a more nationally specific focus than that provided by decolonial thought. Rather than prioritizing one tradition over the other, this book therefore argues that a synergy between CRT and decolonial thought is fruitful because, despite their apparent inconsistencies, they are complementary paradigms of social thought that can be used together to analyze social realities. It is these "complementary inconsistencies" between the two traditions of thought I now discuss.

Between CRT and Decolonial Thought:
Divergences and Convergences

There is an undeniable tension between CRT and decolonial thought's epistemic, empirical, and methodological agendas. Perhaps one of the most significant of these tensions lies in decolonial thought's focus on coloniality and CRT's focus on contemporary racism. As Bonilla-Silva states, CRT focuses on studying the "contemporary foundation" of racial inequality outside of its colonial roots, thus turning away from "the sins [of the] past (e.g., slavery, colonization, and genocide)."[71] This is an important endeavor from CRT. According to the concept of racial interests, reducing racism to a legacy of the past obfuscates how people still benefit from racism in the present day and consequently maintain an interest in reproducing the present racial structure. As Bonilla-Silva clarifies:

> Racial structures remain in place for the same reasons that other structures do. Since actors racialized as "white"—or as members of the dominant race—receive material benefits from the racial order, they struggle (or passively receive the manifold wages of whiteness) to maintain their privileges.... Therein lies the secret of racial structures and racial inequality.... [T]hey exist because they benefit members of the dominant race.[72]

However, in virtue of its desire to study contemporary racism outside of its colonial roots, CRT collides with multiple positions advanced by decolonial thought. First, through attempting to bifurcate the "contemporary foundation" of racial inequality and the "sins of the past," CRT erases the existence of continuing forms of *settler colonialism* that are so central to Indigenous decolonial critiques. As J. Kēhaulani Kauanui puts it, settler colonialism was not merely an "event" that happened in the past; it is an "ongoing structure."[73] This means that settler colonialism is an incomplete, continuing project of eliminating (via extermination, assimilation, or segregation) "the native" to claim ownership over natives' land and "'indigenize' [the] settlers" themselves.[74] This logic of settler colonialism is not a distant memory but something that has been central to the social arrangements of settler states well into the twenty-first century, from the

U.S. state attempting to displace Indigenous people from Bristol Bay (Alaska) in 2010 to build a pebble mine to the finding in 2020 that 73 percent of Canada's First Nations water systems were at risk of contamination.[75] To therefore frame the concept of contemporary racism as being separate from "the sins [of the] past (e.g., slavery, colonization, and genocide)," CRT runs the risk of erasing both continuing projects of settler colonialism *and* different Indigenous groups' ongoing struggles with settler states across the world.

Not only does CRT's bifurcation of contemporary racism from colonial history occlude those instances of *ongoing* colonial rule (i.e., settler colonialism), but it also, therefore, collides with decolonial thought's broad focus on "coloniality." Decolonial scholars have used the concept of coloniality to signal how the power relations born in colonialism *outlived the collapse of colonial administrations*. To such thinkers, *colonialism* refers to a specific political regime, involving "the conquest of a foreign people followed by the creation of an organization controlled by members of the conquering polity and suited to rule over the conquered territory's Indigenous population."[76] By contrast, *coloniality* refers to the broader epistemic and material dominance of the West over the rest of the world, a power relation that was born in the construction of colonial administrations but that outlived their demise. As Nelson Maldonado-Torres clarifies:

> Coloniality is different from colonialism. [Coloniality] refers to long-standing patterns of power that emerged as a result of colonialism, but that define culture, labor, intersubjective relations, and knowledge production well beyond the strict limits of colonial administrations. Thus, coloniality survives colonialism.[77]

To decolonial thinkers, therefore, it is naïve to assume that former colonies gained "independence" from the world order on their decolonization. In this respect, theorists of coloniality offer similar critiques of "decolonization" to Indigenous thinkers such as Glen Coulthard. To Coulthard, decolonization is not properly achieved unless there is "a foundational 'break' with the background structures of colonial power."[78] Decolonization, in this sense, is not a guarantee of decoloniality. Du Bois demonstrated this point when he argued in the

1950s that "there are many countries which have nominal independence which are under almost as complete control by other nations as formerly" and thus that decolonization entailed a "change in method of control . . . but not real change in the facts or rigor of results."[79] Of particular interest to Du Bois, and an issue shared by anticolonial intellectuals throughout the twentieth century to the present day, was how the West, on decolonization of most of the world in the mid-twentieth century, continued to exert economic control—including the control of labor—over formerly colonized nations, meaning that

> [India] must pay prices determined in London and New York and sell for prices set in San Francisco and Paris. She must produce and manufacture not . . . what her people need but what Europe and America want and will buy. . . . World organization of capital will grip and retard India for many decades. The Philippines, Cuba and Puerto Rico; as well as Haiti and the Dominican Republic are at the absolute mercy of American industry, commerce and banking. Cuban sugar, Haitian coffee and Dominican products are sold at prices and in quantities which New York bankers dictate. . . . Tin from Bolivia, coffee from Brazil, gold from South Africa, copper from Rhodesia, and uranium from the Congo are all under foreign control and the native populations have their income and way of life dictated by powers outside their political control.[80]

While CRT seeks to turn the analysis away from "the sins [of the] past," decolonial thought thus uses the concept of coloniality to argue that the past is essential to the contemporary world order. Furthermore, this divergence between decolonial thought's focus on coloniality and CRT's focus on the "contemporary foundation" of racism has methodological consequences. This methodological tension is captured between CRT's presentism and decolonial thought's historicism.

One reason CRT has been so appealing to scholars in the United States is that it provided immediate critiques to the racial status quo. In its first wave, CRT primarily focused on the contemporary U.S. legal constitution and how to instigate sets of laws that provide racially equitable outcomes.[81] As CRT moved into educational studies, scholars made use of qualitative research methods—such as ethnography, autoethnography, and interviews—to "point out the endemic racism that is extant in our schools [and] colleges" and to "deconstruct laws, ordinances, and policies that work to reinscribe racism and deny people their full rights."[82] Even as it moved into sociology, CRT commonly involved using interviews and racial attitudes surveys to show how people explain away contemporary racial inequality (e.g., housing segregation) as being the result of nonracist events (e.g., like-minded people living together).[83] Sociological CRT also investigated how contemporary political moments in the United States emerged from present-day racial ideologies and emotions, such as with President Barack Obama's election emerging from post-racial ideology and Trump's election in 2016 emerging from emotions of white victimhood.[84] In terms of its methodological scope, therefore, CRT has always been geared toward a presentism by virtue of its desire to analyze, and ameliorate, conditions of the here and now.

By stark contrast, decolonial thought denies that the present exists as a discrete temporal event. Instead, decolonial thought embraces a methodological principle from Māori epistemology that "it is impossible to conceive of the present and the future as separate and distinct from the past, for the past is constitutive of the present and, as such, is inherently reconstituted within the future."[85] Thus, through its focus on coloniality, decolonial thought teases out temporal links by analyzing how the logics, processes, and practices put in place during colonialism shape the present and future worlds. This may involve, for instance, linking contemporary events such as the climate crisis, the exploitation of labor in the Global South, or the commercialization of goods such as cotton and coffee with the desire for unlimited capital accumulation and natural resource expropriation set in motion by European colonialism. Moreover, decolonial thought advocates historical methods because of the belief that colonial empires also had deep *epistemological* effects that continue to be "constitutive of the ways we perceive and understand [and act within] the world."[86] For instance, today's bifurcation of the so-called developed and developing worlds reproduces the epistemic principle that European colonialism helped develop "backward" societies.[87] Similarly, the way that contemporary Western discourse Orientalizes regions (e.g., China) and religions (e.g., Islam) as antithetical to modern values directly reproduces the epistemic principle that the West was the heart of modernity, and that it progressed to this modernity through its superior internal characteristics that other cultures lack(ed).[88] Decolonial thought, therefore, interrogates the pasts of empire and colonialism, often through historical methods, because it enables us to make sense of contemporary practices, logics, and principles.

Through such historical interrogation of empires and colonialism, it is also clear that decolonial thought has a more transnational empirical scope than CRT. First, the CRT canon has largely focused on the United States, examining its legal, educational, and social-structural arrangements. Furthermore, such analysis tends to focus on the United States without interrogating its past and present transnational imperial relations. Indeed, this was precisely David Theo Goldberg and Philomena Essed's criticism of especially the first wave of CRT scholarship; as they both argued, this scholarship was

> unfortunately marked by an American parochialism, with being caught up with the more or less restricted considerations of legal structures, conditions, and rationalities in the U.S. context. Scant attention is paid either to the applicability and implications of its key concepts outside of that context, or perhaps more importantly . . . to thinking its central concepts through their globalizing significance and circulation.[89]

Even beyond this first wave, however, CRT scholarship remained similar in its commitment to studying the U.S. racialized social system as a nationally discrete phenomenon. For instance, recently the third-wave CRT scholarship analyzed Trump's election to the presidency in 2016 through focusing on white people's emotions of nonrecognition and devaluation.[90] However, this literature occluded how such feelings of white devaluation fit into wider, transnational discourses, such as the "great replacement" theory spreading across white-majority nations, where it is argued that white people across the West are becoming minoritized in their own lands.[91] Such transnational dynamics are overlooked in CRT's treatment of racialized social systems as nationally discrete phenomena with their own nationally specific mechanisms for reproduction; as Bonilla-Silva explains, "For example, the racial ideology of Canada, Australia, and

the United States is *the direct product of their own racial situations.*"[92]
Even outside of the United States, scholarship drawing on the CRT
canon has been used to study racial structures as nationally isolated
units. In Britain, for instance, CRT has been used almost exclusively
to study the nation's educational inequalities.[93] This creates a situation in which one has comparative studies of different "racialized
social systems"—for example, between the British and U.S. systems—
but such studies do not necessarily seek to show how the different
systems are inherently connected.[94] Using Goldberg's language, CRT
may thus offer insights into comparative studies, but not necessarily *relational* studies; while comparative studies of racialized social
systems do just that (i.e., compare and contrast), relational studies
emphasize how "racial ideas, meanings and exclusionary repressive
practices in one [racialized social system] are influenced, shaped by
and fuel those [in others]."[95] Perhaps, therefore, decolonial thought
would charge CRT with being guilty of methodological nationalism,
described by Go as

> understanding a "society" or its forms, relations, and processes
> by looking only within the spatial confines of that society, i.e.
> the confines of the particular nation-state.[96]

Contrastingly, decolonial thought unearths global and transnational connections. As Go explains:

> Empire was always a transnational and global process . . . and
> as the dynamics and relations of empire always transcended
> the confines of parochial national boundaries, so too should
> our sociological analyses.[97]

Importantly, this difference between global analysis, on the one
hand, and more nationally discrete analysis, on the other hand, does
not necessarily imply that one approach is stronger than the other. In
fact, a CRT advocate might very well argue that, in some cases, decolonial thought is so global that it loses sight of important national
particularities (such as locally embedded ideologies and emotional
repertoires in the racialized social system). As I discuss in the chapters that follow, for example, critical race theorists would say that in

studying phenomena such as educational and housing segregation in the United States, one would necessarily need to adopt a lens that is specific to the nation's social structure. The fact that—ironically—U.S. civil rights laws and cases have been used to justify educational and housing segregation, as CRT argues, is a demonstration that national particularities sometimes need to take center stage in our analysis.

Once again, however, this difference between CRT and decolonial thought is not necessarily a question of one theory "getting one up" on the other. Rather, in this discussion we see the divide that decolonial scholars draw among *colonial difference* and *imperial difference*, and their deliberate focus on the former. As highlighted by scholars such as Mignolo, colonial difference refers to the great divide of coloniality between "the West" and "the rest." By contrast, *imperial difference*— which CRT is perhaps more inclined toward studying—refers to those variations of power *within the West itself.* As Mignolo recounts in his analysis of Western modernity, at various moments in modernity/ coloniality we have seen a large degree of imperial difference in terms of who is the hegemon *within* the West—from the Spanish and Portuguese to the French and British and then the United States.[98] Mignolo's point, however, is that despite all these imperial differences, very little changed in the form of colonial difference—that is, in the realm of the West versus the rest. It did not matter whether an imperial state such as Spain, Portugal, France, Britain, or the United States was the hegemon within the West, and neither did it matter whether the global hegemon was a corporation or multinational organization, as long as those basic relations of exploitation, enslavement, imperialism/neoimperialism, and colonialism/neocolonialism remained in the world system. Indeed, Mignolo points to the case of Ottobah Cugoano, who was enslaved in the 1700s and shipped to Granada before being taken to England.[99] As he comments, Cugoano's experiences of brutality at the hands of the English, *despite the English having condemned the treatment of Indigenous people by the Spanish*, showed that "the distinction between imperial nations makes no sense. . . . For an ex-slave, all cats are black."[100] Following the "all cats are black" line, the decolonial tradition has largely centered analysis on colonial difference to the extent that the particularities of imperial difference are given less analytical attention. It is precisely these particularities *within the West*—that is, particularities of imperial difference—

however, that CRT may be well suited to study in its "quasi" methodological nationalism.

In summary, the difference between decolonial thought's global and CRT's national focus does not necessarily mean one approach is stronger. Rather, it means that they often provide alternative viewpoints of the same social problem. For instance, consider the case of the militarization of the police in the United States, a key issue in contemporary racism. A CRT analysis, as offered by Lisa Long, for instance, pushes us toward viewing police brutality in the United States as a means of using violence to buttress the nation's racial hierarchy.[101] By contrast, as decolonial thought shows, there are also transnational and temporal dimensions at play in such police brutality. For instance, Go points out that the militarization of the U.S. police, beginning in the early twentieth century, involved importing techniques, tactics, and organizational frameworks from the United States' colonial military interventions.[102] In this regard, Go's decolonial approach creates not only a temporal link between a contemporary issue of police militarization with its historical origins but also a *transnational* link between "racism at home" and U.S. "imperialism abroad" in a way that differs from CRT's nation-specific understanding of social processes.

To use another example of such decolonial analysis, we can consider racialized nationalism and national identity. To CRT scholars such as Bonilla-Silva, racialized nationalism—claiming that one's country is a "white country," for instance—is an example of a particular racial ideology rooted in the nation's contemporary racial structure.[103] Decolonial thought, by contrast, views such instances of racialized nationalism through a transnational and temporal lens. In Britain, for instance, one of the symbols of national identity is tea; indeed, as Stuart Hall put it, "What does anybody in the world know about an English person except that they can't get through the day without a cup of tea?"[104] However, as Hall continues,

> Not a single tea plantation exists within the United Kingdom. This is the symbolization of English identity. . . . Where does it come from? Ceylon—Sri Lanka, India. That is the outside history that is inside the history of the English. There is no English history without that other history.[105]

In his analysis of English identity, therefore, Hall's decolonial approach stretches far beyond the temporal limits of the present day, and far beyond the geographical confines of the nation-state. He shows that Britain's historical colonial expropriation, as well as the labor of those colonized by the British Empire, has fundamentally shaped what it means to be "English"—thus the reason Hall refers to himself as "sugar at the bottom of the English cup of tea."[106] In this respect, Hall shows how claims that Britain or England are "white countries" involve a severe distortion of history; the fundamental entanglement between Britain and its colonial territories means that colonized people were in fact *essential* to the making of British identity—the very same identity that nationalists try to protect and define as "white" in the present day.

I have deliberately used these examples from Hall and Go because they speak to topics that are of interest to CRT: racialized nationalism and racial violence. Yet unlike critical race theorists, Hall and Go both show that what may appear to be a particular component of the national order is also connected to historical, transnational processes. In this regard, the decolonial perspective is thus capable of transcending the state-centrism of CRT, instead focusing on "reconstructing global narratives" of the present day "on the basis of the empirical connections forged through histories of colonialism, enslavement, dispossession and appropriation."[107]

A Case for Theoretical Synergy

Nevertheless, just because two approaches are different in multiple ways, this does not mean we ought to simply pick one approach over the other. Furthermore, it does not imply that we need to synthesize the approaches together to make a holistic "theory."

Indeed, there have been attempts to synthesize CRT and decolonial thought. Michelle Christian, for instance, calls for analysis of the "global racialized social system," arguing that "all racialized groups and countries come into existence through a global relational racial field that is hierarchically based."[108] Such a "global critical race theory," Christian argues, enables us to appreciate that between a global white-Black hierarchy there is a range of intermediary groups, such as Brahmin Indians and the Han Chinese, that receive forms of racialized privilege. However, as admirable as Christian's work is, we need to ask why we desire such syntheses of disparate traditions in the first place. Scholars such as Pierre Bourdieu and Giddens, for instance, attempted to synthesize objectivist and subjectivist approaches in their frameworks because they believed each of these two traditions respectively over-emphasized the macro and micro.[109] Similarly, Christian's synthesis comes from the position that CRT is too state-centric, while decolonial thought may be too globally oriented to capture national particularities.[110] Underlying these desires for syntheses, therefore, is a foundational view that the theories at hand are lacking something—they struggle to explain a particular phenomenon. At a more significant epistemological level, therefore, such desires for syntheses are driven by the view that a social theory must be a "theory of everything," and that if a theoretical paradigm cannot explain something, then it needs to be either revised through a synthesis or simply thrown away. Indeed, decolonial thought has critiqued as Eurocentric this very belief that a theory must be a theory of everything.[111] Any such claim to universalism has been more of an uncorroborated and tacit assumption than an actuality. As Raewyn Connell summarizes this assumption:

> In mainstream theory (including methodology), there is little sense of being the product of such a specific milieu. Read a modern classic text like Garfinkel's *Studies in Ethnomethodology*, Coleman's *Foundations of Social Theory*, Bourdieu's *Logic of Practice*, or Habermas's *Theory of Communicative Action* and you will see, rather, an assumption that the thoughts produced here simply apply universally.[112]

With this in mind, what I am calling for in this book is *not* a universal theoretical synthesis but a practice of synergy. The ethos of "synthesis" directly embodies the spirit of having space for only one's own epistemic world. By contrast, synergy involves a practice of lateral thinking, an epistemic humility and pluralism that looks to the prescient forms of analysis that can be opened up by working laterally with multiple traditions of thought. To return to Go's earlier metaphor of theories as maps, if you produce a map of New York, you could draw a map of the roads and walkways (which would be useful for those driving or walking around the city), of the underground system (which would be useful for those taking the subway), or of the main sites and attractions (which would be useful for tourists).[113] None of these maps are "more true" than any other; they just capture different dimensions of reality. Carrying this metaphor to social science, theoretical synergy is beneficial when we are struggling to analyze social phenomena through a singular paradigm—those cases where we are both walking *and* catching the subway and thus require two maps to effectively get around the city. Social reality can be studied from different theoretical viewpoints, and this theoretical pluralism is essential for understanding certain issues, structures, and processes in their full complexity. Within this theoretical pluralism, or "synergy," our aim is not to hierarchize among different theoretical traditions but, instead, to encourage different theories to "meet" one another to reach the common goal of producing "critical . . . knowledge that is rigorous, comprehensive, with a worldly scope."[114]

From the Practice of Synergy to the Requirement for Synergy

Synergizing CRT and decolonial thought is not just "scholastically amusing"; it is *essential* for understanding many of the key crises and disasters facing us in the contemporary world. In particular, this book focuses on four specific case studies to develop the synergy between CRT and decolonial thought: far-right populism in the twenty-first century, global capitalism, the climate crisis, and the COVID-19 pandemic. To understand each of these four cases in its full complexity, we need to use CRT and decolonial thought *together* to sustain transnational, temporally connected analyses that also pay attention to national articulations and particularities.

The key crises of our time—far-right populism stigmatizing, imprisoning, and deporting citizens; global capitalism creating record levels of poverty across the world; the climate crisis making the Earth uninhabitable; a pandemic that is killing people by the millions—all become embodied within particular national racialized social systems, but they also all become entangled in the global process of coloniality. When we look at the climate crisis, for instance, we need to pay attention to the unequal distribution of climate resources—such as clean water and unpolluted air—across national racial hierarchies. In Europe and the United States, for instance, racial minorities disproportionately live in areas with higher levels of air pollution.[115] However, in analyzing the climate, we also need to retain a global focus on coloniality, given that the Global South is already regularly experiencing climate catastrophes and that many Western responses to climate change reinscribe global inequalities (such as veganism and the switch to electronic cars that rely on child labor in the Global South).[116] Similarly, when Jair Bolsonaro's far-right Brazilian government stigmatized Indigenous people and Afro-Brazilians, this action weaponized *both* the ideology of racial democracy (through which investment in racial identities is construed as anti-Brazilian) and the postcolonial project of foregrounding the country's European roots over the nation's Indigenous and Afro-descendant heritage.

Synergizing between CRT and decolonial thought therefore allows us to focus simultaneously on the realities of national racial hierarchies and the transnational, temporally embedded processes of coloniality. This Introduction has attempted to "talk the talk" of showing how decolonial thought and CRT, despite their divergences, offer a fruitful avenue for synergized social analysis. The rest of the book focuses on "walking the walk"—highlighting how this synergy can play out in our analysis of far-right populism, capitalism, the climate, and COVID-19. However, I am not attempting to build a theoretical framework capable of explaining all social phenomena; rather, I show how, through engaging in collaborative conversations between different traditions, we can build critical understandings of the social world. While this book focuses on the synergy and conversation between CRT and decolonial thought, therefore, it is intended to open sociology and social science to the tradition of pluriversality much more broadly.

Outline of the Book

Chapter 1, "Against Zero-Point Epistemology: Delinking, Border Thinking, and Counter-storytelling," presents a more nuanced story of the relations between CRT and decolonial thought. While this Introduction has largely focused on their inherent tensions, Chapter

1 focuses a bit more on some of their shared epistemic ground. In particular, both CRT and decolonial thought critique the notion of purely objective knowledge, and both approaches instead tie together the issue of ontology with epistemology. Sharing in this critique of knowledge, I expand on the discussion by showing how CRT and decolonial thought advocate for a form of delinking from dominant Western social thought. Throughout the chapter, therefore, I stress that both CRT and decolonial thought are forms of "critical knowledge projects," to use Patricia Hill Collins's term, and that it is in virtue of sharing similar epistemic ground that we can use them together in lateral forms of social analysis.[117] The subsequent chapters show evidence of such lateral thinking.

Chapter 2, "When Postcolonial Melancholia Meets Post-racial Ideology: On Right-Wing Populism," turns to the issue of far-right populism in the twenty-first century. The chapter considers how political projects—including Brexit Britain, Trumpamerica, and Bolsonaro's Brazil—have stemmed from both nationally specific racial ideologies and emotions and transnational, historically rooted processes of coloniality. The chapter thus balances a CRT analysis of the national ideologies deployed in such political projects, such as Brazilian racial democracy and the post-racialism of the United States and Britain, with a decolonial focus on how these political projects connect with postcolonial melancholia, as seen in Brexit Britain's and Trumpamerica's attempts to restore the nation to its former imperial greatness, and in attempts to reinstate the "European roots" of Brazil.

In Chapter 3, "National Abjects in the 'Fourth World War': Crises of Neoliberal Capitalism," I examine how CRT and decolonial thought can be used in tandem with studying capitalism and neoliberalism. Despite first evidence, CRT and decolonial thought share elements of epistemic ground with the approach we typically associate with being the primary critical theory of capitalism: Marxism. Both CRT and decolonial thought have put neoliberalism at the heart of their analysis. Critical race theory not only emerged as a critique of the culture of neoliberalism, but it continues to offer ways to think about how neoliberalism relies on the production of *national abjects*—those at the bottom of national racial hierarchies whose exploitation becomes central to the workings of society. Decolonial thought, too, focuses on neoliberalism, and whereas CRT looks at *national abjects*, decolonial thought focuses on the "edge populations" of the world system (whose existence, too, is necessary for the system's reproduction).

Chapter 4, "Environmental Racism and the Logic of Coloniality," turns to the climate crisis. It takes a slightly different direction in that it begins by discussing the "critical legal studies" iteration of CRT—namely, the early CRT critique of the U.S. legal system's nonstructural definition of racism that still resonates in contemporary laws around environmental racism. I then contrast the legal protections of environmental racism in the United States with cases such as Bolivia and Ecuador, where, at least in principle, Mother Earth is ascribed particular sets of legal rights. I then widen the discussion to think about the broader epistemological bases of environmental crises. In particular, Western social thought—through its commitment to a nature-human binary—does not offer an epistemology that would be capable of producing necessary policies and cosmologies to prevent ongoing climate catastrophes. Non-Western and Indigenous modes of thought, by contrast, ascribe agency to what the West declares to be "nature."

Chapter 5, "When Universalism Kills, When Post-racialism Exonerates: COVID-19 and the Myth of a 'Great Reset,'" turns to the last case study: the coronavirus pandemic. Focusing on the United States' and United Kingdom's early handling of the pandemic, I look at how COVID-19 has exacerbated inequalities within national racial hierarchies while such inequalities are then explained away by the respective country's dominant racial ideologies. This includes analyzing how the higher death rate for racialized minorities has been explained away via reference to biological theories of race and genetics, or the racialized pathologization of "cultural lifestyles." However, I then add decolonial thought into the analysis by questioning why so many people died in the United States and Britain to begin with. The logic of Western universalism, or imperial metrocentrisms, shaped the U.S. and British response to the pandemic, seen both in their refusal to move beyond Eurocentric conceptions of exceptionalism, liberalism, and individualism in their virus containment policies and in their collective dismissal of the Global South's more successful responses to the pandemic.

The book concludes with "'A World in Which Many Worlds Fit': Decolonial Thought and Critical Race Theory in the Pluriverse." The effective synergy between CRT and decolonial thought offers an example of pluriversality, a knowledge process that aims to foster conversations among different epistemic traditions. The future of social analysis lies in this pluriversal tradition of theoretical synergy, where the use of disparate theories together can enable better understandings of certain social phenomena. While the notion of synergizing CRT and decolonial thought may be relatively novel in the social sciences, there are various social organizations and movements that have put such synergized analysis to work in their activism. This synergy between CRT and decolonial thought has been articulated by various social groups throughout the twentieth century, including the Zapatistas and the Black Panthers. My aim in examining these case studies is not to produce a historical overview of these groups but, rather, to show that there is a wide range of decolonial and anti-racist social movements from which sociology and the social sciences can learn about the practice of pluriversalism and theoretical synergy. In this regard, I paint theoretical pluralism as something that must be embraced as we collectively move forward in the social sciences.

1

Against Zero-Point Epistemology

Delinking, Border Thinking,
and Counter-storytelling

To survive the Borderlands you must live sin fronteras.

—GLORIA ANZALDÚA,
"To Live in the Borderlands Means You"

Before moving into sociology, I trained in philosophy. The program I studied was quite up-front about the fact that we studied *Western* philosophy, claiming that one could easily study the history and key debates of the discipline simply by focusing on its so called Western expression. "Epistemology"—as it was then taught to us—became at once the central concept, and the concept interrogated the least. On the one hand, we were taught that epistemology, at a base level, is about how we know things. On the other hand, we never took a single minute to discuss who that "we" was. In other words, the "knowing agent" was simply erased from discussion to the extent that knowledge was presented as being disembodied from the social universe. It is this notion of disembodied knowledge that has been the target of critique from so many epistemic positions, including *both* critical race theory (CRT) *and* decolonial thought.

In the Introduction, I deliberately emphasized the divergences between CRT and decolonial thought when making the case for theoretical synergy. Nevertheless, I do think there is a case to be made that these two approaches—despite their differences—are at least epistemic allies in the way they share some central claims about knowledge making. I want to use this chapter to expand on three ways these approaches run close together in their critiques of epistemology.

In particular, I examine how CRT and decolonial thought develop a critique of the "hubris of zero-point epistemology," consequently advocate a turn to alternative epistemologies via border thinking and counter-storytelling, and persuade us to go beyond epistemologies that paint social progress as an inevitable historical force.

The aim of this chapter, therefore, is not simply to compare and contrast the critiques of epistemology developed by CRT and decolonial thought. Neither is it to say that such critiques are essentially the same. Rather, I wish to highlight that—to use Patricia Hill Collins's terminology—both CRT and decolonial thought are *critical knowledge projects* that, despite their central differences, make them sympathetic to each other's aims of building a better world.[1] Indeed, the fact that both CRT and decolonial thought stress that to get to a "better world" we need to transcend dominant knowledge systems shows that both approaches admit that epistemology is integral to producing and legitimating social relations. Again, this is where the critique of disembodied knowledge comes into play, as highlighted in the rejection of the hubris of the zero-point epistemology.

From the Ego-politics to the Geopolitics of Knowledge

The hubris of the zero point, as argued by Santiago Castro-Gómez, is signified by the belief in the possibility of a God's-eye perspective of knowledge.[2] In this hubristic understanding, both the *knower* and the *knowledge* are assumed to be detached from social relations and interests, holding a divine objectivity and rationality. Knowledge, in this understanding, is not produced; it simply "is." This notion of a detached knowledge producer is clearly seen in the well-known Cartesian argument, "I think, therefore I am." As scholars such as Nelson Maldonado-Torres have pointed out, even this simple argument is making a series of assumptions that need to be interrogated.[3] Namely, Descartes was writing in a specific geopolitical region in the world system, at a time of the sixteenth and seventeenth centuries when European colonialism relied on the division between the "thinking" peoples of Europe and the closer-to-animal-than-human colonized savages. As Maldonado-Torres thus points out, even "I think, therefore I am" is an example of a zero-point epistemology that fails to question the conditions of *being* a thinking agent in the first place. As he clarifies: "Beneath the 'I think' we can read 'others do not think,' and behind the 'I am' it is possible to locate the philosophical justification for the idea that 'others are not or do not have being.'"[4]

We have to realize, therefore, that the world is characterized by a deep cognitive injustice that was born in colonialism. Certain colonized peoples—whether Indigenous people across the Americas or enslaved Africans—were denied the status of being "knowing agents." These people, through the relations of colonialism and enslavement, were not allowed to legitimately utter "I think, therefore I am" because—as per the logic of coloniality—they were not "thinking" agents. This is why Maldonado-Torres, for instance, has highlighted the case that it was not really "I think, therefore I am" but, rather, "*ego conquiro* [I conquer], therefore I think, therefore I am."[5] Of course, this debate is about much more than Descartes's *ego cogito*. Really, we are talking about the whole geopolitics of knowledge that underlies the logic of coloniality. Descartes's *ego cogito* is simply an example of this Western geopolitics of knowledge, where it is assumed that if one is speaking from the West, one is able to claim a God's-eye perspective of objective knowledge.

As decolonial scholars have pointed out, it was this supposition of Western objectivity and universalism that was then used in colonialism to commit a mass *epistemicide* of other ways of knowing—an epistemicide that continues into the present day.[6] As previously highlighted, authors such as Boaventura de Sousa Santos have consequently argued that the exploitation of the South, since colonialism, is partly epistemic.[7] As I showed, such an epistemic relation, for instance, includes the Western dismissal of Southern theories and cosmologies as being merely superstition, "magic," tradition, or premodern. Indeed, this divide between the knowledgeable West and primitive rest was taken to be so commonsensical that it was endorsed even by leading critical social scientists. Even Karl Marx and Max Weber, for instance, sounded very similar to the British and German empires in their beliefs that the religious mysticism of India, "the Muslim world," and Confucianism prevented people from such cultures gaining the rational knowledge needed for social development.[8] Furthermore, what we see in this case of Western universalism—the idea that the Western knowledge system is *the* knowledge system—is therefore also a (de)valuation of the people who subscribe to other knowledge systems. As Santos puts it, Western universalism is itself "an epistemology that devalues certain human beings" by dismissing their epistemological worlds.[9] In the case of Marx and Weber dismissing the whole Asian continent as being incapable of social progress due to restrictive religious practices, they are devaluing millions of people as being primitive, stagnant groups in need of Western intervention for their civilizational evolution.

This is all to say that knowledge, therefore, is enunciated from particular positions. In the decolonial tradition, the focus is on examining how knowledge enunciated from the West assumes itself to be objective and universal and, in doing so, supports power relations that enable the devaluation of other ways of knowing and being. Of course, this critique of the geopolitics of knowledge resonates with other critiques of epistemology. Standpoint theorists such as Collins and Sandra Harding have emphasized that all knowledge is socially situated. Thus, to talk about knowledge without talking about where the knowledge is produced from is to miss the whole point about studying epistemology in the first place.[10] Indeed, it is in this tradition of standpoint theory that CRT finds its own critique of zero-point epistemology, complementary to the decolonial project.

White Logic, White Methods, and Racial Knowledge

While decolonial thought focuses on knowledge enunciated from the dominant power in the world system, CRT focuses on knowledge enunciated from the dominant position in the racialized social system. This is the central point made in the CRT critique of white logic, white methods.[11]

Central to this CRT position is that the dominant racial group (whites) has used the pretense of objective knowledge to justify the order of the racial hierarchy. This racialized knowledge, Tukufu Zuberi and Eduardo Bonilla-Silva argue, relies on an "artificial distinction between *analysis* and *analysts*," which again enables knowing agents and their produced knowledge to be presented as disembodied from social relations and interests.[12] Indeed, as Kimberlé Crenshaw and her colleagues describe, this artificial distinction that separates knowledge from the "knowing agent" is indicative of how "mainstream claims to racial and cultural neutrality improperly take as a baseline norm white cultural patterns."[13] In other words, Crenshaw and her colleagues highlight that the very notion of knowledge being neutral and detached from interests is what allows for certain white beliefs about racial superiority/interiority to be legitimated as objective scientific knowledge. For instance, in the nineteenth century, phrenology—the scientific practice based on the idea that "different races" had differently shaped skulls, which tracked on differing levels of intelligence—was disseminated as a "pure" biological science rather than construed as a legitimating force of enslavement.

Just like the decolonial position, therefore, the CRT critique creates a link between ontology and epistemology: those who are deemed ontologically superior (in this case, whites) are the ones capable of producing objective knowledge (that just so happens to rationalize this social hierarchy in which they are the ontologically superior group). Indeed, this critique of "white logic, white methods" has been central to race-critical thinkers throughout the past century. As far back as 1898, for instance, W.E.B. Du Bois criticized his white academic contemporaries for merely reproducing pathological depictions of Black people, arguing:

> It is so easy for a man who has already formed his conclusions to receive any and all testimony in their favor without carefully weighing and testing it, that we sometimes find in serious scientific studies very curious proof of broad conclusions.[14]

A similar critique to Du Bois's was developed by Franklin Frazier.[15] He pointed out that dominant social-science theories of race—from George Fitzhugh's *Sociology of the South* through approaches offered by Howard Odum in social psychology and Robert Park in ethnographic sociology—started from the assumption of Black inferiority and used social-science reasoning to confirm these biases.[16] This is why—as scholars such as Joyce Ladner and John H. Stanfield II have pointed out—dominant theories of race throughout the twentieth century were focused on questions of Black deviance and the possibility of Black assimilation into U.S. society—that is, research focused more on Black folks *as social problems* than on the actual social problems facing Black people.[17] This ethos even carried into the twenty-first century, as Zuberi and Bonilla-Silva point out, with quantitative sociology continuing to treat "race" as an independent variable, thus making it appear as though various inequalities—from health to education—are the result of "natural" differences rather than systemic racism.[18]

We can pause and reflect on this issue of white logic, white methods, by focusing on the ethnographic sociology of Robert Park. He and the Chicago School supposedly pioneered the theory of race relations in the early twentieth century. Studying the dynamics of the so-called Great Migration of Black folks from the U.S. South to the urban North, Park and his colleagues theorized that the racial violence that ensued from this migration was part of an overall race relations cycle.[19] Such a race relations cycle was characterized by *contact* among different "groups," an emergent *conflict* among these groups, with the "winners" of the said conflict *accommodating* the subdominant, followed by *assimilation* of the subdominant into the dominant group.[20]

For many reasons, this model of "racial conflict" put forward by Park has been criticized for both fixing "whiteness" as a norm while legitimating racist violence as a natural byproduct of encountered "difference."[21] In particular, critics have pointed out how Park's theory of race conflict is *astructural*. Conflict among different groups, to Park, is simply a facet of human nature: conflict appears between any two different groups when they come into contact with each other. However, such an analysis radically overlooks the imbalance in power that exists among different racialized groups.[22] Thus, much of Park's writings on the race relations cycle focused on Black Americans moving from the rural South to urban centers in the North in the early twentieth century.[23] To Park, the conflict that subsequently ensued between Black and white Americans was a result not of racism but of human nature. White racist violence was explained as simply being the "conflict" stage in the cycle, merely a *natural* antipathy that a group espouses when encountering difference—or, as Park and Ernest Burgess put it:

A natural contrariety, repugnancy of qualities, or incompatibility [exists] between individuals or groups which are sufficiently differentiated. . . . What is most important is that it involves an instinctive feeling of dislike, distaste, or repugnance, for which sometimes no good reason can be given.[24]

Through Park's understanding, therefore, when Black people moved to the North and were met with job discrimination, poverty, segregation, and violence, this was merely a result of a natural process of conflict. Indeed, taking Park's work to its conclusion, such inequalities were not even the result of a one-way antipathy from whites toward Black Americans; rather, they developed from a struggle between two competing groups. Such analysis, as we can see, does not take into consideration racialized power relations. As Oliver Cox put it, through neglecting the structural process of racialization, Park did not consider the fact that animosities between racial groups are not a natural feature of social life but something that white people themselves created through their asymmetrical racialization of others:

> He assumes that there are fundamental color antipathies between whites, yellows, and blacks. Of course, Park does not demonstrate this; and we might ask the question: what historical evidence is there to show that before the white man made his contact with peoples of colour there existed race prejudice among these peoples?[25]

Cox's comment that "Park does not demonstrate this" is therefore a central problem for the race relations theory: there is no empirical demonstration of the theoretical abstractions. The central premise of Park's race relations model—that we move from contact to conflict, accommodation, and then assimilation, or that the idea that racial groups have natural antipathies to one another—does not stem from empirical research or an engagement with the extant literature. In other words, Park rarely cites previous studies or his own empirical research when making wide generalizations about race relations.[26] This takes us back to the critique of white logic, white methods, developed by Du Bois when he criticized the "broad conclusions" at the heart of supposedly "serious scientific studies."

Of course, advocates of CRT and decolonial thought criticize dominant knowledge systems primarily because they are stressing the necessity to *think* otherwise to create a more equitable society. This is why CRT calls for a project of counter-storytelling, while decolonial thought calls for the global project of border thinking. Just as with their critiques of knowledge, these projects are certainly sympathetic to each other's aims, and the CRT notion of storytelling can itself even be seen as an example of delinking and border thinking, as I now highlight.

Delinking from the Borders

Decolonial thought stresses the need for a delinking from Western universalism and a turn toward border thinking as the epistemic alternative.[27] These border perspectives are, ironically, themselves created by Western universalism; they are epistemologies that have an exteriority in the world system—such as non-Western languages, religions, Indigenous social organizations, and so on—in virtue of Western universalism pushing these knowledges to the exterior. In other words, these perspectives of externality are themselves part of an "outside invented by the rhetoric of modernity in the process of creating the inside."[28] Part of the delinking process involves moving to, and engaging with and among, these positions of exteriority to transcend the material relations that have been produced and sustained through Western universalism. In engaging with these positions of exteriority, we are engaging in the project of *border thinking*.

Border thinking, therefore, necessitates that we engage with those epistemologies that may have been "affected by genocide/epistemicide but not fully destroyed."[29] Such delinking and border thinking are referred to as acts of epistemic disobedience and epistemic refusal.[30] Such border thinking is disobedient to the extent that it *disobeys* the rules and hierarchies of Western knowledge production, and it consequently *refuses* to accept the hierarchies of being and practices that Western knowledge legitimates. In this disobedience and refusal, border thinking thus brings back valuation to those knowledge systems and forms of life attacked by Western epistemicide while consequently opening up new perspectives of social phenomena that have been occluded by the Western lens.

Take, for instance, the notion of "magic." Relations of coloniality have us believe that "magic" is opposed to knowledge: it is traditional, metaphysical, superstitious, and primitive. Indeed, from the colonization of Latin America through the pillaging of the African continent, systems of life, organization, and theology were erased as colonial empires sought to "civilize" those groups said to be practicing magic.[31] However, we can easily delink from this Western rhetoric and engage in a border thinking that gives us a completely different perspective of magic and social life. This is precisely what Jomo Kenyatta did in his 1938 ethnography of the Gikuyu people in Kenya, published in *Facing Mount Kenya*.[32]

In his ethnography, Kenyatta showed that the Gikuyu people's use of magic was an essential means of producing rational social organization and local democracy. In particular, Kenyatta highlights how the rituals and practices in magic directly interrelate with the Gikuyu's economic base. The Gikuyu people run under a system in which land belongs "privately" to each family, but because the whole Gikuyu economy relies on land cultivation, these families always see their land practices as a collaborative, community-based exercise and societal duty. Magic feeds into this economic *mode of production* in that the idea of individualism and opting out of one's group is seen as an example of evil magic. In this regard, the moralism of magic is not evidence of something that is primitive or simplistic but, rather, is a practice and belief that fits directly into the overall running of the Gikuyu economic and social society. In this example alone, therefore, we see a highly complex relationship among economy, magic, and group membership—a level of complexity that we can capture only via border thinking, which goes beyond the myopia of Western epistemicide.

Similarly, we can think of other examples of border thinking and delinking in the twenty-first century, such as Akinpelu Olanrewaju Olutayo's study of West African proverbs as a means of social theorizing.[33] Olutayo points out that while European intellectuals tend to dismiss "proverbs" as traditional—as folklore sayings that are not important to social science—we can find deep social truths within proverbs that are passed through the generations. Olutayo demonstrates this by referencing the Yoruban proverb "A tree does not make a forest" and the Akan proverb "A person is not a palm-tree that he should be self-complete" to show how West African conceptions of agency, which emphasize that individuals attain their social being only through being active members of their group, differ from individualist Western conceptions of agency. Again, what is at stake here is more than just a rejection of Western valuations of knowledge. Not only does Olutayo show us how proverbs themselves are integral to knowledge production in some communities, but we also see how the knowledge produced legitimate alternative forms of life to Western hegemony. In this case, for instance, we see how the differing conceptions of agency produced by the proverbs lay the basis for more collective, cooperative forms of social life than are offered by Western individualism.

To an extent, therefore, everything is at stake in border thinking and delinking. Just as epistemicide legitimates the devaluing of certain forms of *being* through devaluing *knowledge*, border thinking and delinking bring valuation to other forms of knowledge and, in doing so, value those forms of life and being sustained by such knowledge. Border thinking thus becomes a way to build new links between epistemology and ontology, which is exactly what the CRT project of counter-storytelling also aspires to do.

Counter-storytelling and the Unique Voice of Color

Despite race being a social construction, because it is constructed, "race" has a material life. As Bonilla-Silva thus summarizes, race is a "biological myth" but a "social fact."[34] In virtue of race having this social realness, advocates of CRT stress that those racialized downward have a "unique voice of color," whereby, "because of their different histories and experiences with oppression, black, Indian, Asian, and Latino/a writers and thinkers may be able to communicate to their white counterparts matters that the whites are unlikely to know."[35] Indeed, this notion of a unique voice of color is not too dissimilar from Du Bois's notions of double consciousness and second sight. Central to Du Bois's argument was that, in virtue of their subjugation, the racially minoritized develop critical viewpoints toward how the world works in ways that escape the attention of the socially dominant. In this regard, the "second sight," or "unique voice of color," allows the relevant group to see social reality "beyond the veil"—that is, beyond the rhetoric and hidden processes that naturalize racialized inequalities.[36]

Advocates of CRT consequently argue that through engaging with the unique voice of color, one can begin to produce counternarratives to dominant racial tropes and storylines. It is this process of counter-storytelling, advocates of CRT argue, that will enable us to transcend the pathologizing white logic, white methods, that dominates racial knowledge production. Indeed, it was this call for counter-storytelling, Richard Delgado and Jean Stefancic argue, that characterized the first wave of CRT as it emerged in legal studies.[37] Here, the classical CRT methodology involved urging "black and brown writers to recount their experiences with racism and the legal system and to apply their own unique perspectives to assess law's master narratives." This is exactly the point Crenshaw and her colleagues make when they claim:

> Critical Race Theory's engagement with the discourse of civil rights reform stemmed directly from our lived experience as students and teachers in the nation's law schools. We both saw and suffered the concrete consequences that followed from liberal legal thinkers' failure to address the constrictive role that racial ideology plays in the composition and culture of American institutions, including American law school.[38]

Take, for instance, Crenshaw and her colleagues' discussion of how critical legal studies in the 1980s prioritized questions of gender (i.e., white women) over supposedly race-centric analysis.[39] Such discussion begins from the point of Crenshaw and her colleagues' experiences of the legal system, but it also reflected the wider point that since the 1960s, the equal opportunities laws enacted in response to the Civil Rights Movement were largely benefiting white upper- and middle-class women.[40]

Again, therefore, the project of counter-storytelling as an experiential means of social critique and knowledge production connects with the Du Boisian tradition of autoethnography. In this Du Boisian tradition, as later practiced by CRT, we see that autobiography can be an effective mechanism for reflecting on large social-structural relations in a way that provides counter-knowledges to master narratives. As Du Bois commented himself in *Dusk of Dawn*:

> My autobiography is a digressive illustration and exemplification of what race has meant in the world in the nineteenth and twentieth centuries. . . . [The] peculiar racial situation and problems could best be explained in the life history of one who

has lived them. My living gains its importance from the problems and not the problems from me.[41]

Autoethnography thus became a key way for scholars such as Du Bois—and later, the CRT tradition—to reflect on social structures through biographical storylines. For instance, we can see this in the way Du Bois recounts his educational experiences in *Dusk of Dawn*. He recounts his experience of high school, whereupon he was sold a myth of democracy being an American invention:

> I did not understand at all, nor had my history courses led me to understand, anything of current European intrigue, of the expansion of European power into Africa, of the Industrial Revolution built on slave trade. . . . I was blithely European and imperialist in outlook; democratic as democracy was conceived in America.[42]

Such biographical reflection, in this case, leads Du Bois to make structural arguments about how knowledge of the United States' systemic racism was simply erased from the narrative of American state formation. Similarly, Du Bois reflects on his classes at Harvard University to show how the myths of scientific racism and classification were being rationalized through the knowledge production of prestigious institutions, commenting:

> I remember once in a museum, coming face to face with a demonstration: a series of skeletons arranged from a little monkey to a tall well-developed white man, with a Negro barely outranking a chimpanzee.[43]

Central to the methodological enterprise of counter-storytelling, therefore, is the Du Boisian ethos to "[tell] the story of those experiences that are not often told" and to use such counternarratives as a "tool for analyzing and challenging the stories of those in power."[44] Just like with the decolonial project of border thinking and delinking, this CRT project ties together epistemology and ontology. In this CRT frame, the ontological effects of racialization and racism provide the possibilities of a unique voice of color, with this unique voice of color then becoming the foundation stone for alternative standpoints that can provide counter-stories to master narratives about race.

Indeed, once we focus on what exactly characterize these "master narratives," we again see how decolonial thought and CRT converge. Namely, underlying both the master narrative about race and the master narrative of modernity is an assumption of social development being a linear process in which as time moves forward, so does social progress. From their respective positions of externality, both CRT and decolonial thought share in their suspicion of worldviews that assume social progress as an inevitable, linear process, as I discuss as I conclude this chapter.

Against (Inevitable) Progress

Scholars of the decolonial tradition highlight that decoloniality is an option that needs to be won rather than a state of affairs that will naturally follow from history. As Walter Mignolo and Catherine Walsh describe it:

> It has been suggested that decoloniality should be understood as an imperative rather than an option, for option may imply voluntarism. My argument is that in the CMP [colonial matrix of power] there is nothing but options, options within the imaginary of modernity and options within decolonial imaginaries. Accordingly you choose an option in full awareness of the chart or you are chosen by one of the existing options that you take, willingly or not, as the truth, the correct or right one.[45]

For this reason, those in the decolonial school take issue with any theoretical frame that takes progress as a given. Even paradigms such as critical Marxism are rejected due to these terms. As Mignolo argues, any dialectical mode of thought—including Marxism—adopts a view of history as linear, as moving toward some form of development, and any such reasoning is simply an expression of colonial reasoning itself in the way that it "creates exteriorities in space and time (barbarians, primitives and under-developed)."[46] Indeed, the whole concept of coloniality itself is used to help emphasize that what many see as a key moment in the development of world democracy—that is, decolonization of most of the world in the mid-twentieth century—did not amount to any meaningful social progress for the formerly colonized. As Ramón Grosfoguel puts it:

> One of the most powerful myths of the twentieth century was the notion that the elimination of colonial administrations amounted to the decolonization of the world. . . . Although "colonial administrations" have been almost entirely eradicated and the majority of the periphery is politically organized into independent states, non-European people are still living under crude European/Euro-American exploitation and domination. The old colonial hierarchies of European versus non-Europeans remain in place and are entangled with the "international division of labor" and accumulation of capital at a world-scale.[47]

Instead of simply assuming rhetorics of progress and "modernizing" development, therefore, decolonial scholars focus on those continuities of power relations that were born in colonialism. It is through focusing on these geopolitical continuities rather than supposed ruptures that those of the decolonial tradition are able to so neatly pinpoint the extent to which the logic of coloniality continues to be a crucial force in shaping the world system. Coming back to Grosfoguel, for instance, we see that over the past five centuries, the Western world has positioned itself as the heart of God's Earth, the center and incarnation of civilization, the truly "developed" world, and the leaders and warriors of world democracy, thus justifying actions from enslavement and colonialism to the imposition of economic laws and military intervention in the "unruly," backward Global South. As Grosfoguel noted, in 520 years we went from "convert to Christianity or I'll kill you" (1500s) to "civilize or I'll kill you" (1700s–1800s) to "develop or I'll kill you" (1900s) to "democratize or I'll kill you" (today).[48]

Indeed, it is in this regard again that decolonial thought and CRT overlap in their critiques of knowledge. Central to the CRT critique is the notion of racial realism. Coined by Derrick Bell, racial realism was a concept evoked to show how whites—as the racially dominant—make concessions only when it is in their interest to do so.[49] Bell thus argues that "the interest of blacks in achieving racial equality will be accommodated only when it converges with the interests of whites"; consequently, the view emerges that "racial progress is sporadic and that people of color are doomed to experience only infrequent peaks followed by regressions."[50]

Indeed, as recounted in the Introduction, CRT came about in the 1980s partly from the realization that the promise of racial progress offered in the civil rights legislation of the 1960s had not led to any material progress for Black Americans.[51] Bell himself articulated the concept of racial realism when thinking directly about the *Brown v. Board of Education* legislation that supposedly desegregated American education. Central to his argument was that desegregation of education—at that particular conjuncture in the 1960s—served the interests of whites: it allowed them to maintain an international picture of the United States as a leader of world democracy; it enabled them to placate those Black Americans who had fought in the war, only to be discriminated against by the people they protected; and it enabled the South to rapidly industrialize.[52]

Thus, similarly to how the concept of coloniality enables us to move beyond the idea of "decolonization" as a rupture, so does the CRT concept of racial realism allow us to spot the stability of structural racism across time. When we think about moments that many herald as being markers of racial progress in the United States—such as the era of Reconstruction (1865–1877) or the civil rights legislation of the 1960s—all of these moments happened in a context in which whites were the racially dominant group in the structural racial hierarchy. This meant that "whites retain[ed] control during policy transitions (including control of property, law, taxes, corporations, philanthropy, and educational institutions)" and, consequently, that they could construct the so-called policies of racial progress in a way that did not amount to meaningful social change.[53] In the Reconstruction era, for instance, while enslavement was abolished in the U.S. South, the previous slaveholders were richly compensated, while the land given to Black Southerners was quickly taken away by the state.[54] Similarly, as Du Bois remarks on this era of Reconstruction, laws such as "Black Codes" became institutionalized across the U.S. South, where Black folks could be incarcerated for a range of measures, from not being able to provide proof of income for the coming year to sexual intercourse with whites; breach of employment contracts; being drunk; possessing firearms; or even, in some cases, simply questioning a white person.[55] Rather than being an era of progress that afforded Black folks full citizenship, the Reconstruction period reconfigured the already extant practices of racial hierarchy.

Meeting in the Borderlands

When we take a step back, therefore, we see that, despite the divergences between CRT and decolonial thought, they share similar aims in their critiques of knowledge. From their analysis of how knowledge is used to produce and legitimate social relations to their rejection of progress narratives and embracing of border perspectives and counter-perspectives, they share the ethos of needing to "know" otherwise to create a world that can "be" otherwise. In other words, they tie struggles for *cognitive* justice to struggles for *social* justice.

In this regard, it is useful to think of the synergy between CRT and decolonial thought as emerging from these two traditions' "meeting" each other in epistemic space. Gloria Anzaldúa's metaphor of the borderlands is useful here. As she declares: "To survive the Borderlands, you must live sin fronteras, be a crossroads."[56] Here, the Borderlands are a meeting place where we attempt to build dialogue and conversations among multiple epistemological traditions *sin fronteras* (without borders). As Patricia Hill Collins expands on this metaphor, the borderlands are a meeting place within which "the potential for 'democratic' exchanges" is deliberately emphasized and encouraged.[57]

This book, to an extent, is an exercise in showing what happens when we foster meetings, exchanges, and analytical discussions between CRT and decolonial thought *sin fronteras*—without assuming that one approach is superior to the other. The chapters that follow, covering the topics of far-right political projects, capitalism, climate crises, and the COVID-19 pandemic, are all testament to the fact that promoting an epistemic meeting between CRT and decolonial thought offers prescient analysis of some of the key predicaments of our time.

2

When Postcolonial Melancholia
Meets Post-racial Ideology

On Right-Wing Populism

want to begin this chapter by posing a set of questions: What would happen if we considered postcolonial melancholia a "structure of feeling" in which racial ideology finds a home? How does post-racial ideology attach itself to postcolonial melancholia, and vice versa? How do contemporary political movements draw on post-racial ideology to galvanize collective memories of empire? These are all questions that, first and foremost, need to be asked in the context of recent political projects, such as Brexit in Britain, Donald Trump's success in the United States, and Jair Bolsonaro's success in Brazil.[1] Further, these are questions that, in answering them, we see the balance between the national and transnational, and present and historical, that can be achieved when both critical race theory (CRT) and decolonial thought are brought into our analysis. By focusing on the projects of Brexit, "Trumpamerica," and Bolsonaro's Brazil—particularly on their electoral campaigns and immediate aftermaths of electoral success—I use this chapter to show how combining CRT's focus on post-racial ideology and racialized emotions with decolonial thought's emphasis on collective memory and postcolonial melancholia provides an appropriate "conjunctural" analysis of these political projects. Indeed, part of the reason these two approaches balance so well in such case studies is that the concept of postcolonial melancholia itself is attentive to the ideological and emotional dimensions of social life, as I now discuss.

The British Roots of Postcolonial Melancholia

"Empires come and go," Stuart Hall said, "but the imagery of the British Empire seems destined to go on forever. The imperial flag has been hauled down in a hundred different corners of the globe. *But it is still flying in the collective unconscious.*"[2] Indeed, Hall wrote these words in 1982, as a Tory-led government embroiled Britain in a war with Argentina over the Falklands. Hall's argument was that in the midst of the recession of the 1980s, the British government needed to galvanize support and a popular spirit, and instead of doing this by forging a concrete path to utopian futures, it instead turned back to the history of the British Empire to foster a "gut patriotism . . . laced with gut moralism."[3] This gut patriotism, Hall argues, is essentially transnational by nature. It refers to those most precious moments in British history *that actually took place outside of the island called Britain*—whether that was the bringing of democracy to the undeveloped people of Asia, Africa, and the Caribbean; fighting for the abolition of slavery worldwide (because Britain's only role in enslavement seems to be in its abolition); or saving the world from being absorbed into a Nazi world system. In other words, the British gut patriotism/gut moralism that we saw accelerating in the early 1980s was itself a patriotism that celebrated the wide-reaching successes of the British Empire in all its glory. Bear in mind, this is the 1980s Hall is talking about.

Skip forward about forty years, and Hall's remarks around British patriotism remain not just appropriate, but *foundational* for understanding the contemporary British political mainstream. Consider, for instance, the various protests that took place in Britain in the aftermath of George Floyd's murder in Minneapolis in 2020. As I mentioned at the beginning of this book, some of these protests involved the targeting of statues of key figures in Britain's empire, including the statue of the slaver Edward Colston in Bristol. In response to this, the prime minister, Boris Johnson, exclaimed that Brits needed to stop having a "cringing embarrassment" toward its previous empire and needed to stop the ascendant "general fight of self-recrimination and wetness."[4] Along with Johnson's prime ministerial statement, Culture Minister Oliver Dowden organized a summit with British heritage bodies in a bid to "defend our history" against activists who "do Britain down," while Universities Minister Michelle Donelan launched a full-scale attack on those accused of the "decolonisation" of British history, which, she argued, was tantamount to burning books, Sovietesque censorship, and an erasure of Britain's global contributions.[5] It is safe to say, in this context, that while Hall discussed the imagery of the British Empire that still flies in the "collective unconsciousness," the concept of unconsciousness downplays the very explicit and overt articulation of the gut patriotism/moralism through which we are currently living.

Scholars of this British Empire fanaticism have referred to this political rhetoric as being part of an overall "postcolonial melancholia," but it is by no means a structure of feeling isolated to Britain. As it was first termed by Paul Gilroy, postcolonial melancholia in Britain involved an "inability to mourn its loss of Empire and accommodate the Empire's consequences."[6] Building on this definition, Stephen Ashe described this melancholia as involving a "mixture of guilt and pride which prevents Britain from being able to mourn its imperial history without facing up to the barbarity that this entailed."[7] Fundamentally, therefore, postcolonial melancholia is ironically a vision of history that is inattentive to history itself. As Hall describes it, it is a "profound historical forgetfulness—what I want to call the loss of historical memory, a kind of historical amnesia, a decisive mental repression."[8]

While scholars such as Hall, Gilroy, and Ashe have discussed postcolonial melancholia as it developed in Britain, their thoughts on this process most certainly apply to other geopolitical regions. That is true because, as Meghan Tinsley reminds us, what is being described in the concept of postcolonial melancholia is something that is typical to many "post-imperial" nation-states that lost formal ownership of most of their colonial territories in the early to mid-twentieth century.[9] In this regard, at an abstract level, postcolonial melancholia refers to a situation we see across the world where post-imperial nations have no way to understand their present situation and existence outside the memory of their imperial prowess and thus constantly seek to return to the past in the present to reattain this greatness. As Tinsley describes it:

> As the post-imperial nation was left with a sense of loss that it could not name, nostalgia blurred into melancholia, such that an all-consuming sense of longing obscured the object of that longing. So long as postcolonial melancholia endured, the post-imperial nation could neither mourn the loss of empire nor construct any national self-conception apart from empire. Rather, empire remains, even as its memory fades, in collective identity, public policy, and international relations. Yet deprived of imperial glory, and of the national identity that it had entailed, the post-imperial nation continues to long for an unattainable sense of wholeness, self-sufficiency, and home.[10]

Inside Tinsley's description of postcolonial melancholia we see a central point I stress in this chapter: that postcolonial melancholia is a conceptual, ideological, and emotional constellation. It is for this reason, I suggest, that it is useful to think of postcolonial melancholia as being akin to a "structure of feeling."

Postcolonial Melancholia as a Structure of Feeling

When Raymond Williams theorized the "structure of feeling," he was trying to emphasize how emotional repertoires often form the skeleton for conceptual schemes, ideas, arguments, and group identities.[11] In other words, structures of feeling are fundamental for ontological and epistemological dimensions of social life. Central to Williams's theorization, therefore, was that we need to feel things before we can *think* them, and we needed to feel similar things to *be* similar people. As Williams thus shows, we ought not to think that emotions "stand in the way of rationality." Instead, they are the fundamental building blocks of our social lives.[12]

In thinking of postcolonial melancholia as a structure of feeling, we are highlighting how the produced collective memories of empire—those memories that ironically rely on a "loss of historical memory"—provide a skeleton for *thinking* and *being* in particular ways, which achieve and naturalize particular relations of power and social inclusion and exclusion. Again, the work of Tinsley becomes relevant here, as she shows how nostalgia—as an emotional repertoire—becomes a key component of postcolonial melancholia.[13]

The very word *nostalgia*—deriving from *nostos* and *algia*—forces us to confront emotional repertoires.[14] *Nostos* derives from Ancient Greek, referring to the process of returning home, while *algia* refers to a localized pain in the body. Putting them together, Tinsley argues, shows us how *nostalgia* refers to an emotional state of pain, loss, and confusion that derives from a deep-seated desire to return "home." Yet as theorists of postcolonial melancholia stress, this "home" itself is a fiction that is produced by various historical (mis)memories— in this case, of empire. In this regard, the nostalgia of postcolonial melancholia involves "the longing for an idealized 'home' free from longing for any other timespace, coupled with the consciousness of a gulf between past and present."[15] Importantly, this notion of home is

> deterritorialized, drawn from past and present, and projected onto an imagined future—whether or not the nostalgic acts to bring it to fruition. Any other timespace is compared to "home" and found to fall short. For the nostalgic, the ideal timespace is one that is free of references to any other. It is self-sufficient and self-centered, utopian and "authentic."[16]

It is in this imagined conception of home that we see how postcolonial melancholia—as a structure of feeling—promotes social inclusion and exclusion in various ways. To name two in particular, we can consider, first, the imagined conceptions of home that create what Gilroy refers to as "color-coded concepts of national belonging."[17] As Gilroy captures, this refers to how postcolonial melancholia involves a mainstreamed longing for the nation to return to its previous state prior to migrations of people of color and ascendant multiculturalisms. An overt example of this would be the British Conservative Party's election campaign in 1964 (as more citizens from the Commonwealth were moving to the "mother country"), which featured a poster with the slogan: "If you desire a Colored for your neighbour vote labour, if you are already burdened with one vote Tory." More diffused examples of this logic can be seen in the increasing anxiety over Black and Brown Muslim migration to the European continent, leading to a popularization of the great replacement theory (the theory that white people of Europe are going to be replaced by Muslims in the near-future due to migration and its consequent Islamism).[18] In the United States and Canada, we see similar fears over "replacement" conspiracy theories, often articulated in the message that whites in the two countries are now an ethnic minority in their own land. Research has shown how this creates a basis for increased investments in white identity in these nations.[19]

Of course, the fact that whites in Canada and the United States feel like minorities "in their own land" seems to be contradictory, given that the land first belonged to Indigenous peoples. This relates to the second thing we can see in postcolonial melancholia's nostalgia: that it produces bifurcated histories that emphasize the supposed "gains" of empire without thinking about the costs of those so-called gains. In other words, the nostalgia produces accounts of history that overlook the violence of empire, colonialism, and enslavement in a way that erases the very histories, memories, and existence of those nonwhite folks now inside the nation-state. Dancing with the rhetoric of modernity, this nostalgia involves a longing for the nation to return to how it was: a safe space of comfort and peace, free from the contemporary turmoil of globalization. Of course, this vision of home makes sense only if you occlude the existence of people who fall on a different side of the line of the coloniality of being: all those colonized and enslaved people who suffered in the name of this supposedly "safe space" of the nation.

Importantly, both of these elements of postcolonial melancholia's nostalgia provide a skeleton for ideology and identity formation. If you are invested in an idea of returning the nation to its state prior to migrations and multiculturalism, then you would be more likely to follow political projects that restrict immigration and speed up deportation. If you think some people belong in the nation-state while others do not, you are more likely to affiliate yourself with, and form inclusionary relations toward, those who you think belong. If you endorse the rhetoric of modernity and view the history of your nation as being a history of progress, development, democracy, and freedom, then not only are you going to develop a strong affinity toward this imagined space (and, consequently, an affinity toward others who share your collective memory), but you are also going to dismiss any political and social movements for reparations as being, at best, spurious. Postcolonial melancholia may be a structure of feeling—an emotional repertoire built on fictitious memories and symbolic codes—but it has significant material consequences.

Bringing in Racial Ideology and Racialized Emotions

Through the concept of postcolonial melancholia we can therefore see how it is easy to build a bridge between CRT and elements of decolonial thought. In particular, just as postcolonial melancholia stresses the importance of emotional repertoires, so, too, does CRT stress how racial ideology and racialized emotions are key dimensions in reproducing the racial status quo.

Central to the CRT position is that racial ideology is more concerned with *perception* than with deception. Through this lens, racial ideology is akin to a conceptual scheme that produces and mobilizes consciousness rather than being an opaque card that prevents reality from being "known." It is for this reason that Eduardo Bonilla-Silva defines racial ideology as "the racially based frameworks used by actors to explain and justify (dominant race) or challenge (subordinate race or races) the racial status quo."[20] Expanding on this preliminary definition, Ashley "Woody" Doane thus refers to racial ideologies as "an ever-changing collection of components that include frames, narratives, symbols, stereotypes, discursive styles, and a particular vocabulary."[21] Thus, racial ideologies are not "myths" about race that can simply be debunked by logical reasoning. Rather, they encompass various styles, frames, ideas, and schemes of perception that offer a prism for the dominant racial group to rationalize, reproduce, and understand social reality. To this extent, racial ideologies are inherently related to the organization of the racial structure: there is no racial ideology without a racial structure within which it can circulate and become active, but the racial structure itself needs ideologies for its smooth reproduction. Similar to the concept of postcolonial melancholia, a core argument of CRT is that *racialized emotions* are central vehicles for the development and transmission of racial ideologies.

Within CRT, racialized emotions are understood as "the socially engendered emotions in racialized societies."[22] Central to the concept of racialized emotions is the idea that similarly racialized groups "fashion an emotional subjectivity generally fitting of their location in the racial order," meaning that one's racialized emotions are related to, and often reproduce, one's position in the racial hierarchy. Whites, for instance, may have negative emotions such as fear of "Black thugs" and "Muslim terrorists" and indeed—as Pete Simi and his colleagues show in the case of far-right radicalization—negative emotions such as hatred often act as fundamental building blocks for acts of racialized violence.[23] Whites may also have "positive emotions" of pride and joy in reproducing the racial structure (lynching parties being an extreme example of this). Fundamentally, racialized emotions—just like racial ideologies—are not phenomena whose "truth" is up for question. They are instead building blocks of social reality itself. As Bonilla-Silva highlights:

> Analysts who focus on the falsity of Whites' emotions, much like those who interpret ideology as false, miss their true matrix and social power. Whites' emotions, like race itself, are socially real and have a materiality that cannot be ignored or assumed unchangeable.[24]

The CRT position thus becomes similar to decolonial approaches that focus on postcolonial melancholia. Namely, CRT, too, argues that the emotional becomes a necessary skeleton for ideology and identity. By means of example, consider the rise of the "It's OK to Be White" movement in Australia.[25] It is composed of white Australians from a variety of classed and gendered backgrounds, who bind together around the emotional acceptance and pride of whiteness and being white—they share an emotional bond in what W.E.B. Du Bois referred to as a "deep whiteness."[26] What we see in the case of Australia are emotions not just generating a social collectivity but also serving as the basis for transmitting racial ideologies—in this case, the ideology of post-racialism. The reason that white Australians were claiming it is OK to be white is that they believed others disagreed with that fundamental claim; such whites were convinced that antiwhite discrimination was built into the social structure. Plenty of other examples make the same point. With Islamophobia in France, for example, whites need to "feel" Muslims as a threat to think that border control is a good idea.[27] In New Zealand, whites need to "feel" and identify as New Zealanders to think that Indigenous people are not full members of the nation.[28] Rather than theorizing emotions, therefore, as "stand[ing] in the way of rationality," it is more appropriate to see them as in fact being a key component of rationality.[29]

Furthermore, just like with the concept of postcolonial melancholia, the CRT theorization of racialized emotions stresses how the existence of emotions itself is linked to hierarchies of being. With postcolonial melancholia, we showed how the nostalgia built into it created an identification with the state that devalued the existence of nonwhite folks who destroyed the sacred space of "home" in this collective memory. In CRT, too, we see how racialized emotions function to devalue particular people. This is particularly apparent when we consider the reality that different emotions are given different levels of legitimacy and recognition within the racial structure—in other words, the reality that there is a hierarchy of emotional rationality that helps naturalize the racial order. Take, for instance, the "Unite the Right" protest in Charlottesville, Virginia, in 2017, at which white supremacist groups gathered to oppose the proposed removal of a statue of General Robert Lee. When Trump declared, "You had some very bad people in that group, but you also had people that were very fine people, on both sides," we can see that the emotions of those who were protesting against the monument were given greater legitimacy or acknowledgment than those who were affected by the violence of white supremacist activists.

Through these concepts of racial ideology and racialized emotions, therefore, we see that there is another degree of similarity in the frameworks developed by CRT and decolonial traditions. I now want to go beyond recognizing conceptual similarities in the two approaches' repertoires to show the benefits of using them together in the study of right-wing populist projects. Bringing these concepts together, I show that racialized emotions and ideologies have been so powerful in the British, U.S., and Brazilian racialized social systems partly because they have been encapsulated into this "structure of feeling" we have been calling postcolonial melancholia. I demonstrate this in reference to Brexit and Trump's election in 2016 and Bolsonaro's election in 2019.

The Ideological and Emotional of Brexit, Trumpamerica, and Bolsonaro

In all three cases—Brexit, Trump, and Bolsonaro—we see how the various projects built on the dominant racial ideologies and racialized emotions in their racialized social systems. The success of Brexit and Trump, for example, stemmed from the two countries' ideology of post-racialism—an ideology holding that the each country's racial minorities were no longer affected by structural racism. Through this ideological denial of structural racism, post-racialism in Britain and the United States has resulted in many white people claiming that they are in fact the victims of racial inequality as minorities get "special benefits" through affirmative action, antidiscrimination, and equal opportunities legislation. This, in turn, creates racialized emotions of nonrecognition and devaluation.[30]

The post-racial frame of white victimhood took center stage in Trump's 2016 campaign. Arlie Hochschild's *Strangers in Their Own Land*, a book that was retrospectively labeled a key text for understanding the context of Trump's electoral success, helps demonstrate this.[31] Focusing on Louisiana, Hochschild examines how white people (in the working and middle classes) were experiencing growing levels of deprivation and blamed these declining standards on those racialized downward who were receiving preferential treatment in education and hiring. She further argued that such white people construed themselves as being stigmatized through being labeled "rednecks" and "bigoted." Hochschild concludes that this (perceived) combination of material and symbolic exclusion led white folks to construe themselves as "strangers in their own land." The dynamic of white marginality highlighted by Hochschild was further evidenced in Trump's campaign. In his electoral speeches, as Michèle Lamont and her colleagues show, Trump directly drew symbolic boundaries toward lower-income white voters to make them feel valued rather than marginalized in their own nation.[32] This boundary work relied on drawing explicit divisions between white folks—the "true members" of the nation-state—and racialized outsiders. Thus, when addressing low-income white voters at rallies, Trump would often make reference to protecting their jobs from foreign invasion, as he did in West Bend, Wisconsin, saying:

> [Hillary Clinton] is proposing to print instant work permits for millions of illegal immigrants, taking jobs directly from low-income Americans. I will secure our border, protect our workers, and improve jobs and wages in your community.

Trump's campaign thus fostered an image that "hardworking" white American families were being excluded in their own nation *and* that his political program could restore valuation to these groups.[33] It was this logic that underlined Trump's famous response to Hillary Clinton's labeling his supporters "deplorables" by reframing them as "hardworking" patriots:

> While my opponent slanders you as deplorable and irredeemable, I call you hardworking American patriots who love your country and want a better future for all of our people. . . . Every American is entitled to be treated with dignity and respect in our country.

The post-racial ideology underlying Trump's 2016 electoral campaign was similarly expressed in Britain by politicians garnering voter support to leave the European Union. As Satnam Virdee and Brendan McGeever show, a central argument deployed by the "Leave" campaign was that the European Union's policy of open borders was leading to a situation in which racialized outsiders—"the migrants"—were above ordinary Brits in the material hierarchy.[34] Nigel Farage, a key figure in the campaign, captured such reasoning when he said that

> open-door migration has suppressed wages in the unskilled labour market, meant that living standards have failed and that life has become a lot tougher for so many in our country.

Indeed, the concept of indigeneity was directly evoked by another key politician who supported the Leave campaign—Boris Johnson— when he criticized how the union's policy of "open borders" marginalized British workers:

> We also need to ask ourselves some hard questions about the impact of 20 years of uncontrolled immigration by low-skilled, low-wage workers—and what many see as the consequent suppression of wages and failure to invest properly in the skills of Indigenous young people.[35]

Similar to those in the United States, therefore, political figures in Britain presented Brexit as a project that could redistribute value back to those hardworking white families whose social status had been harmed by racialized immigration. In Britain, this narrative was further bolstered *after* the referendum, when Prime Minister Theresa May declared that Brexit ought to be used as an opportunity to build a Britain that values residents of the (almost exclusively white) towns that voted in high numbers to leave the European Union, addressing the "everyday injustices that ordinary working class families feel are too often overlooked."[36] Indeed, as Robbie Shilliam points out, by using the examples of white constituencies and towns—from Margate to Whitby—to refer to the "ordinary working class families" who feel overlooked and face daily injustices, May simply strengthened the already extant ideology that "ordinary" white folks were the new Black.[37] Indeed, May's words show how post-racial ideology and racialized emotions of devaluation were not just a pretext for Brexit but gained legitimacy as the political project developed.

Indeed, May's comments were typical of the fact that post-racial ideology and emotions of white victimhood were further strengthened by media and political discourse in the aftermath of Trump's and Brexit's electoral successes. In this context, such discourses tended to avoid discussing the significant number of white middle-class supporters for both projects and the relatively low number of poor racial minorities who did *not* vote for Trump or Brexit; instead, the discursive attention centered on framing Trumpamerica and Brexit Britain as being driven by a need to redistribute value to the forgotten ordinary white families and the white working class.[38] In Britain there were claims that Brexit voters are not "thick or racist, just poor"; that Brits who demand migration control are *not* motivated by racism; and that "racial self-interest" is not racism.[39] Indeed, David Skelton dedicated a book, *Little Platoons*, to defending the argument that Brexit happened because poor white people in English towns felt economically excluded.[40] Similarly, in the United States Trump's electoral success was described as a "revolt of the masses," in which Trump secured victory "by a . . . wave of support by the white working class" who "were alienated, forgotten by the political establishment [and] their status challenged by the country's growing racial diversity."[41] In both cases, dominant discourse thus framed the success of Brexit and Trump through the very post-racial, emotive logic from which the two projects emerged.

While Trump and Brexit built on post-racial ideology and emotions of devaluation, Bolsonaro's campaign built on an alternative racial ideology that was dominant in Brazil's racialized social system: the ideology of racial democracy. This ideology holds that, due to historical "mixture" among the country's different racialized groups, Brazil is either a race-less or nonracist society.[42] Given the strength of this ideology, as Lamont and her colleagues clarify, even "denouncing racism and emphasizing racial identity [is] seen as unpatriotic not only by the state but by society at large."[43] It was precisely this racial ideology that suppressed discussion and expression of "race" in Brazil that Bolsonaro was able to both propagate and galvanize in his election and political consolidation. For instance, a large part of Bolsonaro's campaign revolved around the desire to "integrate" Indigenous people and Afro-Brazilians into the nation's culture of racial democracy, with the language of integration directly evoked in claims such as, "We are going to integrate them [Indigenous people] into society. Just like the army which did a great job of this."[44] Bolsonaro thus construed Indigenous people as being essentially un-Brazilian, given their failure to "melt" into the racial democratic pot of the nation:

The Indians do not speak our language, they do not have money, they do not have culture. They are native peoples. How did they manage to get 13% of the national territory?[45]

Bolsonaro's iteration of racial democracy thus heavily focused on what he construed as the "problem" of the self-segregation of Afro-Brazilians and Indigenous people, captured in his repeated claims that "not a centimeter will be demarcated either as an Indigenous reserve or as a quilombola."[46] Bolsonaro then immediately consolidated such an ideology of racial democracy by deliberately building an administration that sought to squash a culture of anti-racism in Brazil. This is best signified, perhaps, by his appointment of the anti-anti-racist Sergio Camargo as the head of the Palmares Cultural Foundation (responsible for promoting Brazil's Black presence), who held the view that "Black people complain because they are stupid and misinformed" by "the victim mentality of the left."[47]

Through tracing nationally dominant racial ideologies and emotions, therefore, CRT offers an appealing map for understanding certain right-wing populist projects. Nevertheless, this analysis of Brexit, Trump, and Bolsonaro is actually heightened once we think about the links among these ideologies, emotions, and *postcolonial melancholia*. When we think about slogans such as "Make America Great *Again*" and "Take *Back* Control," we see explicit references to an imagined past in which the nation was great and powerful (and thus also references to imagined futures in which these various political projects could reinstate that greatness). Even if you think about the analysis by Hochschild, who shows the racialized emotions of white Americans who feel like "strangers in their own land," we again see the fictitious representation of "home" that is so central to the nostalgia of postcolonial melancholia. What we see in the electoral campaigns of Bolsonaro, Brexit, and Trump, therefore, is not just a narrative of giving back recognition and valuation to "everyday" people, *but also giving back recognition and valuation to the nation as it stands in the global field.*

The quest to reinstate the United States' imperial greatness, for instance, was one of the key themes underlying the speech in which Trump announced his presidential bid.[48] As he commented:

> Our country is in serious trouble. . . . We don't have victories anymore. We used to have victories, but we don't have them. When was the last time anybody saw us beating, let's say, China in a trade deal? They kill us. I beat China all the time. All the

time.... When do we beat Mexico at the border? They're laughing at us, at our stupidity.... The U[nited] S[tates] has become a dumping ground for everybody else's problems.

In response to this situation of global devaluation, Trump proposed that he could bring recognition back to the nation on a global scale, as he clarified in a later speech at the U.S. Naval Academy:

But we know the truth, we will speak the truth, and we will defend that truth. America is the greatest fighting force for peace, justice, and freedom in the history of the world.... We are going to stand up for our values.... We won two world wars, defeated communism and fascism, and put a man on the face of the moon. We cured disease, pioneered science, and produced timeless works of art that inspire the human soul.

Inside Trump's project, therefore, was a desire to place the United States back into the center of the world system—including the *moral-civilizational* center ("America is the greatest fighting force for peace, justice, and freedom"), the center of power ("We won two world wars, defeated communism and fascism"), and the center of knowledge production ("We cured disease, pioneered science, and produced timeless works of art that inspire the human soul"). Nevertheless, in Trump's inscription of coloniality, we see a key dimension of postcolonial melancholia: the "profound historical forgetfulness" of the horrors and violence of colonialism, imperialism, and empire. Trump's statement "America is the greatest fighting force for peace, justice, and freedom" demonstrates this historical forgetfulness by overlooking U.S. enslavement and segregation and its installation of a military-colonial apparatus across the Americas and Asia. To some, in fact, the United States brought the *opposite* of peace, justice, and freedom.

It is this profound historical forgetfulness we also see running through Brexit's postcolonial melancholia. However, unlike that of the United States, Britain's postcolonial melancholia is expressed through its paradoxical "little Englander" spirit—again, based on the logic of coloniality. This paradoxical little Englander spirit is based on the premise that Britain ought to withdraw itself from international affairs, but it is also crystallized around the belief in British self-determination and Britain being a global superpower despite its "plucky underdog" status. The fact that Britain colonized one-quarter of the world is seen as emblematic of this little Englander spirit, as Britain is represented as a small island that—despite the odds—managed to create a global empire. The empire, therefore, is a source of national pride, as it is said to signal Britain's unparalleled work ethic, philanthropy, and civilizational values. Indeed, it was this little Englander spirit and conviction in self-determination that allowed Leave campaigners to argue that the European Union eroded the strength of British governance. Just as with Trump, the Brexit campaign revolved around the view that Britain was losing its place as a central power in the world system. As Boris Johnson thus claimed, "The independence of this country is being seriously compromised. It is this fundamental democratic problem—this erosion of democracy—that brings me into this fight."[49]

From this moment, the Brexit campaign created its own imagery of Britain itself being a European colony; as Johnson put it, the European Union wanted to "build a country called Europe." It was this logic that allowed for Anne Widdecombe, a Conservative Party member of Parliament, to describe the eventual decision to leave the European Union as a "slave revolt." The Brexit campaign therefore offered imagery of Britain being a European colony while simultaneously claiming that it was a political project that could restore the glory of the British Empire. This is why, for instance, Britain's economic plans in the aftermath of Brexit revolved around creating what the government officially labeled "Empire 2.0," characterized by greater free-trade links with Commonwealth countries.[50] Prime Minister Theresa May claimed that such a turn could help re-create a "Global Britain" that "goes out into the world to build relationships with old friends" and reaps the benefits of its "unique and proud global relationships" with Commonwealth nations.[51] While many commentators thus represented Brexit as a turn away from globalization, what we really see in Brexit Britain is a plea for a postcolonial return to a globalization in which Britain was—as the (mis)representation holds—a benign, democratic empire that was praised in all corners of the world.

Even with Bolsonaro in Brazil—where Brazil was not an empire but a settler colony—we see such a misrepresentation of colonialism, along with a pledge to reinstate colonial projects. Thus, Bolsonaro's political project consistently highlighted Brazil's links to Europe—and Portugal specifically—as a way to highlight the country's supposed civilizational greatness. Of course, this "special link" with Portugal neatly elides the role of the Portuguese in enslavement, with Bolsonaro instead claiming, "The Portuguese didn't even set foot in Africa. It was the Africans themselves who handed the slaves over."[52]

To build explicit links with European culture, Bolsonaro—during and after his campaign—focused on defining Brazil explicitly as a Christian nation, thus relegating Indigenous people, many Afro-Brazilians, and Muslims to the status of "non-citizens."[53] Bolsonaro's campaign slogan was "Brazil above Everything, God above All," while in his inauguration speech he called for the nation to respect "our Judeo-Christian tradition . . . and preserve our values."[54] In doing so, Bolsonaro's project directly built links with far-right parties such as Movimento Brasil Livre (Free Brazil Movement) and Brasil Paralelo, both of which identified "three pillars" of Western civilization built into Brazilian society: Greek philosophy, Roman law, and Judeo-Christian religiosity.[55] Furthermore, not only was Bolsonaro's project of returning to the colonial roots of putative "Judeo-Christian values" connecting with Brazilian far-right parties; it also connected *transnationally* with far-right parties elsewhere fighting for Western values. Bolsonaro's first-choice ambassador to the United States—his son, Eduardo—for instance, was close friends with Steve Bannon, Trump's former chief strategist.[56] Indeed, Bannon even invited Eduardo Bolsonaro to lead the Latin American branch of The Movement, Bannon's far-right organization.[57] The political link between this couple—and, by extension, between far-right politics in the United States and Brazil—is quite clear. Just as Bannon claimed that the United States was in a global cultural war against Islam, Eduardo Bolsonaro evoked this Orientalized imagery of Islam being antithetical to Western values and of Muslims being excluded from the notion of a [Brazilian] "home," claiming: "We respect the women. You have other parts of the world where they didn't grow up with this Jewish Christian mentality, so they don't respect that much the women."[58]

Jair Bolsonaro's political vision not only instigates a return to the colonial roots of "Judeo-Christian values." It is also based in returning to the colonial project of Indigenous erasure and Indigenous land expropriation in the name of capital accumulation.[59] This is captured in his remarks that clearly construe Indigenous people and their reserves as a barrier to Brazil's economic growth:

> There is no Indigenous territory where there aren't minerals. Gold, tin and magnesium are in these lands, especially in the Amazon, the richest area in the world. I'm not getting into this nonsense of defending land for Indians.
>
> [Indigenous reserves] are an obstacle to agri-business. You can't reduce Indigenous land by even a square meter in Brazil.[60]

Again, such a project of Indigenous erasure was embodied in a "historical forgetfulness" of Brazil's colonial past. Much as Brexit construed Britain as a European colony, Bolsonaro ironically construed Brazilians as facing settler colonialism from Indigenous and Afro-Brazilians, accusing the National Indigenous Foundation of deliberately choosing the "richest and most fertile" land to "give away" to "Indians and blacks" and of stealing land from Brazilians who had been "living there for centuries."[61] In this case, Bolsonaro's "attack" on Indigenous people was driven by the ideology of racial democracy, in which such people are seen as anti-Brazilian, as CRT helps analyze, as well as by a construction of Indigenous people as barriers to the nation's economic health through their holding of a vast amount of land—*land that, he argued, does not belong to* them and thus could be expropriated for profit by private and state corporations.

Just as with Brexit and Trump, therefore, it is impossible to comprehend Bolsonaro's electoral success and political project outside of the logic of coloniality and the postcolonial melancholia it expresses. Brexit and Trump's election involved a postcolonial melancholia that sought to return the nation to its imperial glory. Bolsonaro's project iterated melancholia not only to return Brazil to its European Judeo-Christian values, but also to accelerate Indigenous land erasure and redistribute the land to "the Brazilians."

The Binding Power of Postcolonial Melancholia

By just focusing on a handful of right-wing populist projects, we see how a "both-and" approach to CRT and decolonial thought benefits our analysis. If we were only to adopt a CRT position, our analysis would focus on nationally specific racialized social systems' racialized ideologies and emotions but fail to see how these ideologies and emotions were themselves sealed within the skeleton of postcolonial melancholia. We might understand that, for example, white Brits and Americans felt like "strangers in their own land," but we would not fully comprehend how this creation of "their own land" was an expression of postcolonial melancholia rooted in imageries of empire and modernity; we might understand how Bolsonaro wielded the ideology of racial democracy to exclude Black and Indigenous people but fail to fully appreciate how this exclusion related to Bolsonaro's fictitious reworking of Brazil's colonial history. However, if we focused only on postcolonial melancholia—as a structure of feeling—we would lose the focus on national specificity and nationally embedded ideologies and emotions. We would be able to focus on how each of the three national projects endorsed some narrative of colonial/imperial greatness, constellated around a bifurcated account of colonial history, but we would not be able to understand *why* this presentation of history was so appealing to great numbers of voters at those particular conjunctures. In short, such a case of these political projects speaks to the need for the theoretical synergy I advocate for in this book.

Of course, despite the analysis offered in this theoretical synergy, various pundits continue to construe the success of right-wing populist projects a blanket response to the inequalities of neoliberalism and globalization. As mentioned in this chapter, such explanations do not explain *why* the inequalities of neoliberalism and globalization push some people toward overtly imperial/racist projects. Neither do they pay attention to the fact that neoliberalism and capitalist globalization are themselves inherently racialized structures embedded in the colonial matrix of power. To attend to these racialized dynamics, I turn in the next chapter to analyzing how CRT and decolonial thought offer critiques of neoliberalism and capitalism, showing how they converge in the way they analyze neoliberalism's creation of—and dependence on—so-called edge populations.

3

National Abjects in the "Fourth World War"

Crises of Neoliberal Capitalism

> The defeat of the "Evil Empire" has opened up new markets whose
> conquest is provoking a new world war, the fourth. Like all conflicts,
> this one forces nation-states to redefine their identity. The world
> order has returned to the old era of the conquests of America, Africa,
> and Oceania. It is a strange modernity that advances by going back-
> ward. The twilight of the twentieth century resembles earlier barba-
> rous periods more than it does the rational futures described by so
> many works of science fiction.
>
> —Subcomandante Marcos,
> "The Fourth World War Has Begun"

Capitalism is an interesting topic to reflect on the interplay between critical race theory (CRT) and decolonial thought. Especially among certain Marxist circles, both traditions are (inaccurately) critiqued for not putting capitalism at the center of their analysis of national and transitional inequalities. In this chapter, however, I show that CRT and decolonial thought converge in their critiques of capitalism, especially as both traditions have centered neoliberalism in their analyses. In particular, I focus on how both CRT and decolonial thought analyze how neoliberalism produces, and relies on, the exploitation of "edge populations." In CRT, these edge populations are synonymous with national abjects, living at the borders of recognition and citizenship; in decolonial thought, these edge populations live on the borders of the world system, encountering and resisting global proletarianization. Before proceeding to this discussion, it is appropriate to consider some dominant myths about the relationship among CRT, decolonial thought, and Marxism, especially as Marxism is thought to have a monopoly on critiques of capitalism.

Dispelling Discourses: Marxism, CRT, and Decolonial Thought

A first point to consider is that various Marxist scholars have admonished CRT for its "race-centrism," arguing that it truncates the ability to form concrete critiques of material social relations.[1] This has led to quite a mundane "race-versus-class" debate—ironically, an internal debate that is held almost exclusively among the critics of CRT rather than a debate that is held between Marxists and critical race theorists. Of course, as I have highlighted in the past few chapters, it makes no sense to dismiss CRT's ability to form critiques of material social relations. As I highlighted, CRT emerged as a tradition critiquing how the law was reproducing *material relations of inequality* in the face of myths of racial progress. Indeed, I also highlighted how the racialized social system approach's theoretical foundation is built on the idea that racialization and racism are primarily material relations sustained by a variety of micro, meso, and macro social processes. Despite the reality of what CRT actually *is*, and what it *does*, some folks from the Marxist side have convinced themselves that CRT commits itself to a race-centrism that centers identity politics at the expense of concrete social analysis. To these thinkers, CRT raises (at least!) two problems:

1. It analyzes racism as being separate from capitalism and, in so doing, directs our attention away from the mode of production. This is the straightforward claim that CRT prioritizes race over class. Indeed, as Mike Cole put it, CRT is built on the premise that "'race' rather than social class [i]s the primary contradiction in society."[2] While the evidence for this may be thin, scholars such as Cole have argued that "if capitalist modes of production are mentioned, critical race theorists do not analyse their connections with racism. [For instance, David] Gillborn . . . is able to make the case for CRT and 'white supremacy' without providing a discussion of the relationship of racism to capitalism."[3] In contrast to CRT, scholars such as Cole argue, we need to shift our attention away from "racism" and toward "racialization"— that is, "an ideological process that accompanies the appro-

priation of labour power (the capacity to labour), where people are categorized falsely into the scientifically defunct notion of distinct 'races.'[4] To such Marxist scholars, race is largely superstructural, used to naturalize relations of labor exploitation; from this perspective, CRT becomes unable to actually explain such exploitation because it occludes analysis of the root cause (capitalism).

2. In overlooking the mode of production, critical race theorists focus on "white supremacy." However, the concept of white supremacy is said to be unhelpful for social analysis for two particular reasons. First, it homogenizes all white people. As Cole argues, this is problematic because it overlooks the struggles of white workers in the capitalist system. When responding to the works of Charles Mills, for instance, Cole claims: "Mills . . . acknowledges that 'not all whites are better off than all nonwhites, but . . . as a statistical generalization, the objective life chances of whites are significantly better.' While this is, of course, true, we should not lose sight of the life chances of millions of working-class white people."[5] Related to this point, Cole argues that with this generalized conception of white supremacy, social movements have latched on to the concept of "abolishing whiteness" but treat it as synonymous with abolishing white people. Second, the concept of white supremacy is said to elide those "non colour coded racisms."[6] Cole argues that white-skinned folk across the West (e.g., many Jews, Italian, Irish, and Eastern European migrants) historically and currently suffer forms of racism, and the CRT literature tends to center a Black-white binary that prevents such forms of exploitation from being unearthed.

Needless to say, critical race theorists have effectively responded to these Marxist critiques, and these responses have followed different contours. The late Charles Mills, for instance, offered a more "open" reply to the Marxists, holding that CRT was "analogous to feminism: a broad political and theoretical movement within which there are multiple approaches."[7] For Mills, to talk of an antinomy between CRT and Marxism was to misunderstand both approaches, each of which could make space for the other (such that we have Marxist approaches in CRT and critical race approaches in Marxism). Mills's openness to CRT and Marxism is admittedly accurate in its reading of key "classics" in CRT: just as Kimberlé Crenshaw defends a Gramscian critique of liberal ideology, calling for an anti-racist counterhegemony in her canonical *Race, Reform, and Retrenchment*, Eduardo Bonilla-Silva's introduction to *Racism without Racists* freely references Marx's theory of ideology to explain the workings of racialized social systems.[8] While it would be unfair to assert that those from critical race and Marxist positions unequivocally talk past one another, it is perhaps appropriate to appreciate that many within the Marxist camp are relatively myopic in their readings of CRT.

Alongside the Marxist critiques put to CRT, decolonial thought has a slightly awkward relationship with Marxism. However, the issue here is not necessarily Marxist commentators dismissing decolonial thought. Rather, the more significant issue is decolonial thought's rejection of central (classical) Marxist tenets. In particular, this critique includes the following three points:

1. Marx endorsed a linear view of history and development. Decolonial thinkers have focused on the universalism that is implicitly assumed in classical Marxism. To such critics, Marx's account of the development and logic of capitalism relies on a parochial philosophy of history, which assumed that there is only one linear path for societal development (in which class struggle becomes the central "mover" of history). Like Hegel before him, Marx seemed to adopt the view that if you were outside this universal line of historical development, you were outside of history itself. To scholars such as Walter Mignolo, accounts of history offered by Marx thus put those outside the West "outside of history and behind modernity," rendering the colonized "'prehistoric' (or outside history), barbaric, uncivilized savages who should look to Europe for religion, work ethic, language, technology, and knowledge."[9] Indeed, this aspect of dialectical materialism means that decolonial thinkers are even skeptical toward some "Third World" or "Black radical" Marxists, given that they place some faith in a his-

torical teleology in which socialism and communism are necessary, eventual paths. Ramón Grosfoguel, for instance, lamented that Marxist anticolonial revolutionaries such as Víctor Raúl Haya de la Torre were still committed to an orthodox dogma that "all societies had to pass through successive fixed stages to achieve socialism," thus universalizing a model of political-economic development in Europe to the rest of the world.[10] Mignolo spells this critique out perhaps most explicitly when he charges Marxism with being a "modern European invention that emerged to confront, in Europe itself, both Christian theology and liberal economy (that is, capitalism)."[11] Given his claim that Marxism was Eurocentric, Mignolo repeats Grosfoguel's sentiment in the way he argues that "Marxism in the colonies and in the non-European world in general is limited for it remains within the colonial matrix of power that creates exteriorities in space and time (barbarians, primitives and underdeveloped)."

2. This philosophy of history led Marx to endorse a form of "democratic imperialism."[12] Given that Marx saw history and society evolving in one particular way, decolonial thinkers have criticized him for essentially recasting colonial interventions as the West putting the rest of the world on the path of social progress. This is particularly apparent in Marx's journalistic writings, especially on the Asian continent. An often cited example for this is Marx's comment that the British Empire's actions in Bengal brought the only social revolution ever heard of across the entire Asian continent: "English interference having placed the spinner in Lancashire and the weaver in Bengal, or sweeping away both Hindoo spinner and weaver, dissolved these small semi-barbarian, semi-civilized communities, by blowing up their economical basis, and thus produced the greatest, and to speak the truth, the only social revolution ever heard of in Asia."[13]

3. Marx's account of history was *empirically*—not just philosophically—flawed. Decolonial thinkers have pointed out at least two empirical reasons to be skeptical of not just the

philosophical, but also the historical, elements of classical Marxist theory. In particular, such scholars *push back* the origins of capitalism to the "discovery of the new world" in 1492. In doing so, such thinkers revise the classical Marxist idea that primitive accumulation is a precursor to the logic of capitalism, instead arguing that it is central to capitalist social formations. In classical Marxism, primitive accumulation are forms of accumulation—such as enslavement, settler colonialism, land expropriation, and land seizure—that created the basis for the capitalist mode of production *but were still precapitalist moments in history.* Those from the decolonial side stress that such forms of exploitation are still central to capitalism and always have been. Indeed, Utsa and Prabhat Patnaik claim that primitive accumulation is actually a central feature of twenty-first-century neoliberalism, both in the sense of *flow*, "where the average real incomes of the peasants and petty producers are squeezed," and in the sense of *stock*, whereby many are "deprived of their assets, either without any payment . . . or at throwaway prices."[14]

Of course, these three points are not to say that there simply is no room for Marxism in a decolonial tradition. This would go directly against the decolonial mission for horizontal epistemic dialogue. Part of the issue here, of course, is that there is a degree of porosity in the decolonial tradition, where we have the relatively contemporary "decoloniality" theorists (e.g., Maria Lugones, Mignolo, Aníbal Quijano), but we also have a large trajectory of intellectuals, social movements, and political figures who are claimed within this decolonial tradition (e.g., Franz Fanon, Kwame Nkrumah, members of the Bandung Conference, and so on). If we turn to the second of these two groups—the figures incorporated into the decolonial tradition retrospectively—then it is undeniable that there are inherent links between decolonial thought and anticolonial and Black radical Marxist theories. I have already referred to countless anticolonial revolutionaries and intellectuals who, in Fanon's words, "stretched" Marxism to think more precisely about the links among capitalism, colonialism, and enslavement. One such thinker—W.E.B. Du Bois—even went as far as to claim:

I believed and still believe that Karl Marx was one of the greatest men of modern times and that he put his finger squarely
upon our difficulties when he said that economic foundations,
the way in which men earn their living, are the determining
factors in the development of civilization, in literature, religion, and the basic pattern of culture. And this conviction I
had to express or spiritually die.[15]

The relationship between Marxism and decolonial theory may be
one of tension or of reworking, but it is not one of pure antagonism.
One of the most explicit decolonial critics of Marxism, Mignolo, even
makes this concession when thinking about the origins of the Zapatistas in Chiapas, Mexico. As he points out, when Rafael Guillén
helped form the Zapatistas, he came to Indigenous people of Chiapas
as a Marxist intellectual. Yet he realized that these Indigenous groups
already had their own cosmologies, as well as their own concepts and
desires for revolution. Moreover, he realized that "*his* Marxist ideology needed to be infected by Amerindian cosmology."[16] This led to
what Mignolo and others refer to as an epistemic humility:

In contrast to sixteenth-century missionaries who never doubt-
ed that converting people to Christianity was the right thing to
do [Guillén] understood that aiming to convert Amerindians
to Marxism was just a reproduction of the same logic of salva-
tion, albeit with a different content.[17]

From this epistemic humility, we can see an example of double
translation. Guillén, who adopted the name Subcomandante Marcos on the formation of the Zapatistas, encountered Indigenous people in the Lacandon Rainforest and formed a social movement with
them that involved horizontal relationships between epistemologies
and cosmologies. This, in turn, created a powerful blend of Marxist-
Leninist and Indigenous philosophies.

Briefly, therefore, those of the decolonial tradition often position
themselves against Marxist theory, but this does not mean they unequivocally reject Marxism.[18] Inside the decolonial tradition one can
clearly see a rejection of certain aspects of Marxism—in particular,
its story of modernity and capitalism beginning within Europe in

the industrial era and its linear view of "universal" history. However, because Marxist theory has been exported across the world—as
Mignolo states—it makes little sense for decolonial thinkers to neglect its role in the world system and development of anticolonial
imaginaries and movements. What is really being called for from
the decolonial perspective, therefore, is an epistemic humility among
Marxists to listen to and work with alternative cosmologies that have
been peripheralized in the colonial world system.

Broadly, therefore, it is quite evident that there is tension between
Marxism and CRT, and between Marxism and decolonial thought.
While this chapter is not about Marxism per se, this discussion was
worth bringing attention to, given that Marxist theory is perhaps one
of the most common critiques of capitalism flourishing in the social
sciences and humanities. However, this chapter shows how both CRT
and decolonial thought also develop meaningful critiques of capitalism and, specifically, neoliberalism. In particular, bringing these
critiques of neoliberalism together offers a balanced approach that
emphasizes the construction and exploitation of edge populations
nationally and transnationally. My secondary aim for this chapter is
to encourage those from more class-centric, classical Marxist positions to embrace epistemic humility and appreciate the convincing
critiques of capitalism that emerge from other perspectives. We can
begin this discussion by considering how first-wave CRT emerged
as a critique of how neoliberalism sustained the racial order, before
bracketing out the discussion more widely to consider the relation
between national and transitional edge populations.

Critical Race Theory and the "Culture" of Neoliberalism

Critical race theory shows that the culture of neoliberalism, as it developed in the United States, is inherently connected to the racial
ideology of color-blindness (or post-racialism).[19] This was one of the
main points of first-wave CRT in legal studies, and it remains a key
point now with the development of the racialized social systems approach.

When Crenshaw wrote *Race, Reform, and Retrenchment*, one of
her key points was that if neoliberalism is an economic agenda, neoconservativism is the cultural side of the same coin.[20] As she points

out, however, this neoconservativism as it developed in the U.S. post-civil rights era was inherently a racial ideology. It constellated around the ideas that the very existence of civil rights legislation meant that civil rights had actually been attained; that, contradictorily, we therefore no longer needed civil rights legislation; and that "race-specific civil rights policies [were] one of the most significant threats to the democratic political system."[21] In this culture of neoconservativism, emphasis was thus put on

> the need for strictly color-blind policies . . . the repeal of affirmative action and other race-specific remedial policies . . . an end to class-based remedies, and calls for the Administration to limit remedies to what it calls "actual victims" of discrimination.[22]

In this critique of the rising culture of neoliberalism in the 1970s and '80s, Crenshaw reels off multiple examples, including "Reagan's attempt to fire members of the United States Commission on Civil Rights, the Administration's opposition to the 1982 amendment of the Voting Rights Act, and Reagan's veto of the Civil Rights Restoration Act."[23] Most important to her critique, Crenshaw points out that neoconservativism relied on a culture of racial equivalence—the notion that no racialized group was entitled to a "head start" from a social policy and legal perspective. Prominent neoconservative thinkers such as Thomas Sowell argued that "the battle for civil rights was fought and won—at great cost—many years ago" and that anti-racists of the 1980s were shifting the demands away from equal treatment by law to *equal results.*[24] In Sowell's opinion, this was akin to fascism. Indeed, Sowell goes as far as to claim that shifting demands toward equal outcomes fueled antiwhite sentiments among Black folks, which, in turn, justifiably popularized hate-group affiliation among whites.[25]

In short, as articulated by Crenshaw, CRT emerged as a response to the ascendant culture of neoliberalism.[26] It emerged as a means of showing how color-blind, abstract claims of legal universalism would serve only to reproduce the racial order, and how, by sustaining such a color-blind vision of law, *actual pieces of civil rights legislation were being used to reproduce the very processes (e.g., educational segregation) they had been introduced to outlaw.*[27]

This critique of the culture of color-blindness imbued into neoliberal formations was also central to the educational and sociological CRT scholarship. In educational studies, for instance, research examined how neoliberal reforms of schooling were reproducing systemic racism.[28] As Gloria Ladson-Billings argued, since the 2000s schools across various U.S. states have cut spending on public education, meaning that the putative "urban schools" rely on private venture companies (such as Teach for America) to provide reserves of untrained, low-paid teachers.[29] A harrowing example of this neoliberal reform can be seen in the aftermath of Hurricane Katrina, where members of the United Teachers of New Orleans Union were all laid off and replaced by teachers from Teach for America. Similarly, in CRT's racialized social system approach, a large part of Bonilla-Silva's analysis of the "new racism" was the component of *abstract liberalism* expressed in color-blind ideology. As Bonilla-Silva argues, such abstract liberalism involves a commitment to some of the key cultural mores of neoliberalism: individualism and meritocracy, freedom of choice, and a belief in the state's noninterventionism. The commitment to these mores, Bonilla-Silva argues, leads to color-blind rationalizations of racial inequality: whites recast residential segregation as people gravitating toward those like them (individualism and choice); economic inequality is cast as the result of market processes and the failure of those at the bottom to "put in the work" (meritocracy); and equal opportunity laws are said to make affirmative action superfluous (belief in state noninterventionism).[30]

Straightforwardly, therefore, it seems as though neoliberalism has been an underlying current throughout the successive waves of CRT scholarship. I want to now stay with the racialized social system approach to show how CRT unearths the ways that neoliberalism uses racial ideologies and racialized organizations to produce and "fix" national abjects, in turn justifying various sociopolitical policies. My examples are drawn from the United States and Brazil.

National Abjects, Racial Ideology, and Neoliberalism

National abjects are similar to what other theorists have referred to as "disposable populations" or "racialized outsiders."[31] The key point is that as nation-states try to define themselves in particular ways, various populations are pushed to the borders of citizenship, recognition, and belonging—they are in the state but not necessarily *of* the state. Indeed, this was the premise of Du Bois's theory of double consciousness as it analyzed anti-Black racism in the United States and anti-Semitism across Europe.[32] Central to Du Bois's argument was that double consciousness involved a recognition from those racialized downward that they were not included in the spirit of their various social formations. As he summarized this tension:

> When I heard my German companions sing "Deutschland, Deutschland über Alles, über Alles in der Welt" I realized that they felt something I had never felt and perhaps never would. . . . I began to feel the dichotomy which all my life has characterized my thought: how far can love for my oppressed race accord with love for the oppressing country? And when these loyalties diverse, where shall my soul find refuge?[33]

Importantly, occupying the status of an abject population is not something that happens by coincidence. Populations have to be *made* abject or disposable; they have to *become* racialized outsiders. Indeed, this means that who occupies the position of abjection can change over time. Satnam Virdee makes this point presciently when he considers how the racialized outsiders in the British state shifted through the nineteenth and twentieth centuries, moving from Jewish migrants to Irish migrants to migrating citizens from the former colonies.[34] Critical race theory, and especially the racialized social system approach, offers convincing ways to show how racial ideologies produce national abjects, with this abjection then often being fixed by racialized organizations.

Consider, for instance, the rapid acceleration of neoliberalism in the 1980s United States. As scholars such as Angela Davis have shown, mass cuts to social welfare meant that by 1985 welfare recipients (53 percent of whom were Black) received a maximum of $111 a month; subsidized housing was cut by 63 percent while homelessness was rising; one million people were taken off food stamp rolls; and fewer than half of the nation's poor children were being reached by Aid to Families with Dependent Children programs.[35] At the same time, we see the true logic of neoliberalism: a shrinking "left hand" of the state, with a mass expansion of the right hand: between 1981 and 1985, military budgets totaled $1.2 trillion, and the Pentagon proposed $2 trillion more for the next five years.[36] This is a classic example of neoliberalism: shrinking state paternalism and nonin-terventionism in the realm of social welfare, but a commitment to accelerating "defense" spending and militarism. A significant way this neoliberal move was articulated was *through* racial ideology: ste-reotypes, racial meanings, and racialized stories, particularly around Black welfare queens and the related breakdown of the nuclear family.

The notion of "welfare queens" was evoked by Ronald Reagan in his 1976 presidential campaign. He painted a picture of a woman with "eighty names, thirty addresses, twelve Social Security cards . . . collecting veteran's benefits on four non-existing deceased husbands. . . . [S]he's got Medicaid, getting food stamps, and she is collecting welfare under each of her names. Her tax-free cash income is over $150,000." While he did not claim these welfare queens were all Black, race was encoded into the moral panic of welfare fraud and draining of resources. As Gregory Parks and Jeffrey Rachlinski state:

> Voters knew what he meant. . . . [Y]our taxes are high because Lyndon Johnson's programs are funneling your money to undeserving black women. These seemingly race-neutral campaign themes—welfare and crime—carry demonstrably racially loaded undertones.[37]

The racial ideology of Black welfare queens thus served a clear purpose for neoliberal cuts. As Davis summarizes, once the idea is produced that a sector of the population (Black women) is work-shy, draining the state's resources at the expense of the everyday taxpayer and expecting handouts from the state, it becomes relatively straight-forward to persuade people that the way to combat this is simply to stop "wasting" money on these underserving populations.[38] Indeed, this was the logic that underlay Reagan's Family Support Act in 1988, in which former recipients of welfare would be rewarded with "work-fare." In some cases, this involved having women pick up rubbish from the sides of roads in states such as New York for $1 an hour.[39] Thus, we have a straightforward example of how the production of racial imageries (the Black welfare queen), coupled with racial stories (single Black mothers draining the state's resources), connects with neoliberal policies (cuts to welfare, moving money to the right hand of the state) and norms (workfare over welfare, the state shouldn't provide handouts, people should work their way out of poverty).

While the case of welfare queens patently shows how racial ideology creates national abjects in neoliberal formations, I also mentioned that CRT can bring attention to how *racialized organizations* can fix the status of such national abjects. To clarify this, we can move to a different time and space of neoliberalism: Brazil in the twenty-first century. Within this century, Brazil has established itself as a global leading exporter of sugar. Along with beef, sugar has been a central part of Brazil's neoliberal project, as the state has become "one of the most vocal advocates of free market globalisation and the push to expand and liberalise global markets."[40]

Nevertheless, the process of Brazilian neoliberalism is inseparable from the workings of the state's racialized social system. Ian Carrillo demonstrates this in his study of sugar-ethanol mills in northeastern Brazil.[41] Such mills follow organizational patterns that are very similar to the country's long era of slavery, characterized by white owners of the land and organizations overseeing Black laborers working for little pay. Within this relationship of exploitation, not only do the white landowners control the labor time of the Black workers; they also control the *labor conditions.* As Carrillo shows, however, the labor conditions are made secondary to the quest for profit maximization, and neoliberal deregulation of markets means that poor working conditions are part and parcel of "productive" markets. Thus, Black workers are forced into various forms of dangerous labor practices that are said to be the "most productive" for the industry at hand, such as straw burning and manual harvesting. These tasks pose severe health risks to workers, sometimes to the point of death, with Carrillo pointing out that through manual harvesting "on a typical day, a cane-cutter sweats 8 liters, walks 8.8 kilometers, makes 133,332 machete strikes, and does 36,630 body twists."[42]

Importantly, just as with the case of Black welfare queens, these exploited workers of the sugar-ethanol mills *had to be made into national abjects.* This is where racial ideology again enters organizational structures—namely, white landowners are able to exploit these large reserves of Black labor and force these subjects into unsafe labor practices because of dominant representations of Blackness in the Brazilian racialized social system. As Carrillo argues, the white elites of Brazil see Black rural populations as "pre-disposed toward criminality" and argue that this criminality is "an innate tendency that cane work mitigates and suppresses."[43] In his fieldwork in northeastern Brazil, Carrillo recounts a mill director explicitly stating that

> government subsidies [are needed] for the sugarcane industry because of the social role mills played in controlling crime: "And the crime, the hunger, the robberies, the misery, it will all unfold, because the security belt for [the state capital] Recife is the sugar zone. If the mills close, there isn't enough police in the world for that. Everyone would be killed, hundreds killed, dozens every day."[44]

Racial ideology therefore again finds itself at the foundation of a neoliberal social formation. Just as with the case of welfare queens, racial representations (the innately criminal Black Brazilian; the work-shy, scrounging Black woman) and racial stories (if Black people are not doing manual labor, they will commit more crime; Black women are draining the state's resources) provide concrete foundations for justifying neoliberal socioeconomic policies. This is to say not that such policies would simply not be enacted without the construction of such national abjects but, rather, that the construction of such national abjects enables the neoliberal policies to attain greater hegemony.

From National Abjects to "Edge Populations": Capitalism as the Essence of Modernity/Coloniality

National abjects therefore can be thought of as being part of the "edge populations" central to the neoliberalized world system. The way that CRT can discuss such edge populations is focused on the level of the nation-state and nationally specific racialized social systems, thus justifying the focus on *national* abjects. By contrast, when decolonial theory turns analysis toward edge populations, its focus centers on the *transnational* abjects of the neoliberal world system.

In decolonial theory, capitalism is a story of peripheralization—a story of the very creation of edge populations. Indeed, within this approach capitalism is described as "the essence for both the conception of modernity and its darker side, coloniality."[45] Through arguing that capitalism is the essence of modernity/coloniality, decolonial advocates are able to highlight a number of points. One is that the West benefited from capitalism via its relations with (what was produced as) the non-West; these relations become central to the existence and reproduction of global capitalism. Here we have the straightforward "retelling" of the story of capitalism and modernity, as I alluded to earlier in the chapter. The central point that decolonial thinkers are making—which is, at least, sympathetic to the argument made by theorists of racial capitalism or Black radicalism—is that Western capitalism was never the result of "internal" factors of European culture or indigenous European social processes.[46] Rather, Western capitalism was fundamentally based on the West's colonial relations with "the rest" of the world. In other words, there was no "Western capitalism." There was only a global capitalist system *in which the West placed itself in the center,* consequently peripheralizing other geopolitical regions.[47] This origin story of capitalism is why intellectuals such as Fanon have famously claimed that

> Europe has stuffed herself inordinately with the gold and raw materials of the colonial countries: Latin America, China, and Africa. From all these continents, under whose eyes Europe today raises up her tower of opulence, there has flowed out for centuries toward that same Europe diamonds and oil, silk and cotton, wood and exotic products. Europe is literally the creation of the Third World. The wealth which smothers her is that which was stolen from the underdeveloped peoples.[48]

The point made by Fanon has been echoed by multiple decolonial and anticolonial thinkers. Even prior to Fanon's famous intervention, Eric Williams had discussed how colonialism and enslavement meant that capitalism "provided the sugar for the tea and coffee cups of the Western world. . . . [T]he rising capitalist class was becoming used to the idea of sacrificing human life to the deity of increased production."[49] Economists such as Utsa Patnaik have consequently theorized the "colonial drain" as a means of assessing precisely how much wealth (in the form of resources and labor) was transferred from colonies into the metropoles during colonialism.[50] Patnaik, for instance, predicts that in the case of India, more than £9 billion worth of capital was channeled into the British economy between 1765 and 1938.

Second, this organization of capitalism created fundamental relations between the European workers and the global proletariat. When Aimé Césaire declared that Western capitalism created the problem of the proletariat *and* the colonial problem, he was stressing that there was an inherent relation between the workers of Europe and those colonial and enslaved edge populations who had become peripheralized in the world system.[51] This is another point that is central to the decolonial critique of capitalism. Thinkers such as Gurminder Bhambra and Paul Gilroy, for instance, have used the example of cotton in the colonial era to illustrate this story.[52] Cotton and the textile industry are regularly seen as great success stories of British capitalism, wealth accumulation, and modernization; however, this story of cotton is one of transnational relations. The majority of "British cotton" was coming from plantation slavery in the United States. After being shipped to British docks and woven in British factories, the majority of this cotton was then exported to British colonies as a means of destroying indigenous markets. (Just under half of Britain's cotton was exported to India.) What we have here, therefore, is a linking between the labor of the enslaved in picking the cotton, the factory workers in Britain who then turned this cotton into textile commodities, and the exploited textile workers in India who consequently lost their labor because there was no need for cotton production given India's importation of this product from Britain.

This is not to say that decolonial thinkers posit an inherent solidarity between the workers of the West and the colonized and enslaved edge populations. In fact, the analysis points toward quite the contrary. Instead, decolonial thinkers often highlight how an investment in the project of modernity/coloniality has prevented Western workers from striving toward anti-imperialism and anti-racism.[53] As Du Bois commented in *Socialism and the Negro*: "I maintain that the English working classes *are* exploiting India . . . and the working classes of America *are* subjugating Santo Domingo and Haiti. . . . He is a co-worker in the miserable modern subjugation of over half the world."[54] Central to Du Bois's argument, as echoed more recently by Gargi

Bhattacharyya, is *not* that Western workers are prejudiced against the enslaved or colonized—though it may be true—but that the very existence of waged labor in the West, as capitalism developed and develops, relies on the exploitation of laborers in the peripheries of the world system who exist at the very "edges" of waged labor.[55] To clarify with this example: there could not have been exploitation of workers in Manchester's textile factories without first the enslavement of people to pick and process the cotton in the United States and the colonization of territories to which the cotton would be exported.

Third, importantly, decolonial thinkers stress how the former two points did not fundamentally change after "decolonization." In other words, Western-led capitalism *still* relies on relations of coloniality and *still* binds together exploited workers in the West with those edge populations across the peripheries. This is a point I reviewed in the Introduction and Chapter 1, when I analyzed how decolonial thinkers reject the narrative that the "decolonization" of most of the world amounted to a shift away from the colonial matrix of power. Instead of this narrative of progress—itself an illusion of modernity/coloniality—decolonial thinkers stress the continuities in the world system. Thus, when Du Bois wrote in 1954 that a "new phase of colonial imperialism" had emerged, he could have been talking about 2022:

> New York dictates the price of Cuban sugar, Haitian coffee and Dominican products while tin from Bolivia . . . coffee from Brazil, gold from South Africa, copper from Rhodesia, and uranium from Congo are all under foreign control and the native populations have their income and way of life dictated by powers outside their political control.[56]

As Manuela Boatcă argues, the post-decolonization era continued the colonial project of the "development of underdevelopment."[57] The difference mostly resided in which institutions now had the power to produce and legitimate those relations of coloniality. This, of course, is where neoliberalism figures into the decolonial critique of capitalism.

In particular, decolonial intellectuals highlight how multinational institutions such as the United Nations, International Monetary Fund (IMF), and World Bank play(ed) a crucial role in legitimating the colonial matrix of power after decolonization. The IMF and World Bank especially, as Mignolo highlights, became key institutions that "sanction[ed] the legitimacy of economic projects around the world" in Western interests.[58] As economists such as the Patnaiks have highlighted, the result of this mass institutional power given to organizations such as the IMF and World Bank is that the formerly colonized world has been forced into accumulating debt and gotten "caught in the vortex of globalized financial flows," all in the name of neoliberal development.[59] As Ha-Joon Chang has shown, as neoliberalism constellated around the Washington Consensus of free trade and deregulated markets, organizations such as the IMF were offering poor nations across Africa and Latin America loans to develop according to these neoliberal ideals.[60] This created a seemingly paradoxical situation in which poor countries were poor because of colonialism, and instead of reparations they were then offered "loans" to develop, *but* these loans (and, consequently, the vision of development) were conditional on the ideals and interests of the very geopolitical regions that had made these countries poor to begin with. Indeed, given the relations of power that underlay such "structural adjustment" loans, it is no surprise that these enforced economic policies have done little to actually "develop" those poor nations. They have just enabled the cheaper exploitation of already peripheralized regions, as evidenced in the fact that by 2020, the World Bank (ironically) was saying that the "debt burden of the least developed nations" had risen to $744 billion.[61]

The Edge Populations of Neoliberalism: A Conversation with Subcomandante Marcos

Inside the decolonial critique, therefore, is an acknowledgment that neoliberalism maintains relative stability in the global colonial matrix of power. It is for this reason that Subcomandante Marcos, spokesperson for the Zapatistas, has declared neoliberalism the fourth world war—a war "conducted between major financial centres . . . that are global in scale and with a level of intensity that is fierce and constant." As Marcos argues, this fourth world war has given birth to the finance bomb, and unlike the bombs at Hiroshima and Nagasaki, this new bomb does not simply destroy the polis (in this case, the nation) and bring death, terror and misery to those who live there; it also transforms its target into a piece in the jigsaw puzzle of the process of economic globalisation.[62]

I want to provide a brief overview Marcos's comments about this fourth world war to highlight how neoliberalism, as decolonial critique exposes, greatly expands the size of those edge populations in the world system, populations that are pushed further to the edges of wage labor and the edges of humanity and existence. While Marcos's famous polemic was written in 1997, I highlight his conceptual points by also making reference to the twenty-first century.

Central to Marcos's argument was that the fourth world war of neoliberalism involved seven pieces of a puzzle. They include the two-fold accumulation of wealth and of poverty, the total exploitation of the totality of the world, the nightmare of that part of humanity condemned to a life of migration wandering, the sickening relationship between crime and state power, state violence, the mystery of mega-politics, and increasing resistance that humanity is deploying against neoliberalism. I want to expand on Marcos's first two points about wealth, poverty, and exploitation.

When Marcos was writing in 1997, the richest 358 people had a greater combined annual income than half of the world's poorest inhabitants (approximately 2.6 billion people); decades later, in 2020, we see a similar statistic: the world's richest 1 percent own just under half of the total global wealth.[63] This widening at both poles, Marcos argues, is the essential logic of neoliberal "development," whereby "in its 'distribution' of wealth all it achieves is a two-fold absurdity of accumulation: an accumulation of wealth for the few, and an accumulation of poverty for millions of others."[64] As Marcos highlights, this process of wealth inequality happens *within* nations, but it is on a transnational scale that you can patently see how neoliberalism greatly expands the mass of edge populations in the world system. For instance, take a cursory look at the global concentration of poverty. You will see that about 84.3 percent of those in poverty live in "sub-Saharan" Africa and South Asia.[65] Indeed, focusing on sub-Saharan Africa, 40 percent of the population lives in extreme poverty (earning less than $1.90 a day), and the World Bank predicts that by 2030, 87 percent of the world's poorest are expected to live in this region.[66] These straightforward statistics echo Marcos's argument that neoliberalism "involves the exclusion of all persons who are of no use to the new economy"; the neoliberal world system provides no safety net for the vulnerable people of the world who, instead, are pushed to the margins of recognition and existence in global society.[67]

Connected to this polarization of rich and poor we have what Marcos refers to as the "globalisation of exploitation" or the "total exploitation of the totality of the world."[68] Namely, neoliberalism involves a seeming paradox to the bureaucrats of organizations such as the World Bank, United Nations, and IMF: while more people move into poverty, the size of "economically active" populations actually increases. In other words, neoliberalism creates a situation in which labor is not a guarantee of a living (or even surviving) wage. When Marcos was writing in 1997, for instance, he highlighted that, while the number of those living on less than $1 a day had risen from two hundred million to two billion between 1960 and 1990, the economically active population grew from 1.38 billion to 2.37 billion.[69]

Of course, what we then see is that because more people are becoming poor, they are forced into low-paid, dangerous labor in their quest for survival. Marcos's own example of this is child labor, whereby 146 million children in Asia were said to be working in manufacturing by 1997. Again, this is the logic of neoliberalism. What we have is a clear example of what Bhattacharyya describes when she comments on "those on the edge of capitalist formations with occasional entry to insecure waged work . . . unable to gain recognition or secure entry to the terms of capitalist citizenship in that location"—in other words, edge populations.[70] Further, as Bhattacharyya argues, such people are pushed to the edges not just of waged labor but also of *humane* labor. In other words, those pushed to the edges are also pushed toward the very boundaries of humanity. The making of global edge populations is thus structured by what Achille Mbembe terms *necropolitics*, an expression of power that relies on fundamental divisions between those worth and unworthy of life.[71] To stay with Marcos's example of child labor, in 2021 child labor remained concentrated in the Global South and had actually grown to 160 million, with 79 million of those children working in hazardous conditions.[72] Further, these children are not being exploited by local organizations, they are being forced into labor by the mega-multinational corporations of neoliberal finance, such as Mondelēz International (the owner of Cadbury), which employs children in Ghana because it can't afford to hire adults; Tesla, Apple, and Volvo, which rely on child labor in the Democratic Republic of Congo to supply cobalt; and Nestlé and Starbucks, which exploit child workers at the coffee farms of Guatemala.[73]

The edge spaces of neoliberalism, in this sense, are thus spaces of modernity/coloniality. For finance and profit to be funneled into a Western elite, spaces need to be made (and maintained) where people become simultaneously disposable (because they are not given worth or recognition and are dehumanized) and *essential* (because their "cheap" labor becomes the building block for productivity). Even as Mondelēz International saw its net revenues increase by 8 percent in 2021, it claimed it could not afford to hire adult labor in Ghana. Simply put, therefore, neoliberalism is a key site of critique for those of the decolonial tradition because it is in the expansion of transnational edge populations that we see the continuity of modernity/coloniality far into the twenty-first century.

On the National and Global Edges of Neoliberalism

It is evident, therefore, that both CRT and decolonial thought offer strong critiques of capitalism and, specifically, of its neoliberal expression. In short, both offer insights into how neoliberalism creates, and relies on, the existence of various edge populations. However, the way these two approaches actually define and study "edge populations" differs in a way that makes it important to bring CRT and decolonial thought together. While decolonial thought focuses on those edge populations forged via transnational flows of capital across the world system, CRT focuses more inward toward the national abjects of racialized social systems. Importantly, as per the ethos of this book, these approaches do not have to contradict each other.

If we go back to the example from this chapter of the exploitation of Black labor in Brazilian sugar mills, we can see how a both-and approach to CRT and decolonial thought is useful. Namely, while the exploitation of such Black labor is justified via local racial ideologies and organizations, the very industry of sugar itself is a transnational market in which Brazil is dominant. In this case, CRT may highlight the production of Black Brazilians as national abjects who become exploitable, but decolonial thought helps to remind us how these same people are also interpellated into transnational relations of economic and political power. To use another example from this chapter—on so-called Black welfare queens in the 1980s United States—CRT shows how such subjects were produced by racial ideologies to justify neoliberal social policies, but decolonial thought highlights how these neoliberal policies had transnational reverberations. In this case, the United States cut social welfare spending to reinvest in the military. The creation of "national abjects" at home to justify these welfare cuts was thus inherently connected to the United States' subsequent creation of edge populations across the Global South that resulted from its increased military interventions in the 1980s across Libya, Honduras, and the Persian Gulf.

This both-and approach to CRT and decolonial thought therefore gives us an ability to analyze the edge populations of neoliberalism in a way that is attentive to the national and transnational nature of capitalism, exploitation, and dehumanization in the world order. Of course, one key issue concerning this global, neoliberal expansion of capitalism is the acceleration of the draining of the world's natural resources. In the next chapter, I turn to this case to think about how CRT and decolonial thought offer complementary insights into accelerating climate crises.

4

Environmental Racism and the Logic of Coloniality

n 2020, Puerto Rico suffered its deadliest earthquake in one hundred years. In the previous year (2019), Cyclone Idai—the most powerful cyclone recorded in the Southern Hemisphere—swept through southeastern Africa, creating humanitarian crises in Mozambique, Zimbabwe, and Malawi; lack of rainfall created mass water shortages in India; and a record-high heat wave in southern Australia led to the destruction of vast amounts of land, including much of the Tasmanian forest. As the United Nations Climate Change Conference (COP) met in Glasgow in 2021—the twenty-sixth iteration of this conference—the message ought to have been patently clear that things are not going to get better without systemic change. Nevertheless, twenty-six COP conferences in, major geopolitical units were simply repeating the same message as the first meeting in 1995: that climate change threatens the existence of the planet, and this damage ought to be reversed. Why has the message not changed since 1995? Similarly, why have successive climate agreements and pledges—from the Kyoto Protocol in 1992 to the Paris Climate Agreement in 2016—failed to impede rapidly accelerating climate crises across the world?

Hegemonic powers in the world system—whether they are nation-states, the United Nations, super-corporations, or the Group of Seven—have largely sought to tackle accelerating climate crises through the same framework that created the crises in the first place: the framework of modernity/coloniality. None of these major hegemons in the world system, for instance, are going beyond the myopic philosophy of Western anthropocentrism; none are advocating for and implementing a new world system that is not based in capital accumulation; and none are implementing mass demilitarization. Instead, the suggestions for tackling global catastrophe seem to amount to *more capitalism* (under the guise of "green capitalism"), *more technological innovation* (under the justification that it can enable carbon capture), *more regulation of national borders* (because climate crises threaten national security), and *more individual responsibility* (under the slogan "We are all in this together"). This is the paradox that Boaventura de Sousa Santos describes when he comments on how coloniality has "disabled the global North from learning in noncolonial terms": modernity/coloniality has given way to climate crises and yet is also being offered as the solution to this global catastrophe.[1]

Further, while the Paris Agreement in 2016 and COP26 highlighted that the rich nations need to offer assistance to poor nations in their "green development," the systemic environmental racism happening *within* the so-called developed nations often goes unremarked. As COP26 was taking place in 2021, residents of Flint, Michigan, still did not have safe drinking water seven years after the city's water crisis started. In 2020, the year before COP26 took place, Ella Adoo-Kissi-Debrah, a nine-year-old Black girl in London who had died seven years earlier, was declared the first person in the United Kingdom to have air pollution listed as a cause of death, highlighting the poor air quality in the city's Black and Brown neighborhoods. Indeed, as COP26 was proceeding, the Amazon rainforest had just experienced its highest rate of deforestation in fifteen years, destroying wildlife and displacing Indigenous communities.

In this chapter, I want to show how CRT and decolonial thought can be used together to gain prescient insights into contemporary climate crises and environmental racism. This both-and approach is necessary because climate change is rooted in the logic of coloniality while it is also expressed and localized into nationally organized racialized social systems. Furthermore, by taking this both-and approach to CRT and decolonial thought we can pay due attention not just to the material but also to the *epistemic* roots of climate crises.

Indeed, I want to begin this chapter by considering some of these epistemic roots, and it will be a theme I return to at the end of the chapter when considering the mass epistemicide that has helped legitimate Western, anthropocentric humanism.

The "Perpetrator Perspective" of Environmental Racism

In 2022, the Biden administration announced that it would address the disproportionate effect that climate change has on people of color in the United States. Brenda Mallory, who as chair of the White House Council on Environmental Quality is responsible for this agenda, claimed:

> We are trying to set up a framework and a tool that will survive, and one that still connects to what the on-the-ground impacts are that people are experiencing. . . . I feel that we can do that based on *race-neutral criteria*.[2]

Here we have something that is not too dissimilar to the legal framework first-wave critical race theorists were critiquing in the post–civil rights era. Namely, there was federal recognition of racism, yet the legal frameworks used to ameliorate inequalities were ironically color-blind. As scholars such as Kimberlé Crenshaw and Derrick Bell highlighted, the U.S. federal response to racism was not *anti*racism but simply the legal enshrining of race-neutrality.[3] I therefore begin this chapter by reflecting on how the early CRT scholarship on the legal system's epistemology of race-neutrality remains appropriate when looking at how environmental racism works today.

A central avenue for linking first-wave CRT scholarship with the current focus on environmental racism is to consider what Alan David Freeman called the "perpetrator perspective" on racism.[4] Just as Eduardo Bonilla-Silva later critiqued the idea of "racism as prejudice," Freeman highlighted how post–civil rights legislation in the United States adopted a perpetrator perspective: an epistemology that defined "racial discrimination not as a social phenomenon but merely as the misguided conduct of particular actors."[5] Through this epistemology, Freeman argued that the legal system occluded a recognition of how law itself could be an instrument of structural racism and instead decided to focus on overt actions of individuals and institutions that could be labeled explicit, intentional, race-based discrimination.

First-wave critical race theorists stressed how this enshrined perpetrator perspective toward racism worked to reproduce structural racial inequalities. Take, for instance, Bell's criticism of legal reform since *Brown v. Board of Education*, the 1954 case that made it unconstitutional to segregate public schools by race. As he pointed out, a consequence of this case was that U.S. courts were much more concerned with questions of statistical, demographic desegregation (e.g., having schools that broadly represent the racial demographics of their district) than with questions of *educational quality* accessible to Black students. This is important because at the same time civil rights were being legislated, many whites feared the integration of Black folks into their public institutions and consequently took flight from urban areas to create white enclaves. This meant that while educational segregation was de jure unconstitutional, it was de facto still the norm. Indeed, the U.S. legal system was shaped such that such de facto segregation could not be understood as a form of discrimination; schools could be accused of segregation only if plaintiffs could prove that such segregation was itself the result of "discriminatory actions intentionally and invidiously conducted or organized by school officials"— a criterion of evidence that was both equivocal and nearly impossible to attain.[6] This is all testament to Crenshaw and her colleagues' claim that "civil rights reformism has helped to legitimize the very social practices—in employment offices and admissions departments—that were originally targeted for reform."[7]

Building on this early CRT scholarship, it therefore seems appropriate to ask how the legal system can account for processes such as environmental racism if it remains committed to a perpetrator perspective. Indeed, this question was already posed in critical legal studies in the 1990s, with the *Michigan Law Review*, for instance, producing a series of papers on environmental racism in 1992. Central to this legal studies scholarship was a recognition of a fact that remains true in the United States today: that "study after study confirms that poor people and people of color bear the disproportionate burden of not only toxic waste facilities, but air pollution, lead poisoning, pesticide poisoning, and garbage dumps. [I]n California, . . . three Class I toxic waste dumps—the dumps permitted to take almost every chemical known to science—are all situated in communities of people of color."[8]

When Luke Cole wrote the essay from which this quote is taken in 1992, he claimed that despite the evidence of environmental racism, and despite this stratification that seemed to transgress the Fourteenth Amendment, not a single plaintiff had successfully used a civil rights approach in federal or state courts to show the existence of environmental racism.[9] In response to this situation of the 1990s, Cole argued that there are two reasons that the answer to environmental racism does not lie in legal struggles. First, when campaigners against environmental racism place hope in the legal system, they in fact "play right into the polluters' hands":

> Struggles between a polluter and its host community pit the power of money against the power of people. Polluters generally have the money, while communities resisting toxic intrusion have the people. Thus, to take a dispute into court, where the polluters have the best lawyers, scientists, and government officials money can buy, can be a tactical mistake. It will often disempower community activists to take a struggle out of their hands and into court, where they have to rely on "experts" and outside help rather than their own actions.[10]

And second, Cole pointed out that to those seeking refuge in the legal system, "Civil rights law has so far miserably failed to combat racism, so why should we think that it will be better able to combat environmental racism?"[11] In other words, Cole reiterated the central first-wave CRT premise that the legal system, even in its race-equality framework, served to reproduce the racial status quo. If environmental racism is part of the racial status quo, as the evidence suggests, then seeking transformation via the legal system merely takes you around in circles.

While Cole was writing in the 1990s, his first-wave CRT approach still rings true. Laura Pulido, for instance, reiterates Cole's points in the context of the twenty-first century.[12] As she shows, most of the legal options for combatting environmental racism in the United States get dismissed by the various courts. By 2017, for instance, all eight lawsuits against environmental racism that used the equal protection clause of the Fourteenth Amendment had failed. The primary reason these cases failed was that none of them could prove discriminatory intent—that is, they could not satisfy the perpetrator perspective of racism that had been adopted decades previously. Second, various campaigners saw hope in Title VI complaints, given that under the Civil Rights Act public agencies receiving federal funds are prohibited from discriminating. In this remit, campaigners had filed 298 Title VI complaints with the Environmental Protection Agency (EPA) by 2014, but only one has been successful.

Indeed, Pulido shows that the legal system is not just ignoring but actively accelerating environmental racism. For instance, in 1994 President Bill Clinton issued Executive Order 12898, which required all federal agencies to consider the environmental justice implications of their activities.[13] As Pulido shows, a 2003 Civil Rights Commission set out to evaluate how this executive order had been implemented by the EPA, Department of Housing and Urban Development, Department of Transportation, and Department of the Interior. It found that it had not resulted in any change in environmental racism across the United States; in fact, as Elizabeth Gross and Paul Stretesky point out, Executive Order 12898 is not even directly enforceable in the courts.[14] Second, as Pulido shows, various states were actually using the legal system to further legitimate environmental racism in the name of—ironically—fighting climate change. A key example of this is California's Global Warming Solutions Act, passed in 2006. While it attempts to regulate pollution across the state, the act also signaled a commitment to "cost-effective" solutions to private corporations to ameliorate their environmental hazards. As Raoul Liévanos shows, this essentially meant that California had given the go-ahead to private corporations to continue their toxic dumping across the state—primarily in rural Latino/a and Black neighborhoods—if it could be proved to be cost-effective.[15]

Central to Pulido's argument, which itself builds on first-wave CRT scholarship, is, therefore, that the courts are not a straightforward ally in the battle against environmental racism. On the one hand, the legal system's commitment to a perpetrator perspective of racism—which centers intentional discrimination—makes it near impossible to successfully *prove* environmental racism as a structural feature of the U.S. racialized social system. On the other hand, even when executive orders and federal or state laws and projects have been put forward to combat environmental racism, they have tended to either reproduce or augment it.

What we see in this case of environmental racism is thus a central premise of CRT: that legal epistemology is being used to reproduce structural racism. To put it in the language of CRT's racialized social systems approach, legal epistemology is being used to reproduce the unequal distribution of environmental resources across the racial hierarchy. I use this language deliberately because it allows us again to see how CRT—whether from its legal studies or its sociological iteration—can provide prescient insights into the workings of environmental racism. People of color's disproportionate exposure to air pollution, extreme temperatures, toxic dumping, unsafe water, and so on is not an aberration but is built into the workings of the racial structure. In a sense, as Pulido argued, people of color and their neighborhoods across the United States function as a "sink" or "drain" for the disposal of the United States' ever-accumulating environmental waste.

From the Perpetrator Perspective to *Buen Vivir*: Resisting the Environmental Drain

Interestingly, decolonial scholars also have addressed transnational environmental racism through the metaphor of the drain, albeit to highlight a separate process from the one described in the previous section. Prior to Utsa Patnaik's work that lucidly used the metaphor of the drain to signal the draining of the Global South's wealth to the Global North during colonialism, decolonial thinkers had stressed the draining of the Global South's *natural resources* for the West's capital accumulation.[16]

In fact, this concern for the draining of the South's natural resources means that decolonial thinkers were theorizing about environmental catastrophe long before it moved into the mainstream of Western social science.[17] For instance, when Syed Hussein Alatas sketched out why we need an autonomous sociology that breaks from the Western tradition, one of his points was that this would allow us to reflect on issues such as the climate crisis—or the "degradation of the environment"—that are central to the lives of people in the Global South.[18]

Similarly, in calling for a delinking from Northern theory, Raewyn Connell points out that in the Global South it is "hard to get worked up about reflexive modernity or shifting subjectivities" when you are facing daily realities of phenomena such as the "climate disaster."[19]

Part of the reason climate crises have been focused on within the Southern standpoint is that decolonial thinkers spotted the link between modernity/coloniality and the destruction of the environment in the name of capital accumulation. Almost a century ago, W.E.B. Du Bois commented on how the driving logic of neocolonial capitalism was "private profit from low wages of colored workers and low prices for *priceless raw materials* over the earth."[20] As Du Bois argues, modernity/coloniality—fostered through the actions of empires that wanted to hoard, capitalize on, and profit from the world's resources—was always committed to the destruction of the environment in the name of economic growth. Enrique Dussel summarizes this logic of modernity/coloniality and environmental destruction when he comments that

capitalism, mediation of exploitation and accumulation (effect of the world-system) . . . is later on transformed into an independent system that from out of its own self-referential and autopoietic logic can destroy Europe and its periphery, *even the entire planet.*[21]

From a decolonial perspective, therefore, there has long been a recognition that modernity/coloniality—in the form of extractivist capitalism—involves the draining of natural resources from the land of the Global South to the profits of Western nation-states and companies. Indeed, Indigenous communities and scholars have consistently tied their critiques of settler colonialism to capitalist land destruction. The Standing Rock Sioux's resistance to the Dakota Access Pipeline in 2016 and the United Tribes of Bristol Bay's resistance to toxic rock mining are just two examples of Indigenous communities in the Global North having their land drained of its resources, causing dire ecological consequences, all for the sake of capital accumulation.[22] Furthermore, if anything, this draining has accelerated as neoliberalism has ascended. Ironically, even market-based shifts to become more environmentally friendly—such as with the case of electric cars instead of those that use

internal-combustion engines—still rely on the same pattern of draining natural resources from the South (e.g., in the form of cobalt and
the land needed for cobalt mines), with the profits then being taken
by foreign companies (Tesla, Ford Motor, etc.).[23]

Through the Global South's being treated like a drain since the
beginning of colonialism, we have thus reached a situation whereby
a world system created by the West destroys land across the Global
South while the environmental consequences of this system also disproportionately affect those across the South. While organizations
such as the COP repeat slogans that everyone is in the climate crisis together and Western social scientists have woken up to the fact
that humans are now "geological agents" in the so-called age of the
Anthropocene, this all fails to recognize how the Global South is
the least culpable in fueling climate crises and yet faces the greatest
threats of impeding climate catastrophes.[24] As scholars such as Leon
Sealey-Huggins have pointed out, this means that Western-led institutions have produced apparently "global" policies to address climate
change—such as in the pledge to limit global warming to 2 degrees
Celsius by 2050 in the Paris Agreement—that fail to recognize that
these policies would be disastrous to the non-West.[25] In the Caribbean, for instance, temperature increases of 1.5 degrees Celsius by
2050 could spell the end of the entire region.[26] This recognition of the
West's false universalism of the climate crisis was sharply critiqued by
Prime Minister Mia Mottley of Barbados, who addressed the West at
COP26 by stating, "We do not want that dreaded death sentence, and
we have come here today to say, 'Try harder.'"[27]

Nevertheless, unlike the U.S. legal system that adopts a perpetrator perspective on environmental racism, we have seen cases across
the Global South of using Indigenous cosmology—enshrined into
law—to address extractivist capitalism and the environmental consequences it engenders. This is captured in the case of *buen vivir* and
sumak kawsay.[28]

Delinking from "Development"

The notion of *sumak kawsay* derives from the language of the Quechua peoples, an Indigenous community stretched predominantly
across the Andes. According to Santiago Garcia Álvarez, *sumak kaw-*

say is a cosmology based in three principles: relationality (the inter-connection of all beings in and to the world), reciprocity (the duty of all these relational parts to care for one another), and connection (the idea that all relational parts can fit together in a harmonious whole).[29] Drawing on this Indigenous cosmology, *sumak kawsay* in Bolivia is said to entail the philosophy of *vivir bien* (living well); similarly, in Ecuador it is said to entail *buen vivir* (good living).

Central to *sumak kawsay*, therefore, is a recognition that—in vir-tue of the recognition, reciprocity, and connection among all things—humans have a fundamental duty to look after the natural world (just as the natural world looks after us). Taking this Quechua cosmology seriously, Ecuador used the position of *sumak kawsay* in 2008 to en-shrine the "rights of nature" in its constitution; this was then followed by Bolivia making the same addition to its constitution in 2009. Ar-ticle 10 of the Ecuadorian Constitution holds that the universal rights extended to "persons, communities, peoples, nations and communi-ties" are also extended to nature. Articles 71–72 hold that nature has the right to integral respect and the right to be restored. Following this, Article 73 gives the state the ability to "apply preventive and restrictive measures on activities that might lead to the extinction of species, the destruction of ecosystems and the permanent alteration of natural cycles," while Article 74 returns to *buen vivir* to claim that "persons, communities, peoples, and nations shall have the right to benefit from the environment and the natural wealth enabling them to enjoy the good way of living."

While the 2009 Bolivian Constitution recognized the importance of protecting nature, it was not until the Law of the Rights of Mother Earth was enacted in 2010 that nature was formally recognized in law as having particular rights. As Paola Villavicencio Calzadilla and Louis Kotzé show, through the Law of the Rights of Mother Earth and the later Framework Law 300 of Mother Earth and Integral De-velopment for Living Well (2012), Bolivia stressed various principles of note, including:

> *Harmony*, requiring that "human activities, within the frame-work of plurality and diversity, must achieve a dynamic balance with the cycles and processes inherent in Mother Earth."

Defense, requiring that the "state and any individual or collective person . . . respect, protect and guarantee the rights
of Mother Earth for the well-being of current and future
generations."

Anti-commercialization, requiring that "neither living systems
nor processes that sustain them . . . be commercialized or
serve anyone's private property."

Multiculturalism, stating that "the exercise of the rights of
Mother Earth requires the recognition, recovery, respect,
protection, and dialogue of the diversity of feelings, values,
knowledge, skills, practices, transcendence, transformation, science, technology and standards of all the cultures
of the world who seek to live in harmony with nature."[30]

Taking the Bolivian and Ecuadorian cases together, we thus see a
completely different legal framework from that, for instance, of the
United States. As the CRT literature highlighted in the case of the
United States, while federal and state laws maintained some commitment to protecting the environment, the commitment to a color-blind
epistemology and perpetrator perspective of inequality meant that it
often reproduced rather than ameliorated environmental racism. By
contrast, the Bolivian and Ecuadorian cases show at least the foundations—if not yet realized—of a legal framework that does not just
allow for, but actively encourages, a delinking from the extractivist
global economy that is destroying the planet.

In Ecuador, for instance, the constitutional protection of nature,
and *buen vivir*, directly translates into political rhetoric and attempted economic policies to delink from extractivist capitalism. As the
preamble to the 2008 Constitution reads: "We . . . [h]ereby decide to
build a new form of public coexistence, in diversity and *in harmony
with nature*, to achieve the good way of living, the *sumak kawsay*"
(emphasis added). In this enshrining of coexistence and harmony,
Ecuador used the constitution to justify a plan to move away from a
petroleum-exports model of economic development toward a "post-
petrol economy" that generates wealth through "biodiversity applica-
tions, bio- and nano-technology, and a vibrant ecological and com-
munitarian tourism sector."[31] A good example of this can be seen,
for instance, in President Rafael Correa's campaign against the en-

vironmental damage Chevron-Texaco did to the Amazon between 1964 and 1990, which resulted in two Ecuadorian courts ordering the company to pay $18 billion and $9.5 billion in reparations. We see a similar shift in political rhetoric and economic policy in Bolivia, where under the presidency of Evo Morales gas and mineral companies were nationalized to protect Bolivia from foreign extractivism, allowing the state to maintain sovereignty over resources and return the profits to the people. This has reduced the proportion of people living in poverty from 60.6 percent of the population in 2005 to 43.4 percent in 2012, while the disparity in income between the richest 10 percent and the poorest 10 percent has narrowed from a ratio of 128:1 in 2005 to 60:1 in 2012.[32]

Of course, I do not want to give the impression that the enshrining of the rights of nature in Bolivian and Ecuadorian law has been unequivocally successful in its mission. Since the two states adjusted their constitutions in 2008 and 2009, environmental activists and Indigenous groups have constantly had to hold them to account for transgressing their own frameworks of *sumak kawsay*.[33] Indeed, Indigenous activism against the two states especially has highlighted how the constitutional and legal enshrining of *sumak kawsay* amounts to a form of epistemic colonization, whereby the commitment to living in harmony with nature runs in direct contradiction to the states' ongoing practices of extractivism.[34] The Yasuní-ITT initiative is a case in point. In 2007, the Ecuadorian government claimed it would stop exploiting the oil reserves in the Amazon's Yasuní National Park but went directly against this promise when it recommenced oil extraction in 2016.[35] Similarly, in Bolivia Morales went directly against the rights of nature when the government secured a highway that ran through the biodiverse Isiboro Sécure National Park and Indigenous Territory in 2017.

However, despite the contradictions that continue to run through Bolivia and Ecuador, I have included them as examples because they provide insights into *possible futures*. As Adriana Angel and Luis Miguel López-Londoño argue, these two cases are part of a wider trend on the Latin American left that involves attempting to create "an alternative and Indigenous model . . . independent of multilateral organizations, participating in environmental summits, rejecting neocolonialism, adopting practices of good living, and exercising sovereignty over resources" in a context in which this has been denied to the Americas—first by colonialism and then by neoliberalism (implemented by the likes of the United Nations, World Bank, and International Monetary Fund).[36] While Bolivia and Ecuador have not fully detached from the destructive practice of extractivism, they show where the possible delinking may come from. In particular, by building a constitution or legal framework around Indigenous cosmology/cosmologies, such states bring valuation to those knowledges that have been devalued via epistemicide and show how epistemological alternatives to Western universalism offer alternate models of existence and social, political, and economic life to Western-led capitalism. Centering these Indigenous cosmologies—and, more important, honoring them—offers a way to reconceptualize the currently exploitative relationship between humans and "nature" that exists in our current global economy. It is for this reason that I now turn toward a greater engagement with epistemology, highlighting, in particular, how climate crises cannot be prevented in a world system that gives primacy to Western anthropocentrism.

Human-Nature Binaries and the Coloniality of Knowledge

I began this chapter with a discussion of epistemology, to which I now return. In particular, I looked at how *legal* epistemology in the United States was allowing for the reproduction of environmental racism. Indeed, epistemology then implicitly ran through the chapter as it looked at how the Western epistemology of development—centered on extractivism and draining resources for profit—remains hegemonic in the world system, despite its environmental consequences, which are felt most intensely across the Global South. The case of *sumak kawsay* was then introduced as an example of how an alternative epistemology can help tackle accelerating climate crises by enshrining legal rights to nature. In this penultimate section of the chapter, I center the discussion of epistemology by focusing on the coloniality of knowledge, analyzing how the cosmology of Western humanism and anthropocentrism provides an immutable barrier to addressing climate crises.

Through the coloniality of knowledge, not only has the binary of humans and nature been reproduced, but a hierarchical relation between the two has become the basis for social, political, and economic life. Indeed, part of the reason that Black people were exploited and enslaved, for instance, was that European theology and science had decided they were closer to animals (and thus of the "natural world") than humans.[37] Inside the human-nature binary, therefore, is first a supposition of a hierarchy whereby humans are at the top of the chain. In this hierarchical relationship, nature is construed as a "resource to be exploited for profit." In other words, nature is constructed as an *instrument* for humans to use to enrich their own lives and maintain their superiority.[38]

As Dipesh Chakrabarty shows, it was particularly around the time of the Enlightenment, in the eighteenth century, that the nature-human binary of Western social thought came to the fore.[39] Particularly in political theories of that era, Western intellectuals became fixated on questions of freedom and liberty but failed to recognize that the environment was a key *agentic* subject in the distribution of freedom and liberties.[40] Neither were these intellectuals recognizing how, at this time of Enlightenment, the rise of capitalism meant that human-made processes were rapidly damaging the environment in a way that would constrain the liberties and freedom of many people in the present and future. As Chakrabarty put it:

In no discussion of freedom in the period since the Enlightenment was there ever any awareness of the geological agency that human beings were acquiring at the same time as and through processes closely linked to their acquisition of freedom. Philosophers of freedom were mainly . . . concerned with how humans would escape the injustice, oppression, inequality, or even uniformity foisted on them by other humans or human-made systems. Geological time and the chronology of human histories remained unrelated.[41]

Not only, therefore, was there a human-nature binary in this era, but, importantly we see an (erroneous) overlooking of nature to think about issues pertinent to humans. Importantly, this bifurcation and—to an extent—ignorance also influenced post-Enlightenment critical social thought in the West. For example, while there was a recognition of humankind's desire to control nature in Marxism and the subsequent critical theory of Max Horkheimer and Theodor Adorno, they still insisted on starting with a binary between humanity and nature.[42] Indeed, even within those critical Marxist traditions that recognized that the geological could constrain human action and life, this recognition was seen as describing more of a hypothetical state of affairs than something that was being actualized. This is perhaps best captured in the philosophy of Stalinism, which recognizes geological power but simultaneously rejects that that power can ever be realized. As Stalin commented:

> Geographical environment is unquestionably one of the constant and indispensable conditions of development of society and, of course [it] accelerates or retards its development. But its influence is not the determining influence, inasmuch as the changes and development of society proceed at an incomparably faster rate than the changes and development of geographical environment. In the space of 3000 years three different social systems have been successfully superseded in Europe: the primitive communal system, the slave system and the feudal system. . . . Yet during this period geographical conditions in Europe have either not changed at all, or have changed so slightly that geography takes no note of them. And that is quite natural. Changes in geographical environment of any importance require millions of years, whereas a few hundred or a couple of thousand years are enough for even very important changes in the system of human society.[43]

What we see in the case of Western social thought, therefore, is that the binary of humans and nature, where agency is only properly ascribed to the former, significantly constrains the possibility of creating a new epistemic basis for a world system that doesn't rely on destroying natural resources for its reproduction. This is why decolonialists have called for us to learn collectively from, for instance, Indigenous people who have been dealing with climate crises from the birth of colonialism.[44] For centuries, Indigenous people across the world have had to deal with the destruction of their environments by settler colonialists in the name of capital accumulation, and they are therefore the best placed people from whom we can learn about how to deal with climate crises. As Franco Cassano puts it, "A world suffocated by unlimited growth needs to *discover the wisdom of a way of life that does not seek to violate the earth but rather recognizes the limits of exploitation.*"[45] Part of learning from this wisdom, decolonial thinkers emphasize, involves acknowledging the importance of fostering a new form of planetary universal humanism in which we recognize the shared existence between humans and the natural world as finite beings. As Namita Goswami puts it:

> Climate change, as the singular crisis putting at risk the very possibility of human culture, as we have known it, is the ground upon which a new understanding of global multicultural reality and postcolonial antiracist theory must be developed. I argue that this *global multicultural reality must include the cultural reality of our lives as animals.*[46]

What is partially ironic, importantly, is that outside of the epistemic confines of the West it is incredibly common to view humans as *one of many* agentic beings on the planet. In this infinite number of "border perspectives," realizing a "global multicultural reality" is facilitated by the recognition that humans are not the only beings with subjectivity and agency and that *all* beings on the planet are fundamentally linked to one another. Walter Mignolo and Catherine Walsh summarize the varying iterations of this view as it gets articulated from Indigenous epistemologies in the Andes to Daoism and Taoism in China:

> Now, taking a cursory look at Daoism, one finds that the concept of *nature* in Western (west of Jerusalem) medieval Christianity, and in Western civilization after it, hides more than it reveals. . . . *Qi* cannot be translated as "nature"; it must be translated as "energy": the energy of the living *in the* living universe, named *Pacha* (cosmos) and Pachamama (Earth) in the Andean civilizations and Gaia (the Earth) and Cosmos in ancient Greece—it is the energy that enables living organisms that are able to define themselves in relation to all other organisms in *Convivencia*. . . . Qi is the energy that must be governed by the complementarity and harmony of *yin-yang*. . . .

Like *tinku* in Andean philosophy and other Indigenous cosmologies in the great civilizations of the Americas shattered by European invasions, yin-yang involves the constant search for harmony and equilibrium, and is the goal of living organisms endowed with the capacity to define themselves/ourselves as particular entities in convivial or antagonistic relation to other living organisms. In Taoist or Daoist philosophy, the diversity of living that Western epistemology reduced to *nature* does not exclude the spiritual and the social.[47]

Indeed, it is not a coincidence that Mignolo and Walsh can move from a discussion of Andean cosmologies to Daoism *without* imposing any universalism or homogenization. They can do this because there are numerous border perspectives that, while articulated in their own locales, can *relate to one another* in the way they conceive of agency and the various forms of social organization that can be based on the recognition of nonhuman agencies. The examples briefly mentioned by Mignolo and Walsh, for instance, can easily be put into conversation with a disparate cosmology we see in Hawai'i. Native Hawaiian cosmology centers on *aina*, which translates roughly as "land that feeds." The very view of "land" espoused here, as Jennifer Darrah-Okike reminds us, is "akin to a familial elder that nurtures humans and binds them in relationships of caretaking."[48] In virtue of viewing land as a nurturing elder, this means that *aina* is something that has to be treated with respect and recognition and, indeed, is something with which humans are in an ongoing relationship of coexistence and conviviality. As Manulani Aluli Meyer summarizes, even the Hawaiian greeting *aloha*—which translates literally as "to share breath"—is part of a way of life that constantly situates humans as being parts within a larger, natural environment.[49] Through this constant acknowledgment of *aina* and our relationship and duties toward it, Meyer clarifies,

> Indigenous people are all about place. Land/*aina*, defined as "that which feeds," is the everything to our sense of love, joy, and nourishment. Land is our mother. *This is not a metaphor.* . . . Because of the high mobility of Americans and billboards as childhood scenery, many find this idea difficult to compre-

hend. Land/ocean shapes my thinking, my way of being, and *my priorities of what is of value.*[50]

From just this cursory overview of Hawaiian cosmology, along with Mignolo and Walsh's comment, we see that there are border perspectives that acknowledge the agency of things Western social thought simply relegates to the static concept of "nature." Remember, these perspectives are *border perspectives* because Western universalism and the coloniality of knowledge have pushed them to the peripheries of the world system. Importantly, given that there are so many border perspectives that center nonhuman agency—whether it is the Andean conception of *achachilas*, the Hawaiian concept of *aina*, or the Shi'a Islamic principle of "oneness"—it means that there are an infinite number of possibilities for these border perspectives to help displace the current centralized Western epistemic core. My question—or, perhaps, my point—therefore is to ask: "What would happen if all of these border perspectives that were devalued in the name of epistemicide came together to displace Western universalism?" and "What kinds of social and economic organization can we build once we have a pluriversal recognition that humans are only one of many agentic beings?" The answer is straightforward, of course: if we genuinely committed to the view of (what we refer to as) "nature" as being a nurturing, agentic entity with which we have a communal bond, then we probably would not seek to use this nurturing agent as a source of ever increasing capital accumulation until its (and our) collective death. Yet what we have at the present time is a *minority epistemology*—an epistemology that is almost exclusive to the West—at the very core and foundation of our world system. Perhaps by realizing that this is a minority position—as I come to in the Conclusion—we can start to imagine various possible futures in which the majority of the world's peripheralized people can help sustain a more harmonious form of social, economic, and political life. For the time being, perhaps, this may remain little more than wishful thinking.

Returning to the Call for Theoretical Synergy

It may seem as if, in this discussion of non-Western ways of thinking about the environment, we have traveled quite far away from the chapter's beginning focus on the U.S. legal system and environmental racism. To an extent, this is the whole purpose of the book, and it is certainly the purpose of the chapter. When we take a concrete global social problem such as climate crises, both CRT and decolonial thought help us to understand different dimensions of the overall phenomenon. We are able to see, for instance, how environmental catastrophes get buried in racialized social systems and in the overall world system in a way that disproportionately affects those at the bottom of the respective hierarchies. Similarly, we are able to see how the epistemological frameworks developed by the dominant—whether via legal epistemology in the United States or the commitment to a static view of nature in Western social thought—help to reproduce the existence of climate crises and the inequalities they further engender.

Of course, one thing that is particularly ironic is that, despite all of the inequalities we have discussed in relation to climate crises, a regular message that gets recirculated by organizations such as the United Nations is that we are all in this together. Through this universalist discourse we hear a subsequent call for all humans, nation-states, geopolitical regions, and so on to come together to battle one of the greatest existential threats of our age. Indeed, such universalist calls to "come together" also came to the fore during the emergence of the COVID-19 pandemic in 2020. In that case, various organizations and political leaders called for a "great reset" in which we could "build back better." But as the next chapter explores, that great reset did not, and was never going to, materialize.

5

When Universalism Kills,
When Post-racialism Exonerates

COVID-19 and the Myth of a "Great Reset"

When the COVID-19 pandemic spread into the West in early 2020, myth and rumor took center stage. Indeed, some of the rumors pertained to the virus itself: how it spread, its origins, why it was so lethal (and *whether* it even was lethal), what the best methods of containment were, how to tell if someone had it, and so on. Alongside these rumors were potent myths: that the global spread of a virus required nations to adopt stricter border controls; that the virus was brought to the world by China (or Chinese culture); that the virus did not even exist; and, perhaps one of the most potent myths of all, that the pandemic would allow, in the words of the World Economic Forum of 2020, for a great "reset" of national and global distributions of wealth, welfare, and work.

The motto "Build Back Better" became one of the key points of political convergence at the 2021 Group of Seven (G7) meeting of Canada, France, Germany, Italy, Japan, the United Kingdom, the United States, and the European Union. Underlying the call to build back better was, first, an argument that *the world* needs to be better prepared for future global crises; and second, that COVID presented the perfect opportunity to hit a reset button on global and national governance. Of course, the irony of the G7 endorsing a Build Back

Better World initiative *even though there is only one non-Western na-tion* in this organization did not seem to occur to any of the group's members. Indeed, the fact that the West was able to admonish the whole world for not being well prepared for a global crisis seemed to be a crude application of Western universalism: it overlooked a whole range of cases across the Americas, Asia, and Africa in which the pandemic was being handled much more appropriately than within the West.

This chapter challenges the narrative that any reset, let alone a "great reset," was facilitated by the crisis of the pandemic. In fact, this chapter will take the opposing view—namely, that the pandem-ic managed to simply expose and exacerbate existing inequalities globally and in national racialized social systems. Focusing particu-larly on the emergence of the pandemic in early 2020, I look spe-cifically at the United States and the United Kingdom, showing a double process in both cases. First, in both countries existing racial inequalities were exacerbated by the emergence of the pandemic, which is patently clear when one looks at the high COVID-19 death rates of people of color. I show how key organizations and institu-tions in these two nations drew on post-racial ideology to exoner-ate the state from responsibility for these inequalities by arguing that the high death rates of people of color had to do with cultural or "natural" factors. Second, I show how both the United Kingdom and the United States adopted an expression of Western universal-ism, or imperial metrocentrism, that led them to reject the possibil-ity of learning from other geopolitical regions (especially across the non-West) that were protecting their populations much more ef-fectively from the virus. It was largely due to this refusal to learn from the non-West that the United Kingdom and the United States suffered high rates of COVID cases and deaths in the first place, exacerbating their extant inequalities. Coming back to the theme of the book, therefore, I show how a balance between decolo-nial thought and critical race theory (CRT) shows the connections between a transnational, historical process (Western universalism) exacerbating inequalities at a more local level (of the nation's ra-cial order), then being explained away by a dominant racial ideology (post-racialism).

"Certain Ethnicities Are More Susceptible to Coronavirus": On the Search for the Elusive White Gene

In January 2021, the United Kingdom had the highest COVID-19 death rate in the world.[1] Home Secretary Priti Patel was interviewed in the national press about why this death rate was so high. Among her answers, she said that "certain ethnicities are more susceptible to coronavirus."[2] Of course, what this answer seemed to curiously overlook were the millions of people, spread across hundreds of nations, who were classified as "not white" and yet were not dying at disproportionate numbers, as was being recorded in Britain. Shortly before Patel's comment, Donald Trump had pondered the same issue, asking:

> We're seeing tremendous evidence that African Americans are affected at a far greater percentage number than other citizens of our country. But why is it that the African American community is so much, numerous times more than everybody else? We want to find the reason to it.[3]

Across the United Kingdom and the United States there was a recognition that people of color were dying of COVID at higher rates than whites, but very little attention was paid to how social factors and structural racism explained this "medical" finding. Instead, more attention was paid to a mythical "white gene" that allowed for whites to significantly bypass COVID mortality at higher rates than people of color; to the various comorbidities that put people of color at risk (without attention to why various comorbidities exist in the first place); and to various cultural deficiencies, which implied that people of color were partly to blame for their high death rates. As Britain's Health Secretary Matthew Hancock summarized, there was simply a recognition that *not racism* but "being Black, or from a minority ethnic background, is a major risk factor."[4] In short, what we saw in the United States and Britain was the exposure and a deepening of the racial hierarchy, with key organizations and institutions drawing on post-racial ideology to explain away inequalities as "just the way things happen." In this chapter, I focus on two articulations of this

post-racial rationalization of the COVID death rate: cultural pathologization and historical displacement.

Sending Structural Racism to History, Bringing Comorbidities to the Present

A body of literature in the United States theorizes that structural
racism is a "fundamental cause" of medical disease.[5] Central to this
literature is the notion that the material inequalities shaped by structural racism—including occupation, housing, poverty, and underemployment and unemployment—are essential variables in individuals'
and groups' health. The argument developed by this literature is that,
if socioeconomic inequality is a fundamental cause of disease—as has
long been recognized in medical professions—and if racial inequality is largely socioeconomic, then racial inequality also should be acknowledged as a fundamental cause of disease.

The coronavirus pandemic clearly bolsters this "fundamental
cause" approach. Take Britain as the first example. Statistics from
the first wave of the pandemic in March 2020 suggested that all "ethnic minority" census groups were more likely to die from COVID-19
than white Brits, with the death rate for Black people being four times
higher than that for whites.[6] The material context for this death rate
is marked by structural racism: Black, Asian, and minority ethnicity (BAME) people are disproportionately represented in poor housing, unemployment, underemployment, and poverty.[7] As researchers
such as Yang Hu have shown, as Britain experienced its first national
"lockdown" in March–July 2020, BAME Brits were 1.2 times more
likely than white Brits to experience household income loss.[8] In this
same time period, as Lucinda Platt and Ross Warwick show, only 30
percent of Bangladeshis, Black Caribbeans, and Black Africans had
enough savings to cover one month of income in the case they were
laid off (compared with 60 percent for the rest of the population).[9]
As Platt and Warwick continue, this racialized differential in savings and accumulated capital was especially pertinent in the period
in which COVID emerged, as BAME workers were disproportionately employed in industries that were closed during the lockdown.
Indeed, it is predicted that Bangladeshi men were four times more
likely; Pakistani men, nearly three times as likely; and Black African

and Caribbean men, 50 percent more likely than white British men to work in such shut-down sectors. What we see in Britain, therefore, is that the death rate of people of color rose in a context in which such people were already suffering major material inequalities that were exacerbated in the early stages of the pandemic. This is the same picture one sees in the United States.

In the United States, the Color of Coronavirus Project found that by December 2020 Latino, Pacific Islander, Black, and Indigenous people were all dying at higher rates than whites.[10] Just as it did in Britain, this statistic needs to be contextualized with reference to structural racism. Similar to the picture in Britain, there was the issue of liquid savings: while the average American had thirty-one days' worth of savings, the typical Black household had just five days' worth. Further, while the rate of food insecurity for whites fluctuated from 7 percent to 10 percent from 2001 to 2016, for Black people and Latinos it ranged from 17 percent to 27 percent.[11] These conditions are coupled with the copious amount of research that has documented structural racism in the United States across the areas of employment, housing, debt, and incarceration.[12] As in the British case, the United States presents a clear example of structural racism creating conditions in which many people of color entered the pandemic unable to cope materially with the various stay-at-home orders that were issued across the states.

In truth, there is a huge body of other statistics one can use to show the existence of structural racism prior to the pandemic. This is a relatively uncontroversial point in critical social science. However, these statistics, as well as (m)any others one can imagine, were largely ignored in favor of more "naturalistic" interpretations of the COVID-19 death rate when it came to people of color.

A large, overarching frame that was deployed in both the United States and the United Kingdom was historical displacement, in which post-racial ideology construed "structural racism" as a historical rather than a contemporary reality. Through this displacement, deaths of people of color could be described as, at best, a legacy of something that no longer existed, if not simply the result of natural factors that no one could do anything about.

This post-racial frame was clearly articulated in a report by Public Health England (PHE), which was commissioned by the British government to study the disproportionate COVID-19 BAME death rate.[13] In multiple places, the report cites historical racism as a reason for the disproportionate number of deaths of BAME people. On page 5, for example, it states, "Historic racism . . . may mean that individuals in BAME groups are less likely to seek care when needed or as N[ational] H[ealth] S[ervice] staff are less likely to speak up when they have concerns about Personal Protective Equipment (PPE) or risk." This statement is largely repeated on page 13 ("Historic negative experiences of healthcare or at work may mean that individuals in BAME groups are less likely to seek care when needed or as NHS staff less likely to speak up when they have concerns about PPE or testing") and on page 23 ("Historic racism and poorer experiences of healthcare or at work may mean that BAME individuals are less likely to seek care when needed or as NHS staff less likely to speak up when they have concerns about PPE or testing").

Such temporal displacement occludes the contemporary practices that reproduce negative health outcomes for BAME people, and through these occlusions, state actors and institutions exonerate themselves from playing any role in racial inequality. For instance, in these quotes the report mentions that "historic negative experiences of healthcare" and "historic racism . . . may mean that individuals in BAME groups are less likely to seek care when needed." However, we can respond that it was not a historical circumstance but a *current reality* when Kayla Williams, a Black woman from South London, died after medical professionals continually dismissed the severity of her COVID-19 symptoms. Such cases highlight a structural problem in the NHS's diagnosis procedures.

Similarly, while the PHE report claimed that "NHS [staff were] less likely to speak up when they ha[d] concerns about PPE," one can ask why BAME people were disproportionately represented in those "key worker" positions that disproportionately exposed them to the virus. A report by the Runnymede Trust suggests that 34 percent of Black people and 28 percent of BAME people—compared with 23 percent of white people—are classified as "key workers."[14] Moreover, to get to work, BAME people are more than twice as likely as white Brits to rely on public transport (which poses a high risk of coronavirus transmission), and BAME people, *despite, on average, living in smaller properties than white Brits*, are more than twice as likely as white Brits to live in households of four or more people.[15] Rather than questioning whether key workers are comfortable with speaking up about their concerns, it is more prudent to critique the structural relations that relegate BAME people to low-paying jobs and reliance on public transport, both of which make them more vulnerable to viral exposure, as well as to overcrowded household conditions that make them more likely to pass the virus on to family members.

Similar frames of historical displacement were expressed in the United States. While the PHE's overt language of "historic racism" was not used, there are still examples of shunning the discussion of social factors in favor of focusing on more natural explanations of COVID mortality. Dr. Anthony Fauci, a key figure on Trump's COVID-19 task force, summarized this approach in his response to a question in April 2020 about why Black Americans were dying at such high rates:

> We've known literally forever that diseases like diabetes, hypertension, obesity and asthma are disproportionately afflicting the minority populations, particularly the African-Americans. Unfortunately, when you look at the predisposing conditions that lead to a bad outcome with coronavirus, the things that get people into [intensive care units] that require intubation and often lead to death, they are just those very co-morbidities that are unfortunately disproportionately prevalent in the African-American population, so we're very concerned about that. It's very sad. *It's nothing we can do about it right now except to try and give them the best possible care to avoid those complications.*[16]

Fauci's explanation shows a notable lack of discussion of social factors. His statement "It's nothing we can do about it right now" ceases to make sense if one recognizes that the death rate itself emerges from social factors. Nevertheless, Fauci and the Trump administration continued with this post-racial argument, with Fauci paraphrasing the claim of another White House COVID task force figure, Dr. Deborah Birx, that

> it's not that [Black Americans] are getting infected more often, it's that when they do get infected, their underlying medical

conditions—the diabetes, hypertension, the obesity, the asthma—those are the kind of things that wind them up in the ICU and ultimately give him a higher death rate.[17]

Replicating this post-racial ideology, Surgeon General Jerome Adams expressed perhaps the more liberal version of this argument when he claimed:

> We do not think people of color are biologically or genetically predisposed to get COVID-19. There is nothing inherently wrong with you. But they are socially predisposed to coronavirus . . . and to have a higher incidence of the very diseases that put you at risk for severe complications of coronavirus.[18]

Even as Adams states that there is no specific gene that makes people of color predisposed to dying from COVID, however, he argues that the reason for African Americans' death rate lies in so-called natural features of biological life. When Adams mentions being "socially predisposed to coronavirus," he is not talking about material conditions of inequality so much as preexisting medical conditions (which, of course, have no links to material context).

As in the case of Britain, therefore, these post-racial rationalizations miss the central crux of structural, racial inequality that the pandemic exacerbated. As Eduardo Bonilla-Silva highlights, putting comorbidities at center stage in one's analysis of COVID mortality grossly overlooks not only that people of color entered the pandemic in vulnerable positions (due to such factors as employment and housing) but also, contrary to Fauci's and Birx's claims, that their position of vulnerability *did* increase their risk of exposure to the virus. As Bonilla-Silva puts it:

> Our racialized class structure leads Black and Brown workers to be in jobs more exposed to COVID-19 than Whites. Black and Brown workers represent 50 percent of janitors, the bulk of nurses in supportive positions (those more exposed to hazardous conditions and receiving less protection), 44 percent of construction workers, 50 percent of correctional officers, 52 percent of bus drivers, a whopping 70 percent of graders and

sorters of agricultural products (these are the workers at Tyson, Smithfield, JBS, and other meat-packing companies), and 30 percent of police and sheriff patrol officers.[19]

Furthermore, we need to appreciate how the idea that COVID mortality is closely connected to "historic racism" (or present co-morbidities) lays the groundwork for more culturalist explanations that pathologize people of color and their lifestyles. Indeed, cultural pathologization during the coronavirus pandemic followed the path of many previous pandemics.

Cultural Pathologization and Abstract Liberalism

Throughout history, health crises often have been construed as moral crises. Charles Briggs highlights this by commenting that racial hier-archies lead to a construction of epidemics and pandemics "in such a way that getting cholera or living in an infected neighborhood consti-tutes natural proof of a moral failure to conduct oneself in a rational, informed manner."[20]

Indeed, reading "health crises" through the prism of race is part of the reason we have the word *ghetto* in our lexicons. As Richard Sen-nett illustrates in his work, when Venice suffered a severe outbreak of syphilis and leprosy in the 1500s, the Venetian state blamed the area's Jewish population for it. This led to the successive creation of authorized areas, or ghettos, in which Jewish people were segregated as a way to contain the viruses.[21] In short, Jewish people were not just seen as carriers of the virus, but through this frame they came to be equated with the virus itself.

This racialized reading of health crises is similar to the Sinopho-bia of the coronavirus pandemic. In Britain, for instance, Grace Gao and Linna Sai showed how the rise of Sinophobic violence in February 2020 resulted in Chinese Brits' being "the most common victims" of racist hate crimes.[22] Similarly, in the United States hate crimes toward Asian Americans are estimated to have increased by 339 percent in 2020.[23] Indeed, this rise in anti-Chinese violence was saliently linked to cultural pathologization. Discourses about "kung flu" and "the Chinese virus" became global in scope—uttered by the prime minis-ter of Britain and the president of the United States alike—and were deployed to portray COVID-19 as a *biological* virus that had emerged from Chinese *culture*. A more explicit example of this racialized reading can be seen in the widespread understanding—later proved incorrect—that COVID-19 emerged from someone eating an unsanitary animal (likely a bat) from a food market in Wuhan. This is why, as Gao and Sai recount, white consumers avoided eating Chinese food as the coronavirus was spreading across the West in early 2020: they feared that they could catch the virus from poor hygiene practices. Further, they note that "maskophobia" caused those "perceived to be Chinese people" who wore face coverings to be othered and vilified.[24]

The everyday reading of the COVID pandemic in the West, especially in the early days, very clearly took place through a pathologized imagery of race. Indeed, cultural pathologization was a key way post-racial ideology was expressed when it came to explaining away the death rate of people of color. Here, explanations of the death rate centered on putative moral deficiencies of people of color themselves rather than on the structural realities of their material conditions. Consider, for instance, the PHE report commissioned by the British government. Rather than focusing on how BAME people are disproportionately exposed to air pollution that weakens lung capacity and increases the likelihood of asthma, or their poor economic and housing situations, the report instead focused on BAME people's purported fear of being tested:

> Fear of diagnosis and death from COVID-19 was identified as negatively impacting how BAME groups took up opportunities to get tested and their likelihood of presenting early for treatment and care. For many BAME groups' lack of trust of NHS services and health care treatment resulted in their reluctance to seek care on a timely basis, and late presentation with disease.[25]

By understanding racial inequality as rooted in "culture," it becomes be something that can be cured with cultural, not material, solutions. Thus, if the problem of high COVID-19 death rates emerges from BAME people's cultural values and practices, then a way to address this inequality is to change their cultural values and practices. Indeed, the PHE report proceeds down this route, proposing to tackle coronavirus's impact on BAME people not through material measures such as improving housing conditions, tackling local pollution, or increasing the availability of testing in areas with large BAME populations, but through "community programs" and "social cohesion." It states, for example,

> Faith communities played a vital role in engaging with communities and were a trusted source of information, leadership and engagement with many BAME groups and needed to be better engaged in future efforts to build community resilience.[26]

The government endorsed this PHE message. For instance, it spent £4 million to create messaging tailored to BAME Brits asking them to stay at home; to advertise stay-at-home messages in six hundred publications with large BAME readerships; and to fund an "ethnic minority influencer" program to spread lockdown messaging. As BAME people disproportionately died from coronavirus, the state thus prioritized cultural pathologization over effective material restitutions, even though it had no evidence to suggest that BAME people were especially flouting public health guidance.

This reality is also obvious when we consider the cultural pathologization of British Muslims. In the run-up to Eid al-Fitr in late May 2020, for instance, the government made use of its daily 5 P.M. briefings to encourage Muslims to abide by social distancing rules, with Chief Medical Adviser Chris Whitty using a public address to emphasize:

> People will have to adapt these celebrations—the joyful celebrations—around the current social distancing rules. Everybody knows what those rules are and they remain the same for every community. This is to protect the whole community. All communities.[27]

Beyond these public broadcasts, the government launched a social media campaign titled "Celebrate Eid at Home this Year and Help Control the Virus." Commentators pointed out the hypocrisy of the government's focus on Eid, given that at the same time images were circulating of Victory in Europe Day street parties, visits to the beach, and gatherings that were held earlier in May at which mainly white participants flouted social distancing guidelines; indeed, it is also worth noting that the British government later temporarily relaxed coronavirus restrictions for those celebrating Christmas. Nevertheless, despite this inconsistency, the government further accelerated its focus on Muslims on July 31, 2020, the eve of another major holiday, Eid al-Adha, when it imposed lockdown restrictions on a series of northern towns and cities that had large Muslim populations (including Greater Manchester and parts of West Yorkshire and East Lancashire). Health Secretary Hancock claimed the lockdowns were needed because "households [were] gathering and not abiding by the social distancing rules."[28] While Hancock denied that Muslims were being deliberately targeted, one can wonder why measures were put in place that prevented some people from meeting in one another's homes (at a time that many Muslims would want to celebrate with their families), but others were allowed to meet in indoor restaurants, bars, and pubs. While Muslims were not explicitly mentioned in the justification for the local lockdowns, therefore, the timing and application of the policy suggests that "race looms large in these seemingly nonracial discussions."[29]

As this example of Muslim-focused social policy shows, cultural lifestyles were considered a key dynamic in the state's understanding of the BAME COVID death rate. Through this focus on cultural lifestyles, moreover, the myth could be reproduced that the high COVID-19 death rate resulted from BAME people's *biological* composition—that is, their rates of disease such as diabetes and obesity, their diet, and so on, all of which relate to their "deviant" or different cultural lifestyles. At its very extreme, this post-racial rationalization makes it appear as though BAME people simply have a secret "race gene" that makes them more likely to die of COVID-19. Such reasoning is evident in the many times medical experts, politicians, and journalists treat "race" as an independent variable in their analysis of COVID-19 mortality rates. The PHE report, for instance, claimed that ethnicity is "independently associated with COVID-19 mortality."[30] This led to an essentialist understanding of race that, in turn, enabled the journalist Beth Rigby to ask, "[Should] BME people be shielding as they are potentially more vulnerable and at greater risk of catching and dying from coronavirus?"

By adopting such an essentialist concept of race, the state exonerates itself from having to provide socioeconomic restitution to racialized people whose *material circumstances* put them at risk of disease.
Thus, by June 2020 Hancock had suggested that prioritizing BAME
people in a vaccine rollout would likely be a successful policy for addressing the COVID death rate among BAME people, while Equali-
ties Minister Kemi Badenoch called on employers to carry out "risk
assessments" of their BAME staff, thus reproducing the idea that the
problem was caused by something inside BAME people rather than
by factors related to their social location.[31] Connectedly, underlying
such a call for risk assessments was a view that BAME people's cultural lifestyles have certain biological consequences that make them
more prone to dying of coronavirus. Such reasoning is adopted in the
PHE report through its claims that diabetes, obesity, and high blood
pressure put BAME people at higher risk of dying from COVID-19.
Even after it issued this report, the PHE reproduced the idea that diet
and lifestyle factors made BAME more vulnerable to dying from the
virus by citing that Asians and Black people, respectively, were 43
percent and 45 percent more likely than whites to have comorbidities
such as diabetes and hypertensive disease.[32]

A similar focus on the cultural lifestyles and choices of people of
color rather than the material conditions of their existence was also
visible in the United States. Surgeon General Adams, for instance,
highlighted this when he commented that people of color needed to

> avoid alcohol, tobacco, and drugs. And call your friends and
> family. Check in on your mother; she wants to hear from you
> right now. . . . And speaking of mothers, we need you to do this,
> if not for yourself, then for your abuela. Do it for your grand-
> daddy. Do it for your Big Mama. Do it for your Pop-Pop. We
> need you to understand—especially in communities of color,
> we need you to step up and help stop the spread so that we can
> protect those who are most vulnerable.[33]

As Bonilla-Silva argues, Adams's statement is not far divorced
from the "culture of poverty" thesis, which places the explanato-
ry emphasis on deficiencies within cultural groups. Consequently,
policies to ameliorate the inequality focus on addressing those defi-

ciencies—in this case, avoiding alcohol, tobacco, and drugs; calling friends and family; and so on.[34] Bonilla-Silva points out that such culturalist explanations even leaked into more liberal media outlets—for example, the *CNN Tonight* special episode "The Color of COVID." Ironically, the show was intended to shed light on the relationship between structural racism and COVID mortality, yet its understanding of "structural racism" was severely lacking. This is best summarized by the former professional basketball player Charles Barkley, who claimed in his interview for the show:

> We as Black people, we have to accept the fact there is systematic racism. But that does not give you a reason to go out and be overweight, have diabetes. . . . We got to eat better, we need better access to health care, we need better access to being able to work out, and things like that. But unless we get better health care which is part of the system, unless we learn to work out better and take better care of our bodies, we are always going to be at a disadvantage.[35]

As Bonilla-Silva argues, Barkley's comment may be so pernicious because he actually expresses recognition of structural racism, yet the deeper grammar of how he understands it vis-à-vis COVID mortality points to cultural lifestyles of Black people. Indeed, Bonilla-Silva points out that a week before the special episode aired, Van Jones, who cohosted "The Color of COVID" with CNN Anchor Don Lemon, had already made a similar point when he stated that Black people need "to take more responsibility for [their] individual health choices" in the face of their mortality rates.[36]

Indeed, such culturalist explanations gained speed as the United States transitioned from the Trump administration to the Biden administration in 2021. In a bid to get more people of color vaccinated, for instance, President Joe Biden famously declared: "It's awful hard, as well, to get Latinx [people] vaccinated. . . . Why? They're worried that they'll be vaccinated and deported." He also acknowledged skepticism among Black people, saying, "They're used to being experimented on—the Tuskegee Airmen and others. People have memories. People have long memories."[37]

While Biden was certainly right to shed light on the U.S. deportation machine and the history of exploitation of Black people in the name of "medicine," such comments amounted to very little when one looks at what Biden actually did about any of the problems he mentioned. First, Biden's rhetoric on so-called illegal immigration was (and is) almost identical to Trump's (meaning that the Biden administration was part of the reason people may have been scared to be "vaccinated and deported").[38] Second, while he was right that there is a legitimate mistrust among Black Americans of medical institutions, Biden failed to acknowledge that across the United States the majority of vaccine centers were located in suburban areas and were accessible only by making appointments online. Biden's comments about mistrust of the vaccine among African Americans thus completely overlooked two significant issues in the American racialized social system: mass ghettoization of Black Americans and high rates of internet poverty in Black neighborhoods.[39] In fact, studies from California and Pennsylvania show that mobile COVID vaccine centers that go *into* Black neighborhoods drastically reduced the vaccine gap between Black and white Americans—again, suggesting that while there may be mistrust of medical institutions, *structural factors* of segregation and poverty were central in explaining putative "vaccine gaps."[40] Simply calling on Black people—as Biden and Vice President Kamala Harris did—to get vaccinated without addressing these structural issues simply shifts responsibility from policy makers onto individual groups and people.

Underlying these culturalist iterations of post-racialism across the United States and the United Kingdom is therefore a commitment to what Bonilla-Silva has referred to as "abstract liberalism."[41] Even when political and media figures mention *structural racism* as a factor in COVID mortality, the interpretations of what the term means—and, consequently, their suggestions for overcoming the inequality—are framed almost exclusively around culturalist understandings of racial group "types" and lifestyles. Thus, we know that one reason people of color have higher blood pressure than whites—a dangerous comorbidity in the pandemic—is their exposure to everyday stress associated with racism.[42] Similarly, we know that people of color in the United States and the United Kingdom live in neighborhoods with poorer air quality and thus suffer at higher rates with cardio-vascular conditions.[43] Saying that people of color are dying because of such comorbidities *without thinking about the material conditions that engender those comorbidities* means, simply, that you do not understand what structural racism means. Thus, when commentators discuss structural racism and COVID mortality, they ironically give us a definition of *structural racism* in which there is no *racism*. In other words, comorbidities are construed as "structural" factors in COVID mortality but are not themselves interrogated as having material roots. This is all to say that in the United States and United Kingdom, we see the state—with the assistance of the overall bureaucratic field—largely exonerating itself from high COVID mortality rates facing people of color via the deployment of post-racial ideology.

Nevertheless, the very fact that so many people of color have died from COVID-19 in the United Kingdom and the United States is representative of the fact that these two countries handled the pandemic especially poorly. While CRT enables us to analyze how this poor handling of the pandemic, with its disproportionate effect on people of color, is explained away via post-racial ideology, to fully comprehend why the states' handling of the pandemic was so poor, we also need to incorporate elements of decolonial thought. In particular, we need to focus on Western universalism, or imperial metrocentrism.

(Not) Learning from Others: Universalisms, Metrocentrisms, Fatalities

In 2019, prior to the emergence of COVID-19, the Global Health Security Index measured which countries were best prepared to deal with an outbreak of a pandemic.[44] At the top of the list was the United States, followed by the United Kingdom in second place. Earlier in 2019, the *British Medical Journal* had published a similar study on the levels of pandemic preparedness across the world, finding that "the most prepared countries were concentrated in Europe and North America."[45] Skipping forward to 2022, as I was writing this chapter, the United States had the seventeenth-highest COVID death rate in the world (measured per million of the population), and the United Kingdom ranked twenty-sixth.[46] Of the twenty-six countries with the highest death rates, only seven were from the Global South—the very areas that the Global Health Security Index told us were not prepared to cope with a pandemic. Centuries of being at the epistemic center of the world system led to this supposition of Western superiority when it came to dealing with viral outbreaks. Centuries of this coloniality of knowledge meant that those policy makers *within* the metropoles of the United States and the United Kingdom endorsed this view of Western superiority, and when it came to the pandemic, it became obvious that this universalism had fatal consequences.

Of course, one might rightfully point out that what is really being expressed in the United Kingdom's and United States' coloniality of knowledge is not just a broad Western universalism but more specific iterations of *imperial metrocentrisms*. These imperial metrocentrisms work *within* the context of Western universalism: while Western universalism places Western knowledge and cosmologies at the center of the world system, imperial metrocentrisms can help us to think about the struggle(s) for epistemic centrality *within* the West (and, consequently, the world system) itself. In other words, this reiterates the division highlighted earlier in the book between *colonial difference* (the West versus the rest) and the *imperial difference within the West* (who has hegemony within the West).[47] Compared with the broad geopolitical bifurcation between the West and the non-West, imperial metrocentrisms are founded even more strongly on an arrogant insistence on the superiority of one's particular geopolitical region in the West and the subsequent "assumption that the experiences and categories of one small place and peoples should be the basis for theorizing and analyzing all other places and peoples."[48]

Within both the United States and the United Kingdom, this ethos of metrocentrism is fairly explicit. To an extent, I discussed such metrocentrisms earlier in the context of how postcolonial melancholia works in the two nations. For instance, Trump's claim in the 2016 electoral campaign that the United States "won two world wars, defeated communism and fascism, and put a man on the face of the moon. We cured disease, pioneered science, and produced timeless works of art that inspire the human soul" was taken as relatively uncontroversial because it told a story of U.S. (epistemic) superiority. Prime Minister Boris Johnson's similar claim that the United Kingdom "is a freedom loving country. . . . [I]f you look at our country over the past three hundred years, virtually every advance, from free speech to democracy, has come from this country" was also relatively uncontroversial, as it likewise told a story of British epistemic superiority (or what other commentators have referred to as "little Englander universalism").[49] Within the context of COVID, these metrocentrisms expressed themselves in the form of both the United States and the United Kingdom rejecting other geopolitical regions' strategies for dealing with the pandemic.

Take, for instance, Britain's policies on face coverings. Throughout the first wave of the pandemic (March–June 2020), the wearing of face coverings in public was never mandatory in Britain, aside from on public transport and inside shops—despite evidence that the COVID-19 virus is airborne and wearing a face covering can effectively reduce its transmission.[50] Yet if one looks at countries that kept their COVID-19 death rates relatively low in the same time period— most of them from the Global South—each made face coverings a key priority in the early stage of their response. For instance, Vietnam (which had no recorded deaths) and Venezuela (which had recorded only eighty-nine deaths) mandated the wearing of face masks in public in March 2020 and South Korea (with 289 recorded deaths) mandated masks in May. Taiwan (with seven deaths) even created a nationwide app that helped citizens locate where to buy face masks. Indeed, in countries such as China and Hong Kong, face masks were provided for free to make them easily accessible. By contrast, even as face coverings were made mandatory on public transport and in shops in Britain, the onus remained on individuals and workers to buy these resources themselves.

Part of the reason it took so long to enact policy to mandate wearing face coverings in shops was the British government's insistence that there was "no evidence" that masking reduced the transmission of coronavirus. Dr. Jonathan Van-Tam, a key scientific adviser to the British government, claimed that the wearing of such masks was based more on Southeast Asian cultural norms than any scientifically rational studies and cited a claim by the executive director of the World Health Organization (WHO) in March 2020 that "there is no specific evidence to suggest that the wearing of masks by the mass population has any potential benefit."[51] This shunning of face coverings happened in a context, however, in which Dr. George Gao, director-general of the Chinese Center for Disease Control and Prevention, had already advised the United States and European countries to mandate face coverings.[52] Moreover, it is here that we see the added problem of "little Englander" metrocentrism: while the WHO originally dismissed the value of face coverings, and while most European countries endorsed this rejection, both the WHO and the European countries changed their policy on emergent evidence. In April 2020, the WHO, for instance, revised its statement to declare that "the use of masks, both home-made and cloth masks, at the community level may help with an overall comprehensive response to this disease."[53] In response, countries such as Belgium, France, Germany, Greece, Italy, and Spain all mandated the wearing of face masks in public spaces, but Britain continued to reject the efficacy of such advice. Not only did Britain turn its back on the face-covering strategies endorsed by countries from the Global South, but it equally shunned "Western" approaches.

The shunning of face coverings, backed-up by vehement metrocentrism, was equally expressed in the United States. South Dakota's Governor Kristi Noem summarized the national approach well when she declared that face covering was a question not of public health but of individual autonomy:

> If folks want to wear a mask, they are free to do so. Those who don't want to wear a mask shouldn't be shamed into it, and gov[ernmen]t should not mandate it. We need to respect each other's decisions. In [South Dakota], we know a little common courtesy can go a long way.

This issue of individual autonomy was a key driver in the rejection of face masks, especially among conservatives, across the United States. In their aggregation of tweets criticizing mask mandates across the United States, Mohammed Al-Ramahi and his colleagues found that constitutional rights and freedom of choice were the most cited reasons for not wearing masks.[54] Such shunning of public health advice in favor of a gut patriotic commitment to American conceptions of liberty is reflected in comments on Twitter such as:

> I am an American citizen with constitutional rights. I have the right & freedom to choose #NoMask. If u try to enforce this

ridiculous order, I will sue your ass 2 hell & back. Kentucky is a #redstate & you don't belong. GTFO [Get the fuck out]. Signed a pissed of[f] Kentucky girl.[55]

Indeed, although the U.S. Centers for Disease Control (CDC) recommended the wearing of face coverings in March 2020, the advice was by no means accepted across the various states or incorporated into the overall national repertoire. From a federal perspective, President Trump started to advise the use of face coverings only in July 2020. However, he continued to reiterate his belief that the wearing of masks was an individual choice and that he would not commit to a federal mandate because, he said, "I want people to have a certain freedom."[56] Thus, via Trump the U.S. federal government responded to the CDC's advice for everyone to wear masks by directly contradicting it. As Trump commented:

I don't agree with the statement that if everybody wear a mask everything disappears. . . . Dr. Fauci said don't wear a mask, our Surgeon General, terrific guy, said don't wear a mask. Everybody was saying don't wear a mask. All of a sudden everybody's got to wear a mask, and as you know, masks cause problems too.[57]

Interestingly, what we may well be seeing here is an epistemic connection between "pissed of[f] Kentucky girl" on Twitter and the president of the United States: they shared a commitment to an idea of American liberty that, they argued, trumped public health guidance. It was this same commitment to "liberty"—albeit a British conceptualization of this concept—that underscored Britain's handling of the early stages of the pandemic.

Consider Britain's delayed imposition of a lockdown (i.e., its stay-at-home order). After Wuhan, China, was locked down in January 2020, countries across Asia rapidly introduced similar measures to reduce the transmission of COVID-19. They included both full-scale lockdowns and policies such as those instituted in South Korea and Hong Kong in which large gatherings were banned and educational institutions moved classes online. Eventually, European nations recognized the value of lockdowns, with France, Italy, and Spain all issuing stay-at-home orders in early March. Concurrently, however, the British government dismissed lockdowns as draconian and unnecessary, with senior members of the government arguing that such measures were driven by populist politics rather than scientific evidence.[58] Indeed, when the British government decided weeks later that a lockdown was necessary, Prime Minister Johnson again referred to the measures as "draconian." However, between this first dismissal of a lockdown and the eventual realization that taking such a measure might indeed be effective, the British government allowed coronavirus to spread through the country. Thus, so-called freedom from government restriction was thus perceived as more valuable than the actual lives threatened by the virus. Boris Johnson directly evoked this concept of liberty when he was probed on the possibility of a lockdown in England, saying, "We live in a land of liberty, as you know, and it's one of the great features of our lives that we don't tend to impose those sorts of restrictions on people in this country."[59]

Again, the link between coloniality and Britain's handling of the coronavirus is evident. Stemming from little Englander universalism, Britain has always seen itself as a champion of "liberty" and freedom—though this "liberty" has always been unequally stratified according to different valuations of different people's lives. In the nineteenth century, for instance, Britain construed itself as a champion of liberty through its taking the lead in the abolition of enslavement—even as it was simultaneously accelerating the reach of its empire.[60] Similarly, in the postwar period, Britain saw itself as saving the people of the world from the evils of Nazism while practicing the same "tactics" as the Nazis on their colonized subjects.[61] Since its construction as an empire, in fact, Britain has claimed to be a defender of liberty and freedom; however, its definition of the terms *liberty* and *freedom* has always been provincial, whereby the liberty of a few champions the death of others. This is the same logic that underlined Britain's slow response to the first wave of the pandemic, whereby the most vulnerable members of society—the disabled, the poor, those living in overly crowded homes, the elderly, those with health conditions—had to face the threat or reality of death so that others could retain their individual liberties.

Importantly, it was this metrocentrism that prevented Britain from learning from other regions'—whether Western or non-Western

—handling of the pandemic. This rejection of learning from others was not even implicit. It was often overtly articulated by key personnel. For example, in mid-March 2020, the WHO was pushing the message "Test, Test, Test." However, Britain rejected its call, with Deputy Chief Medical Officer Jenny Harries defending the position that the organization's advice was only for poor countries:

> The clue for WHO is in its title. It is a World Health Organisation and it is addressing all countries across the world with entirely different health infrastructures and particularly public health infrastructures. We have an extremely well-developed public health system in this country and in fact our public health teams actually train others abroad.[62]

Of course, what Harries's comment missed was that those "poorer," "less developed" countries—which Britain actually helps train—*were* implementing testing protocols and, in so doing, were suppressing the virus at greater rates than Britain.[63] Indeed, when it comes to the strategy of "testing and tracing," we again see that it was not just Britain, but also the United States, whose metrocentrism occluded better avenues for virus suppression.

In the United States, for instance, there was wide consensus in 2020 that the majority of state "track and trace" programs were not properly operational. As Dyani Lewis has shown, these issues spoke to both the U.S. medical infrastructure *and* the method of contact tracing itself.[64] In terms of the medical infrastructure, the United States—along with many other Western nations—simply did not have a reserve of trained contact tracers when the pandemic emerged in March 2020. This meant that in April 2020, when the CDC projected that the United States would need a labor force of 100,000 contact tracers, it only had 2,200 across the whole nation (and by the end of that year, it still only had 50,000). Moreover, the method of contact tracing the United States used was not efficient. Unlike in South Korea, Singapore, and Vietnam, which made use of social media and Bluetooth technology in tracing contacts easily and efficiently, so that those who tested positive for COVID-19 would not have to report lists of contacts themselves, the United States adopted a process in which virus-positive people had to report all contacts they had had in a specific period of time. Of course, this resulted in large numbers of contacts never being told they had been exposed to the virus, because the virus-positive person either was not acquainted with many of their contacts (e.g., fellow public transport riders, restaurant guests, and so on) or did not wish to disclose names of contacts they did know. According to CDC data, for example, just 49 percent of cases between July and November 2020 were contacted in New Jersey, and only 31 percent of those provided any contact details.[65] In fact, while those countries across the Global South were using digital technology to assist with contact tracing, and effectively suppressed the virus in doing so, U.S. states such as Washington were doing contact tracing via fax and wired telephone.

In terms of the method of contact tracing itself, we therefore also see serious faults. Not only were people simply not being traced in the United States, but large sectors of the population could not even be tested. While countries such as China, Japan, and Singapore administered free mass testing, delivered to one's door, throughout 2020, the United States was charging an average of $100 per test.[66] Moreover, when the U.S. states *were* contact tracing, they were focusing on individual contacts rather than on the so-called K number, as in South Korea. The K number is essentially the virus's dispersion value—that is, the consistency with which the virus spreads from one person to another. In 2020, according to research conducted across Asia, COVID-19's K number was a fairly low 0.1 (compared with 0.22 for measles). This meant that the majority of people contracting COVID were not passing it on to others and that most people who contracted the virus did so while attending "super-spreader" events.[67] In countries such as South Korea, therefore, the aim of contact tracing was to work backward to potential super-spreader events, such as public gatherings, crowded restaurants, and so on, so that all attendees could be told they had been exposed to the virus. By contrast, the United States rejected such information in its policy of merely tracing individuals who were named by people who had contracted COVID and paid to be tested.

Back to Theoretical Synergy

When it comes to the early stages of the COVID-19 pandemic, therefore, the issue is not simply that CRT helps us to address national concerns while decolonial thought allows us to think about transnational relations. Rather, in line with the overall thesis of the book, when we look at the United States and Britain's handling of the pandemic in its early stages, we see a simultaneous interplay of national racialized social systems and the logic of coloniality. The pandemic clearly exacerbated the hierarchies of the racialized U.K. and U.S. social systems, with these inequalities (especially pertaining to high mortality rates) then explained away by the dominant racial ideology of post-racialism. Even as these inequalities were being exacerbated, their respective metrocentrisms emerge as a significant explanation for *why* states of affairs vis-à-vis COVID-19 were so bad in the United States and the United Kingdom. The United States and the United Kingdom did not simply shun non-Western strategies of viral management; they were largely committed to sticking with their own, "superior" public health strategies, even as it became clear that those strategies were not effective. Just as with the other cases examined in this book—from populism and capitalism to climate crises—the need to balance insights from CRT with decolonial thought to understand the COVID-19 pandemic becomes clear. As I now turn to in the Conclusion, this ability to balance insights from CRT and decolonial thought has been achieved in practice by various activists and social movements. We should take inspiration from them in our social-science analysis.

Conclusion

"A World in Which Many Worlds Fit"

*Decolonial Thought and Critical Race Theory
in the Pluriverse*

When I was a graduate student in sociology, I had the opportunity to attend a series of lectures by Loïc Wacquant, who was
a visiting professor in our department for that academic year.
The underlying theme of his series was a complaint that people were
speaking "Bourdieu-ese" without necessarily needing to. Carrying on
with the argument developed in *An Introduction to a Reflexive Sociology*, Wacquant argued that we should never use theory for theory's
sake; theoretical models and concepts, he said, should be used only
when they help us understand something concrete that we otherwise
could not properly comprehend.[1] I recall this anecdote because, while
I went to those lectures hoping to learn about urban marginality,
neoliberalism, and the carceral state, I ended up being much more
inspired by and interested in the question surrounding "theory" and
its (mis)uses.

Indeed, this question about the status of "theory" has preoccupied
intellectuals developing both critical race theory (CRT) and decolonial thought. In decolonial thought, of course, theory has served an
important purpose for anticolonial movements, in which "scholar-
activists" have used speeches and writings to provide *theories* of social
structure and coloniality and effective means by which to resist them.
The writings and speeches of Suzanne Césaire, Frantz Fanon, and

Kwame Nkrumah, among others, are examples of this.[2] The underlying ethos here is that theory is not an abstract process divorced from lived realities. Instead, it is something that develops from material struggle. As Amílcar Cabral put it: "Every practice produces a theory, and . . . if it is true that a revolution can fail even though it be based on perfectly conceived theories, nobody has yet made a successful revolution without a revolutionary theory."[3] Still within decolonial thought, other figures have also stressed the need to avoid theory for theory's sake and instead develop *theories* (plural) that can help us to delink from Western epistemology. Speaking directly to those working within the confines of Western educational institutions, for instance, Catherine Walsh comments:

> The challenge is to not look for theory first. It is also to move beyond a simple reading of and about, toward a thinking from and with, a thinking-doing that requires contemplation of one's own place of enunciation and relation (or not) with the so-called universality of Western thought. I am referring to a thinking-doing that delinks, that undoes the unified—and universalizing—centrality of the West as the world and that begins to push other questions, other reflections, other considerations, and other understandings.[4]

As Walsh highlights, this notion of theory in decolonial thought itself reconstitutes what we typically think of as theory from the Western standpoint. From the decolonial position, the binaries of rational and emotional, theory and feeling, thinking and doing, and so on are not as rigid and stable as one finds in the project of Western universalism. Theory is important, Walsh highlights, because it is inherently connected to "doing" (and "doing" itself is also constitutive of theory). Importantly, this is not a recapitulation of the Western discussion of "theory in practice" (or the concept of *praxis*). It is, instead, an epistemology that does not divorce between theory and practice in the first place.

These decolonial approaches to "theory" also bear similarities to what we see in sectors of the CRT canon. Indeed, as Tanya Golash-Boza has aptly put it: "The purpose of a critical theory of race and racism is to move forward our understanding of racial and racist dynamics in ways that bring us closer to the eradication of racial oppression."[5] As summarized here, the purpose of social theorizing is to help us achieve material change—it is not a chin-stroking exercise that one can do vacuumed away from the empirical world in which one lives. This ethos is summarized well by Stuart Hall when he claims that "theory is always a detour on the way to something more important."[6] Theorizing is an important activity, but as an activity, it engages with and emerges from lived worlds and social realities. Those within the critical race canon, such as Patricia Hill Collins, make a similar argument to those from the decolonial tradition in the way that they reject what is termed the *elite social theory* of the West. As Collins highlights, within the West the concept of "theory" has been defined within the interests of elites, meaning that elites "possess the power to legitimate the knowledge that they define as theory as being universal, normative, and ideal [while they] derogate the social theory of less powerful groups who may express contrary standpoints on the same social issues by labelling subordinate groups' social theory as being folk wisdom, raw experience, or common sense."[7] Critical race theory, however, proposes a different understanding of "theorizing" that transcends this legitimated concept of "elite theorizing" and, instead, stresses the importance of theorizing "about the social in defense of economic and social justice."[8]

In plain terms, therefore, we see that both decolonial thought and CRT place emphasis on the importance of "theory," but their understandings of theory are inherently connected to struggles for cognitive and material justice. A corollary of this, therefore, is that we *also* need to widen our scope regarding who and what counts as a theorist or as theorists. We can certainly discuss decolonial and critical race theorists by referring to various scholars and their prolific publication records—for example, Eduardo Bonilla-Silva, Kimberlé Crenshaw, María Lugones, or Walter Mignolo. However, all of these "theorists" also saw theory as deriving from a range of people, especially from within resistance and social movements, who were not university professors and in many cases did not have university educations. This means that, while concern with theory from "decolonial gurus" such as Mignolo, Aníbal Quijano, and so on may be growing, these criticisms overlook that decolonial theory—according to those so-called gurus—derives not just from the halls of Duke University but, as I said in the beginning of the book, dates all the way back to the beginning of colonialism in 1492.[9] Remember, as Walsh reminds us, that "with colonialism and coloniality came resistance and refusal. Decoloniality necessarily follows, derives from, and responds to coloniality and the ongoing colonial process and condition."[10]

Bearing in mind, therefore, that both CRT and decolonial thought offer "practical" views of theorizing, in which theory ontologically relates to resistance and struggle, I want to use this Conclusion to look at a few examples of resistance groups that have offered forms of analysis similar to those offered in this book. In particular, I highlight how these groups worked laterally through drawing connections between their own national predicaments and wider transnational processes. I start the discussion with the Black Panthers' notion of "intercommunalism" and how it traveled into the Black Lives Matter movement.

From the Black Panther Party to Black Lives Matter

> We see very little difference in what happens to a community here in North America and what happens to a community in Vietnam. We see very little difference in what happens, even culturally, to a Chinese community in San Francisco and a Chinese community in Hong Kong. We see very little difference in what happens to a Black community in Harlem and a Black community in South Africa, a Black community in Angola and one in Mozambique. We see very little difference.
>
> —MALCOLM X, *Racial Separation*[11]

The Black Panther Party (BPP) is an interesting starting point for our discussion, given that the movement shifted its focus from Black nationalism and radical nationalism in the late 1960s to a practice of intercommunalism in the early 1970s.[12] Upon the BPP's formation in 1966, its commitment was sided toward Black nationalism. Drawing partly on Malcolm X's engagement with the Nation of Islam, Black nationalism was based in the premise that Black people in the United States were a dispersed colony in need of self-determination through the creation of their own Black nation. As Malcolm X described this philosophy in his 1963 address at Berkeley:

We must have a permanent solution. A temporary solution won't do. Tokenism will no longer suffice. . . . Twenty million ex-slaves must be permanently separated from our former slave master and placed on some land that we can call our own. Then we can create our own jobs. Control our own economy. Solve our own problems instead of waiting on the American white man to solve our problems for us.[13]

As the party's co-founder Huey Newton then noted, however, the BPP quickly realized that Black nationalism was only the beginning of the answer. The *proper* answer, the Panthers thought, lay in "revolutionary nationalism, that is, nationalism plus socialism."[14] However, by the early 1970s the BPP had again revised this commitment to "revolutionary nationalism." First, as signaled by Angela Davis, there was the Black feminist critique that the BPP's commitment to nationalism was based in a masculinist notion of the nation-state.[15] As Davis argues, there were certain "male supremacist ramifications of black nationalism," meaning that the BBP's theories of Black and racial nationalism were still steeped in patriarchal notions of control and violence.[16] Second, as Newton argued, there was a recognition in the BPP that a revolution that afforded equality to only a sector of the population (i.e., Black people in the United States) would be only a partial revolution. As Newton put it:

How can we say that we have accomplished revolution if we redistribute the wealth just to the people here in North America when the ruling circle itself is guilty of *trespass de bonis asportatis*. That is, they have taken away the goods of the people of the world, transported them to America and used them as their very own.

It was this recognition of the need to "go global" that pushed the BPP toward what was subsequently termed *intercommunalism*, which revolved around the straightforward belief that "the world is hooked up."[17] Importantly, however, this theory of intercommunalism stressed that the world was hooked up because the global system was no longer composed of interlocking nation-states. Instead, it was becoming a single world system being absorbed into U.S. hegemony. As Newton summarized it:

> We sought solidarity with what we thought were the nations of the world. But then what happened? We found that because everything is in a constant state of transformation, because of the development of technology, because of the development of the mass media, because of the fire power of the imperialist, and because of the fact that the United States is no longer a nation but an empire, nations could not exist, for they did not have the criteria for nationhood. . . . But since no nation exists, and since the United States is in fact an empire, it is impossible for us to be Internationalists. These transformations and phenomena require us to call ourselves "intercommunalists" because nations have been transformed into communities of the world. The Black Panther Party now disclaims internationalism and supports intercommunalism.[18]

Through this shift to intercommunalism, the BPP thus recast various forms of anti-imperial resistance for self-determination as being only a small part of a much more global struggle. In contrast to unequivocal support for self-determination, the commitment to intercommunalism saw the BPP prioritize the creation of a world socialist system in which the United States and Europe returned stolen resources from imperial-colonial plunder, and the subjugated of the world system—the so-called communities of the world—took control over their own means of production. As Newton summarized:

> So how do we define certain progressive countries such as the People's Republic of China? How do we describe certain progressive countries, or communities as we call them, as the Democratic People's Republic of Korea? How do we define certain communities such as North Vietnam and the provisional government in the South? How do we explain these communities if in fact they too cannot claim nationhood? We say this: we say they represent the people's liberated territory. They represent a community liberated. But that community is not sufficient, it is not satisfied, just as the National Liberation Front is

not satisfied with the liberated territory in the South. *It is only the groundwork and preparation for the liberation of the world- seizing the wealth from the ruling circle, equal distribution and proportional representation in an intercommunal framework.* This is what the Black Panther Party would like to achieve with the help of the power of the people, because without the people nothing can be achieved.[19]

Advocating intercommunalism therefore offered a framework for the BPP to think through the connections that existed between the United States' racialized social system and the global process of colo- niality. It allowed the BPP, for example, to connect police brutality en- acted toward Black people in the United States with various military interventions and coups the United States was supporting across the Global South (e.g., in Angola, Ghana, and Vietnam). After all, as the BPP noted, the same military equipment was being used "at home" and "abroad."[20]

Indeed, the emergence of the Black Lives Matter (BLM) social movement in 2014 saw a potential revival of this commitment to in- tercommunalism in the United States. Angela Davis articulated this spirit of intercommunalism well in her discussion of the emergence of BLM in the aftermath of the police murder of Michael Brown in Ferguson, Missouri.[21] As Davis notes, the BLM protests in the after- math of Brown's murder "ha[ve] become synonymous with progres- sive protest from Palestine to South Africa, from Syria to Germany, and Brazil to Australia."[22] Moreover, as she clarifies, BLM was not just becoming synonymous with progressive protest across the world; it was also drawing intercommunal relations between the United States' systemic racism and the coloniality being enacted across the world. This is particularly apparent in Davis's discussion of the connections between violence toward Palestinians in occupied Palestine and the police brutality being used to maintain the racial order in the United States. As she wrote in 2014:

Palestinian activists noticed from the images they saw on social media and on television that tear-gas canisters that were being used in Ferguson were exactly the same tear-gas can- isters that were used against them in occupied Palestine. As a matter of fact, a U.S. company, which is called Combined Systems, Incorporated, stamps "CTS" (Combined Tactical Systems) on their tear-gas canisters. When Palestinian activists noticed these canisters in Ferguson, what they did was to tweet advice to Ferguson protesters on how to deal with the tear gas. . . . There was a whole series of really interesting comments for the young activists in Ferguson, who were probably confronting tear gas for the first time in their lives.[23]

Expanding on this example, Davis thus comments on the "connections between the militarization of the police in the US" (a key working of the racialized social system) and the "ongoing proliferation of racist police violence, and the continuous assault on people in occupied Palestine" (a key working of coloniality).[24] Recognizing these links, BLM started sending delegates to Lebanon in 2015 to work with Palestinian activists and reiterated its support for Palestinian liberation in 2020 in the aftermath of George Floyd's death.[25] This focus on the links between U.S. racism and settler colonialism in Palestine led BLM to focus on, among many things, the shared training of police officers across the United States and Israel via organizations such as the Anti-Defamation League.

In a sense, therefore, we see that elements of the BLM movement—picking up speed in 2014 and further accelerating in 2020—reinvigorated the intercommunality of the earlier BPP. In an ethos similar to my book's argument, this intercommunalism balanced an appreciation of how the United States' own organizations and institutional apparatuses were reproducing the logic of the racialized social system while also appreciating how these organizations or processes were linked to the logic of coloniality more broadly. It is this both-and approach of resistance that we also see coming to the fore in the philosophy/philosophies of the Zapatistas, to which I now turn.

The Ethics of Double Translation

Formed largely by Indigenous people in eastern Chiapas, Mexico, in 1994, the Ejército Zapatista de Liberación Nacional (Zapatista Army of National Liberation [EZLN]), or the Zapatistas, is both the product and the leading advocate of pluriversalism. It is undeniable that, like the BPP, the Zapatistas had self-determination in the forefront of their aims when they emerged in their 1994 uprising. As they wrote in the First Declaration of the Lacandon Jungle: "We are the true inheritors of the true builders of *our nation*."[26] Indeed, a significant reason the Zapatistas began this uprising in 1994, specifically writing this first declaration on January 2, was to respond to what they saw as an illegitimate government in Mexico accelerating the program of neoliberalism. It is no coincidence, therefore, that their first declaration was made precisely one day after the North American Free Trade Agreement came into effect, an agreement that lowered tariffs to permit free trade among the United States, Canada, and Mexico in a way that benefited U.S. industries at the expense of workers in Mexico.[27] Indeed, over the next decade the Zapatistas claimed that the Mexican Congress had failed to recognize the Indigenous rights enshrined in the Mexican Constitution and consequently took it upon themselves to guarantee Mexico's Indigenous peoples' right to autonomy and self-determination. This meant that through the 1990s into the 2000s, the Zapatistas secured "rebel territories" across Altamirano, Chanal, Comitán de Domínguez, Huixtán, Ocosingo, Oxchuc, and many more places, which became constituted as autonomous municipalities.[28] In these autonomous regions, they created *juntas de buen gobierno* (councils) formed by the locals, sticking to the Zapatistas philosophy of non-vanguardism and "commanding by obeying."[29]

However, unlike the BPP, the Zapatistas, from the very beginnings of their formation, thought of Indigenous self-determination in Mexico as being linked to global processes and global resistances elsewhere. This is evident in both the practice and in the political rhetoric of the Zapatistas. Consider, for example, Subcomandante Marcos's address "In Our Dreams We Have Seen Another World" (1994).[30] In it, Marcos began by addressing not just "the Mexican people" but also "the people and governments of the world."[31] In the address, Marcos calls not just for reforms to the Mexican system of economic and political governance but for worldwide shifts to create a world with "no need for armies," where "peace, justice and liberty were so common that no one talked about them as far-off concepts."[32] Importantly, this desire for a peaceful world beyond inequality was not just an abstract philosophy for the Zapatistas. It was a guiding principle in their struggle and resistance. In July 1996, the Zapatistas organized the First Intercontinental Encuentro for Humanity and against Neo-liberalism, where thousands of people across the world gathered in Chiapas.[33] Within the meeting, the Zapatistas shared with everyone that they were all part of a similar struggle for humanity in a context in which the global system of neoliberalism was dehumanizing millions of subalternized people. As the Zapatistas declared in the final remarks at the meeting:

> Millions of women, millions of youths, millions of Indigenous, millions of homosexuals, millions of human beings of all races and colors only participate in the financial markets as a devalued currency worth always less and less, the currency of their blood making profits. . . . The globalization of markets is erasing borders for speculation and crime and multiplying them for human beings. Countries are obligated to *erase their national borders when it comes to the circulation of money but to multiply their internal borders*. . . . National governments are turned into the military underlings of a new world war against humanity.[34]

As emphasized in this quote, the Zapatistas recognized something that the BPP also recognized through the concept of intercommunalism—namely, that the "internal borders" within nations, whether created by racism, sexism, or any scheme of inequality, may immediately present themselves as national problems with national solutions, but the reality is that they are *national problems underscored by global social processes*. As the Zapatistas reiterated in the closing remarks: "National repression is a necessary premise of the globalization neoliberalism imposes."[35]

A central commitment of the Zapatistas, therefore, was to create a "world, with the many worlds that the world needs"—or, put another way, a world in which many worlds fit.[36] This meant that at the First Intercontinental meeting, they were not trying to convince the attendees, who came from more than forty different countries, that their struggles were all the same. But neither were they advocating that each of their struggles was independent and geopolitically isolated. Instead, their answer stemmed from pluriversalism, a recognition that Aimé Césaire had described decades earlier when he stated:

I'm not going to confine myself to some narrow particularism. But nor do I intend to lose myself in a disembodied universalism. There are two ways to lose oneself: through walled-in segregation in the particular, or through dissolution into the "universal." My idea of the universal is that of a universal rich with all that is particular, rich with all particulars, the deepening and coexistence of all particulars.[37]

By stressing this "universal rich with all that is particular," the Zapatistas encouraged people across the world to see how their struggles might be interconnected without stressing the need to lose any specificity. As they declared in the closing remarks, struggles against military interventions across the Global South, the rising use of private security firms and prisons in the United States and Europe, the denial of health care and land to Indigenous peoples of the world—these were all *particular* social problems in *particular* social contexts, but they could also be connected so that "the multiplication of resistances, the 'I am not resigned,' the 'I am a rebel,' continues."[38]

Throughout their existence, the Zapatistas have continued their rebellion against the Mexican state while also involving themselves in resistance struggles across the world. These involvements include writing to the Supreme Court of Pennsylvania in 1999 about Mumia Abu-Jamal, who was unjustly sentenced to death in a case that appeared fabricated by the police; calling on the North Atlantic Treaty Organization (NATO) in 1999 to withdraw from its military interventions in the Balkans (As the Zapatistas put it, "If we don't say 'No!' to Kosovo today, tomorrow we will be saying 'Yes!' to the horrors that Money now prepares all over the world"[39]); addressing the National Indigenous Congress in 2014 to condemn the murder of Palestinians;[40] and launching the self-proclaimed "Zapatista invasion" in 2020, in which Zapatistas are traveling across five continents to "carry out meetings, dialogues, exchanges of ideas, experiences, analyses and evaluations among those of us who are committed, from different conceptions and from different areas, to the struggle for life."[41]

Just as the BPP eventually came to realize, therefore, the Zapatistas now situate their local struggle in the context of wider, transnational social processes. They view their freedom and self-determination as part of a much wider struggle that transcends the nation-state—indeed, a struggle that itself is composed of multiple interlocking struggles. Thus, we see again how the ability to think about the specificity of the nation-state while also forging transnational analysis—a central theme of this book—is a way of thought that has been commonplace in resistance movements. In other words, while I have written this book to focus explicitly on the potential of using *both* decolonial thought *and* CRT to balance the study of the national and the transnational, this way of thinking is useful not just for abstract social theorists in their armchairs. Rather, it is a way of thinking that—as history proves—is essential in struggles for material and cognitive justice.

Following from this balance between the national and transnational, what appears to be essential to the Zapatistas' philosophy is a stringent commitment to "double translation," or "diversality."[42] This ethic of double translation means that the Zapatistas are not interested in producing a theory or resistance and revolution from their own contexts that can simply be exported elsewhere in the world. Rather, double translation involves a bidirectional process of dialogue between different cosmologies, cultures, knowledges, and traditions in which the dialogue itself acts as a *connector* between different struggles. This is why the Zapatistas are currently traveling across the world to foster "dialogues, exchanges of ideas, experiences, analyses and evaluations among those of us who are committed, *from different conceptions and from different areas*, to the struggle for life."[43] Indeed, it is this commitment to creating dialogue between different knowledge systems that sparked my primary interest in writing this book. Thus, I return to the discussion of CRT and decolonial thought and how the project of synergy draws on the epistemic ethics developed by the Zapatistas.

"Walking While Asking Questions": Lessons for Social Theory

In their endorsement of double translation, the Zapatistas call for an ethic of "walking while asking questions." As Ramón Grosfoguel has commented about this Tojolabal philosophy, walking while asking questions involves never assuming the universalism of one's own theory or cosmology and, instead, seeking to foster horizontal dialogue among different approaches. I conclude by reviewing the thoughts in this book about CRT, decolonial thought, and the horizontal connections we can build between the two approaches. In particular—so I do not simply repeat the arguments already made in the book's chapters—I focus on three important thinking points as we seek to move forward in our dialogue between CRT and decolonial thought. Moreover, I address these points directly to those working in CRT and decolonial thought, given that these epistemic communities have been so foundational to this book.

To Those in CRT

First, to those working in CRT, particularly within the United States, I encourage a recognition that a "transnational turn" does not mean that one must lose a focus on national particularities. The BPP and the Zapatistas, for instance, did not sacrifice their focus on state racism and Mexican neoliberalism, respectively, when they focused on processes that have had effects elsewhere. So, too, can those working in CRT engage in some form of transnational analysis—indeed, they may find that it enriches their understanding of the process at hand (as per the premise of this book). The way for those in CRT to engage in transnational analysis nonetheless requires a recognition that—to come back to a metaphor from the Introduction—CRT provides only *one map* of social reality: it tells only a fraction of the total story. Working *with* elements of decolonial thought can be one beneficial way that critical race theorists can (literally) broaden the horizons of their analysis; this both-and approach to CRT and decolonial thought is a powerful way to balance the commitment to national particularity while also thinking about transnational reverberations.

Consider, for example, the Thirteenth Amendment to the U.S. Constitution, which prohibits slavery unless as punishment for a crime. It is undeniable that this specific working of the Constitution is tied to the racialized social system, as it provides a basis for legitimating mass incarceration under the "New Jim Crow" of Black Americans who end up providing masses of reserve labor for big corporations.[44] However, if you think about the corporations that benefit from the cheap labor provided by prisons, some of them are not even based in the United States (e.g., Nintendo, whose headquarters are in

Japan). In other words, a CRT analysis would do a perfect job of telling us the relation between the Thirteenth Amendment and the racial order, but a decolonial analysis would add to this map the global flows of labor and capital also engendered by this legal framework in the United States. Neither of these "maps"—of CRT and decolonial thought—is more true, but looking at the maps simultaneously can tell us something about the world that we could not see as clearly if we looked only at one.

To Those in Decolonial Theory

Second, turning to the decolonial theorists: it is perfectly feasible to focus on colonial difference *and* imperial difference. At a time when scholars are calling into question decolonial thought's generalizing binary between the West and the rest, it is important for decolonial thinkers to study the variation *within* the West and the rest.[45] I believe this is what Satnam Virdee was alluding to when he criticized the decoloniality program by stressing that there has always been "an East within the West and a South within the North."[46] Virdee's comment has at least two generative implications for decolonial thinkers. First, it can encourage them to analyze how struggles *within* the West (i.e., in the sphere of imperial difference) have significant implications for how these respective regions actually articulate coloniality. This came to the fore in the discussion of the United States and Britain and their early handling of the COVID-19 pandemic (see Chapter 5). Both nations endorsed an imperial metrocentrism that meant they were shunning strategies not only from the Global South but also from other Western regions. In this case, the logic of coloniality—that is, Western universalism—is being articulated not in a grand West-versus-the rest binary but in a way that stresses a national, imperial metrocentrism.

Second, by studying these "withins," decolonial thinkers may also realize that struggles within the West for hegemony have significant implications for the colonial world system. In other words, imperial difference is inherently connected to colonial difference. In some accounts of decoloniality, such links between imperial and colonial difference seem to be downplayed. Take again Mignolo's example of Ottobah Cugoano (see the Introduction), who experienced brutality by the English even as Britain was condemning Spain for its treatment of Indigenous people. Imperial nations, Mignolo points out, share in their upholding of coloniality.

Yet Mignolo overlooks some central moments in which imperial difference has created seismic shifts in the overall coloniality of power. Take, for instance, the Haitian Revolution (1791–1804). The Haitians could not have fought the French empire for so long had they not been given equipment and food by the British and Spanish empires.[47] Neither the British nor the Spanish wanted to help Haiti for a charitable reason; they both wanted to damage the French empire and hoped to claim Haiti as their own. Regardless of the fact that both Britain and Spain were thus clearly enacting coloniality, their struggles for dominance *within the West* (i.e., in the sphere of imperial difference) were a key resource in Haitian revolutionaries' being able to declare Haiti the First Black Republic of the world. To go even further, given that Haitian revolutionaries then helped anticolonial resistance movements across Barbados, Bolivia, Brazil, Cuba, Jamaica, and Saint Lucia, we see that struggles within the sphere of imperial difference, by contradiction, related to a wide range of anticolonial movements across the modern world.

This is all to say, therefore, that decolonial theorists may find it beneficial to sometimes look inward to the diverse worlds *within* the metropoles and peripheries. In fact, doing so would likely enrich the decolonial project of showing how fundamentally interlinked the world is via the colonial matrix of power. Let us not forget, to come back to the example of this chapter, even the Zapatistas—whom the decolonial thinkers revere—have balanced a focus on transnational processes of coloniality with the specific economic, political, and legal frameworks in the Mexican nation-state.

To All of Us

Finally, to all of us working in this broad field of "critical" social science: we need to embrace lateral ways of thinking so that we avoid the traps of theoretical myopia. Such lateral ways of thinking take inspiration from the ethics of the Zapatistas when they stress double translation—that is, *horizontal dialogue* rather than *vertical hierarchies* among different theoretical traditions. Indeed, it is this ethic of lateral thinking that is the foundation of the book, as I have tried to show how thinking with both CRT and decolonial thought can offer prescient insights when looking at particular social phenomena.

Especially with the lateral thinking between CRT and decolonial thought we gain insights into the relations that exist between racialized social systems and coloniality. Again, the relations are precisely what so many social movements—from the BPP to BLM and the Zapatistas—have highlighted in their analysis. If one considers neoliberalism, to use an example from earlier in the book, one can very easily see how this "strain" of capitalism brings coloniality and the racialized social system into the same analytical space. As we discussed, neoliberalism involved/involves the construction of "national abjects" within the racialized social system—such as Black welfare queens in the 1980s United States or poor Black folk in rural Brazil. However, the creation of these *national* abjects is related—in virtue of coloniality—to the various states' *transnational* projects, whether the project is the United States using racial stereotypes of Black welfare queens to justify rolling back welfare spending and thus freeing up capital for military expansion or white Brazilian elites securing maximum profits in the world market through cheap labor via the sugar trade.

What this case of neoliberalism shows is precisely what lateral thinking—or "theoretical synergy"—is about. Importantly, I am not asserting that either CRT or decolonial thought is better suited to understanding the process at hand. Rather, I am acknowledging the relatively uncontroversial points that most social processes get articulated at different levels of the social universe and, consequently, different theoretical approaches will be more or less suited to addressing these specific articulations. Decolonial thought may not be as well suited as CRT to studying something like the stigmatization of Black women in the United States in the 1980s, but not because it is "inferior" to CRT. Rather, it addresses different sets of questions and social problems. Likewise, when CRT looks at neoliberalism, it is not necessarily looking at the creation of edge populations in the world system. This means not that it is a weaker approach than decolonial thought but, rather, that it is more concerned with *other*, albeit related, dimensions of neoliberalism.

To Dwell in Epistemic Disobedience

The whole project of theoretical synergy, therefore, is to acknowledge that different—sometimes conflicting—theoretical approaches can exist, but they can still work together laterally. These approaches and their insights do not have to be reducible to each other; instead, they can help us to focus on multiple aspects of the same social phenomena. They help to build more useful maps of social reality.

Yet even thinking in these lateral terms is to counter what we are regularly taught in our educational training. In the social sciences we are taught about putative great figures—Bourdieu, Foucault, Habermas, Marx, and so on—who infamously synthesized disparate streams of thought into one universal theory. We are taught about the insurmountable differences among traditions such as structuralism, existentialism, symbolic interactionism, functionalism, critical realism, and Marxism, and we are encouraged to align ourselves with specific intellectual groupings. An ethic is given to us from very early in our intellectual journey that our theories must be universal or they cease to be proper social theory.

To an extent, therefore, even to think in terms of the lateral connections between CRT and decolonial thought is to signal some form of epistemic disobedience. We are rejecting the need for universalism, for synthesis, or for a vertical hierarchy among different traditions. We are rejecting the logic that a drawback (e.g., CRT's methodological nationalism) constitutes a reason to disregard a theory. We are rejecting the point that theories in tension cannot be epistemic allies. We are embracing, however, a humbler approach to social theory that gives us more prescient insights into social phenomena.

With this in mind, let us conclude by reminding ourselves that both CRT and decolonial thought emerged out of refusal and disobedience. Those in CRT refused the liberal rhetoric of civil rights reformism, and the culture of liberalism in critical legal studies more broadly, with sociologists then refusing and disobeying the logics of color-blind social science. As of this writing, in August 2022, seven states in the United States have banned the teaching of CRT, with sixteen more states having bills passing through state legislatures of the same effect. Even thinking with CRT, in such contexts, demonstrates a refusal and disobeying of dominant frames. Likewise, decolonial thought emerged as a refusal of Western hegemony and a disobeying of the epistemic rules of Western power and social thought. As Walsh reminds us, this disobedience is a productive disobedience, it is "a form of struggle and survival, an epistemic and existence-based response and practice . . . *for* the possibilities of an otherwise."[48] Through our own disobedience of using CRT and decolonial thought in tandem, I hope that this book has pointed toward merely a handful of cases where such synergy and lateral thinking is not just beneficial, but essential.

Notes

Introduction

1. Du Bois 2007 [1940].
2. Weiner 2018.
3. Ibid.: 3.
4. Other social scientists—such as Gurminder Bhambra (2007, 2014) and Julian Go (2016a)—have also articulated an idea of "three waves" of decolonial thought as it proceeded from anticolonial intellectuals in the early twentieth century through postcolonial scholars in the humanities (such as Homi Bhabha, Edward Said, and Gayatri Spivak) to social-science critiques of the rhetoric of modernity.
5. Fanon 1963 [1961]: 209
6. Du Bois 1967 [1899]: 386–387.
7. Du Bois 2007 [1947].
8. Guaman Poma de Ayala 2009 [1615]; Mignolo 2011c.
9. Nkrumah 1970, 1971.
10. Nkrumah 1971.
11. Quijano 2007: 168–169.
12. The Global South here is being defined in terms of the geopolitical regions of the world that were under European colonial occupation or were directly or indirectly controlled via Western imperial projects.
13. Mariátegui 2014.
14. Bhambra 2007.
15. Alatas and Sinha 2017.
16. Weber 2002 [1905].

17. Marx 2007 [1932].

18. Marx 1973 [1939]; Weber 1959, 2000 [1958].

19. Mignolo 2011a.

20. Bhambra 2014: 130.

21. Dussel 2002.

22. Patnaik 2017.

23. Fanon 1963 [1961]: 102.

24. Eurocentrism here is understood as "a particular position, a perspective, a way of seeing and not-seeing that is rooted in a number of problematic claims and assumptions" (Alatas and Sinha 2001: 319).

25. Beck 2000; Giddens 2002; Mann 2012. See also Connell 2007b; Go 2016b.

26. Cabral 1969: 62–64.

27. Césaire 2010 [1956]: 147.

28. Mignolo and Walsh 2018.

29. See Meghji 2020; Mondon and Winter 2020.

30. Meghji 2020.

31. See Fúnez-Flores 2022; Hall 1992; Said 1978, 1989.

32. Go 2011; Gopal 2019.

33. Chang 2002.

34. Grosfoguel 2017: 158.

35. Santos 2014.

36. Mignolo and Walsh 2018: 148.

37. See Getachew 2019.

38. Santos 2014: 207.

39. Quoted in Desai 2020.

40. Du Bois 2014 [1935]: 56–57.

41. Du Bois 1954: 2–3.

42. Du Bois 2008 [1920]: 308.

43. Connell 1997, 2007b; Go 2014.

44. Drake and Clayton 1962; Frazier 1957 [1955].

45. Wright 2002.

46. Bobo 2000; Bonilla-Silva 2015; Emirbayer and Desmond 2015; Feagin 2006; Golash-Boza 2016; Omi and Winant 2015.

47. Crenshaw 1988.

48. Delgado and Stefancic 2000 [1995].

49. Ibid.: xvi.

50. Ibid.: xvii.

51. Bell 1992.

52. Ladson-Billings 1999; Parker et al. 1999.

53. See Meghji 2022a.

54. Bonilla-Silva 1997.

55. Ibid.: 469.

56. Ibid.: 469–470.
57. Bonilla-Silva 1997, 2015, 2017a.
58. Bonilla-Silva 2015: 75.
59. Du Bois 2014 [1935].
60. Bonilla-Silva 2017a: 15.
61. Meghji and Saini 2018: 673.
62. Bonilla-Silva 2012: 174.
63. Ibid.
64. Bonilla-Silva et al. 2006: 231.
65. Bonilla-Silva 2019a: 3.
66. Ibid.
67. Lamont et al. 2017.
68. For a discussion of how reactionary politicians in the United Kingdom, the United States, and Australia have used "CRT" as a straw figure for any critical work on race and racism, see Meghji 2022a; Ray 2022. The quote is from Treviño et al. 2008: 9.
69. Go 2020b: 14.
70. Ibid.: 14.
71. Bonilla-Silva 2015: 74.
72. Bonilla-Silva 2017a: 15.
73. Kauanui 2016.
74. Darrah-Okike 2020.
75. Beardall 2021.
76. Steinmetz 2014: 79.
77. Maldonado-Torres 2007: 243.
78. Coulthard 2014: 39.
79. Du Bois 1954: 1–2.
80. Ibid.: 2.
81. Bell 1980; Crenshaw et al. 1995a.
82. Ladson-Billings 2013: 45.
83. Bonilla-Silva 2017b; Bonilla-Silva et al. 2006; Lewis 2004.
84. Bonilla-Silva 2017a, 2019b; Bonilla-Silva and Ray 2015.
85. Stewart-Harawira 2005: 42.
86. Go 2018: 441.
87. Rodney 2018 [1972].
88. Bhambra 2007.
89. Goldberg and Essed 2002: 4–5.
90. Bonilla-Silva 2019a, 2019b.
91. Mondon and Winter 2020.
92. Bonilla-Silva 2000: 192, emphasis added.
93. See Warmington 2020.
94. Meghji 2021, 2022a.

95. Goldberg 2015: 254.
96. Go 2009: 783.
97. Go 2018: 447.
98. Mignolo 2005.
99. Mignolo 2011a, 2011b.
100. Mignolo 2011b: 59.
101. Long 2018.
102. Go 2020a.
103. Bonilla-Silva 2000.
104. Hall 1991: 49.
105. Ibid.: 49.
106. Ibid.: 48.
107. Bhambra 2014: 149.
108. Christian 2019: 174.
109. Bourdieu 1990; Giddens 1984.
110. Christian 2019.
111. Bhambra 2014; Connell 2007b.
112. Connell 2018: 401.
113. Go 2020b.
114. Grosfoguel 2017: 163.
115. Fecht et al. 2015.
116. Meghji 2020.
117. Collins 2019.

Chapter 1

Epigraph: Anzaldúa 2006 [1987]: 317.
1. Collins 2019.
2. Castro-Gómez 2021.
3. Maldonado-Torres 2007.
4. Ibid.: 252.
5. Ibid.
6. Santos 2014.
7. Ibid.
8. See Meghji 2020.
9. Mignolo and Walsh 2018: 148.
10. Collins 1986; Harding 2004.
11. Zuberi and Bonilla-Silva 2008.
12. Ibid.: 4.
13. Crenshaw et al. 1995a: 314.
14. Du Bois 1898: 13–14.

15. Frazier 1947.
16. Fitzhugh 1854; Odum 2010 [1910]; Park 1914.
17. Ladner 1973; Stanfield 2011.
18. Zuberi and Bonilla-Silva 2008. See also Zuberi 2001.
19. Park 1950.
20. Ibid.
21. See Meghji 2022a.
22. Park 1928a, 1928b.
23. Park 1950.
24. Park and Burgess 1921: 631.
25. Cox 1944: 454.
26. For evidence of this criticism, see Park 1914, 1928a, 1928b; Park and Burgess 1921.
27. See Mignolo 2011a.
28. Mignolo 2007: 472.
29. Grosfoguel 2013: 87.
30. Mignolo 2011a; Simpson 2017.
31. Kenyatta 1979 [1938].
32. Ibid.
33. Olutayo 2014.
34. Bonilla-Silva 2015.
35. Delgado and Stefancic 2001: 9.
36. Du Bois 2007 [1903].
37. Delgado and Stefancic 2001: 9.
38. Crenshaw et al. 1995b: xix.
39. Ibid.
40. Crenshaw 2011.
41. Du Bois 2007 [1940]: 221.
42. Ibid.: 32.
43. Ibid.: 98.
44. Solorzano and Yosso 2001: 475.
45. Mignolo and Walsh 2018: 224.
46. Mignolo 2011c: 281.
47. Grosfoguel 2007: 219.
48. Ibid.: 158. On this quote, see also the Introduction in this volume.
49. See Bell 1992.
50. Bell 1980: 523; Delgado and Stefancic 2001: 154.
51. Crenshaw 1988.
52. Bell 1980.
53. Seamster and Ray 2018: 327.
54. Du Bois 2014 [1935].

55. See Davis 2006; Du Bois 2014 [1935].

56. Anzaldúa 2006 [1987]: 317.

57. Collins 2019: 32.

Chapter 2

1. Of course, this is part of a wider trend toward authoritarian populism that we have seen at the same time in contexts such as France (with rising support for Marine Le Pen), India (under Narendra Modi's regime), Israel (under Benjamin Netanyahu and now Isaac Herzog), and Viktor Orbán's regime in Hungary—to name a handful of cases.

2. Hall 2017: 200, emphasis added.

3. Ibid.: 203.

4. Quoted in Waterson 2020.

5. Dowden, quoted in Moore 2021; Donelan, quoted in Stubley 2021.

6. Gilroy 2004: 111.

7. Ashe 2016.

8. Hall 2017: 145.

9. Tinsley 2020.

10. Ibid.: 2336.

11. Williams 1977.

12. Bonilla-Silva 2019a: 9.

13. Tinsley 2020.

14. Ibid.

15. Ibid.: 2328.

16. Ibid.: 2331–2332.

17. Gilroy 2001.

18. See Davey and Ebner 2019.

19. See Jardina 2019; Outten et al. 2012.

20. Bonilla-Silva 2017a: 15.

21. Doane 2017: 977.

22. Bonilla-Silva 2019a: 3.

23. Simi et al. 2017.

24. Bonilla-Silva 2019a: 8.

25. See Sengul 2021.

26. Du Bois 2007 [1940].

27. Beaman 2021.

28. Kukutai and Didham 2012.

29. Bonilla-Silva 2019b: 9.

30. Song 2014.

31. Hochschild 2016.

32. Lamont et al. 2017.

33. Ibid.; Meghji 2022b.
34. Virdee and McGeever 2018.
35. Johnson 2016.
36. May 2017.
37. Shilliam 2020.
38. Bhambra 2017.
39. See Dixon 2017; Kaufmann 2017; O'Neill 2016.
40. Skelton 2019.
41. Fallows 2016; Jardina 2019: 91.
42. See Silva 2016.
43. Lamont et al. 2016: 128.
44. Bolsonaro 2018.
45. Quoted in Marques and Rocha 2015.
46. Seen in speeches such as the one at the Hebrew Club (Bolsonaro 2017). *Quilombola* refers to a resident of a quilombo, a settlement formed by escaped enslaved people in Brazil.
47. Watson 2020.
48. As argued in Schaefer 2019.
49. Johnson 2016.
50. See Virdee and McGeever 2018.
51. May 2017.
52. Quoted in Watson 2020.
53. Leal 2017.
54. Phillips 2019.
55. Pachá 2019.
56. Eduardo Bolsonaro chaired the International Affairs and National Defense Committee.
57. Goldhill 2019.
58. Ibid.
59. It should be noted that *Judeo-Christian values* is a term used by Bolsonaro and other media and political figures; it is not a term I find useful for describing geopolitics and power. Anya Topolski (2020), for instance, has highlighted how the term *Judeo Christian* is often used as an exclusionary boundary against Muslims while providing no concrete support or inclusive boundary toward the Jewish diaspora.
60. Jair Bolsonaro, quoted in Marques and Rocha 2015.
61. Leal 2017.

Chapter 3

Epigraph: Marcos 1997.
1. See Cole 2009a, 2017; Cole and Maisuria 2007.

2. Cole 2009b: 247.

3. Cole 2017: 9. See also Gillborn 2005, 2006; Mills 1997: 37.

4. Cole 2009a: 114.

5. Cole 2009b: 249. See also Mills 1997: 37.

6. Cole 2009b.

7. Mills 2009: 270.

8. Bonilla-Silva 2017a; Crenshaw 1988.

9. See Mignolo 2011a; Weiner 2018.

10. Grosfoguel 2008.

11. Mignolo 2011c: 281.

12. Meghji 2020.

13. Marx 1853.

14. Patnaik and Patnaik 2021: 275.

15. Du Bois 2007 [1940]: 151.

16. Mignolo 2002: 247, emphasis added.

17. Ibid.: 247.

18. See Asher 2013.

19. Other scholars, such as Alana Lentin (2020), refer to this ideology as one of "not racism."

20. Crenshaw 1988.

21. Ibid.: 1337.

22. Ibid.

23. Ibid.: 1338.

24. Sowell 2009 [1984]: 116.

25. Ibid.

26. Indeed, neoliberalism was so essential to the maintenance of the racial order that other scholars outside of the CRT tradition began to theorize "racial neoliberalism" as means of explaining how increasing individualism and state retrenchment were fundamentally expressions of racialized power (see Goldberg 2009; Kapoor 2011).

27. An example of this could be in *Milliken v Bradley* (1974), in which the U.S. Supreme Court refused a remedy for racial segregation in Detroit (where the whites had fled to the suburbs, leaving Black people concentrated in urban areas, de facto segregated both residentially and educationally in poorer social and educational spaces). Despite the district court proposing a scheme that would integrate across the urban and suburban schools, the Supreme Court, to battle educational segregation, directly evoked the antidiscrimination law that "an inter-district remedy might be in order where the racially discriminatory acts of one or more school districts caused racial segregation in an adjacent district, or where district lines have been deliberately drawn on the basis of race." However, it found no evidence of either of these violations.

28. See Gillborn 2005.

29. See Ladson-Billings 2011. For instance, by 2015, twenty-nine states were still providing less total school funding per student than they were in 2008.

30. See Bonilla-Silva 2021.

31. See Giroux 2006; Virdee 2015.

32. See Du Bois 2007 [1903]; Thomas 2020.

33. Du Bois 1968: 127; see Thomas 2020.

34. See Virdee 2015.

35. Davis 1984.

36. Ibid.; Wacquant 2010.

37. Parks and Rachlinski 2013: 201.

38. A story and justification which, as Michael Omi and Howard Winant (2015) show, carried on through the successive administrations.

39. See Bezusko 2013.

40. Hopewell 2013: 605. Such neoliberalization of Brazil involved the privatization of large economic sectors (transport, steel, petrochemicals, public utilities), low tariff trade with the (over)developed countries, and increasing foreign capital investment (see Amann and Baer 2002).

41. Carrillo 2021.

42. Ibid.: 60.

43. Ibid.: 61.

44. Ibid.

45. Mignolo 2005.

46. On racial capitalism, see Go 2021. On Black nationalism, see Robinson 1983.

47. This is the point made by Immanuel Wallerstein (2000: 87) when he commented that "capitalism was from the beginning an affair of the world-economy and not of the nation-states. It is a misreading of the situation to claim that it is only in the twentieth century that capitalism has become 'worldwide.'"

48. Fanon 1963 [1961]: 101, emphasis added.

49. Williams 1944: 5. Of course, this quote itself echoes in Stuart Hall's (1991: 48) later declaration half a century later that he is the "sugar at the bottom of the English cup of tea."

50. Patnaik 2017.

51. Césaire 2001 [1950].

52. See Bhambra 2007; Gilroy 1993.

53. From the more critical race theory side parallel arguments are developed in Bonilla-Silva et al. (2006), Du Bois (2014 [1935]), Lipsitz (1998), and Roediger (2007 [1991]), among others, in the way they discuss a possessive investment in the wages of whiteness. They highlight how poor white workers in the United States have often supported policies and projects that are bad for them (such as Jim Crow) if those policies allow them to maintain a degree of racial superiority.

54. Quoted in Desai 2020: 144.

55. See Bhattacharyya 2018.

56. Du Bois 1954: 2.

57. Boatcă 2021.

58. Mignolo 2005.

59. Patnaik and Patnaik 2021: 258.

60. See Chang 2002.

61. See World Bank 2020. Of course, this begs the questions as to whether they are the "least developed" nations or, instead, *underdeveloped*, as Walter Rodney (2018 [1972]) reminds us to always question.

62. Subcomandante Marcos 1997.

63. TRTWorld 2020.

64. Subcomandante Marcos 1997.

65. World Vision 2021.

66. Roser and Ortiz-Ospina 2013.

67. Subcomandante Marcos 1997.

68. Ibid.

69. Ibid.

70. Bhattacharyya 2018: 26.

71. See Mbembe 2000.

72. Unicef 2022.

73. See Doward 2020; Pattisson 2021; Ungoed-Thomas 2022.

Chapter 4

1. Santos 2014: 9.

2. Friedman 2022, emphasis added.

3. See Crenshaw 2011.

4. Freeman 1995.

5. Ibid.: 30.

6. Bell 1995: 24.

7. Crenshaw et al. 1995b: xv.

8. Cole 1992: 1992.

9. The Fourteenth Amendment states, "No State shall make or enforce any law which shall abridge the privileges or immunities of citizens of the United States; nor shall any State deprive any person of life, liberty, or property, without due process of law; nor deny to any person within its jurisdiction the equal protection of the laws."

10. Cole 1992: 1996.

11. Ibid.: 1996–1997.

12. Pulido 2017.

13. As the order read, it called on federal agencies to "make achieving environmental justice part of [their] mission by identifying and addressing, as appropri-

ate, disproportionately high and adverse human health or environmental effects of its programs, policies, and activities on minority populations and low-income populations."

14. Gross and Stretesky 2015.

15. See Liévanos 2012.

16. See Patnaik 2017; Patnaik and Patnaik 2021.

17. And indeed, as Kyle Whyte (2018) argues, outside of academic journals Indigenous people had been theorizing the same phenomena since their experiences of it beginning with settler-colonial projects in the late 1400s.

18. Alatas 2006: 20.

19. Connell 2018: 403.

20. Du Bois 1954: 3, emphasis added.

21. Dussel 1999: 17, emphasis added.

22. See Whyte 2017, 2020.

23. Prause 2020.

24. For a critique of this realization, see Chakrabarty 2009; Saldanha 2020. See also Roberts and Parks 2006.

25. Sealey-Huggins 2017.

26. Ibid.

27. See Sultana 2022.

28. *Buen vivir* is commonly translated as "living well" or "good living."

29. See García Álvarez 2013.

30. Villavicencio Calzadilla and Kotzé 2018: 408–409.

31. Radcliffe 2012: 241.

32. See Fuentes 2014.

33. See Lalander 2016; Radcliffe 2012; Rodriguez Fernandez 2020; Villalba 2013; Villavicencio Calzadilla and Kotzé 2018.

34. See Radcliffe 2012.

35. Villavicencio Calzadilla and Kotzé 2018.

36. Angel and López-Londoño 2018: 58.

37. See Hund 2015.

38. Darrah-Okike 2020: 4.

39. Chakrabarty 2009.

40. Coupled with the rise of "natural science" as a discrete subject in its own right.

41. Chakrabarty 2009: 208.

42. Adorno and Horkheimer 2002 [1944].

43. Stalin 1938.

44. See Figueroa Helland and Lindgren 2016; Whyte 2017, 2018.

45. Cassano 2010: 214, emphasis added.

46. Goswami 2013: 106, emphasis added.

47. Mignolo and Walsh 2018: 167

48. Darrah-Okike 2020: 4.
49. Meyer 2008.
50. Ibid.: 219.

Chapter 5

1. The rate was 17.47, measured in deaths per million people.
2. Quoted in Almeida 2021.
3. Cited in Bonilla-Silva 2020: 5.
4. Hancock 2020.
5. See Laster Pirtle 2020; Link and Phelan 1995; Phelan and Link 2015.
6. Public Health England 2020.
7. See Brynin and Longhi 2015; Li and Heath 2020.
8. Hu 2020.
9. Platt and Warwick 2020.
10. Egbert and Liao 2020.
11. Bonilla-Silva 2020.
12. Alexander 2012 (employment); Charron-Chénier and Seamster 2021 (debt); Gilmore 2007 (incarceration); Pattillo 2013 (housing).
13. Public Health England 2020.
14. Haque et al. 2020.
15. Ibid.
16. CNN Newsroom 2020, emphasis added.
17. Nelson 2020.
18. Frakt 2020.
19. Bonilla-Silva 2020: 345.
20. Briggs 2005: 273.
21. See Sennet 2002. The Ghetto Nuovo was created for seven hundred Jews in 1516; Ghetto Vecchio was created in 1541; and Ghetto Nuovissimo was created in 1631.
22. Gao and Sai 2020: 2.
23. Yam 2022. For a discussion of Korean Americans being afraid of wearing face masks because it attracts racist violence, see Hong 2021.
24. Gao and Sai 2020.
25. Public Health England 2020: 7–8.
26. Ibid.: 8.
27. Quoted in Rodger 2020.
28. Quoted in ITV News 2020.
29. Bonilla-Silva 2020: 345.
30. Public Health England 2020: 23.
31. Hancock 2020.

32. Public Health England 2020.

33. Quoted in Bonilla-Silva 2020: 348.

34. Ibid.

35. Lemon 2020.

36. Lemon 2020.

37. Of course, Biden was referring to the Tuskegee syphilis study. The Tuskegee Airmen were military pilots.

38. Not mentioning, of course, that millions of Latinx were U.S. citizens. Biden thus conflated a racialized group with a stereotype of being "illegal."

39. Bateman et al. 2021.

40. Abdul-Mutakabbir et al. 2021 (California); Mintz et al. 2021 (Pennsylvania).

41. Bonilla-Silva 2003.

42. Jackson and Stewart 2003.

43. Fecht et al. 2015.

44. See Cameron et al. 2019.

45. Oppenheim et al. 2019: 1.

46. Data retrieved from Statista 2022.

47. Mignolo 2005.

48. Go 2016b: 98.

49. Quoted in BBC News 2020. On "little Englander universalism," see Meghji and Niang 2021.

50. Greenhalgh et al. 2020.

51. Bloom and Shadwell 2020; Howard 2020.

52. Cohen 2020.

53. Ting 2020.

54. Al-Ramahi et al. 2021.

55. Cited in ibid.

56. Robertson 2020.

57. Ibid.

58. McGuinness 2020.

59. Quoted in O'Donoghue 2020.

60. Gopal 2019.

61. Getachew 2019.

62. Quoted in Staunton 2020.

63. See Meghji and Niang 2021.

64. Lewis 2020.

65. John Oeltmann, head of contact-tracing assessment at the CDC, quoted in ibid.

66. Kliff 2020.

67. Barrett 2021.

Conclusion

1. Bourdieu and Wacquant 1992.

2. I use the term *scholar activist* to highlight intellectuals who have not confined themselves to ivory towers. The term has often been used in discussions of Du Bois (see, e.g., Itzigsohn and Brown 2020).

3. Cabral 1966.

4. Mignolo and Walsh 2018: 21.

5. Golash-Boza 2016: 129.

6. Hall 1991: 42.

7. Collins 2019: 92.

8. Collins 1998: xiv.

9. See Lehman 2021.

10. Mignolo and Walsh 2018: 17.

11. Newton 2002: 170.

12. See Narayan 2019; Rodriguez 2006.

13. Malcolm X 2013 [1963].

14. Newton 2002: 169.

15. See Davis 1998.

16. Ibid.: 281.

17. Newton 2002: 172.

18. Ibid.: 169–170.

19. Ibid.: 170, emphasis added.

20. Ibid.: 253. See also Go 2020a.

21. Davis 2016.

22. Ibid.: 83.

23. Ibid.: 139–140.

24. Ibid.: 140.

25. See Naber 2017. Black Lives Matter (2021) tweeted, for example, "Black Lives Matter stands in solidarity with Palestinians. We are a movement committed to ending settler colonialism in all forms and will continue to advocate for Palestinian liberation. (always have. And always will be)."

26. Subcomandante Marcos 2002a: 13, emphasis added.

27. See Chang 2008.

28. See Mora 2017.

29. Grosfoguel 2017.

30. Subcomandante Marcos 2002a.

31. Ibid.: 18.

32. Ibid.

33. Including people from both the metropoles, such as Austria, Canada, Denmark, Italy, France, Germany, Great Britain, Portugal, Greece, and the United States, and the postcolonies, such as Argentina, Bolivia, Brazil, Chile, Colombia,

Costa Rica, Cuba, Ecuador, Guatemala, Haiti, Iran, Ireland, Kurdistan, Mauritania, Mexico, Nicaragua, Paraguay, Peru, the Philippines, Puerto Rico, South Africa, Uruguay, Venezuela, and Zaire.

34. Subcomandante Marcos 2002a: 117, emphasis added.

35. Ibid.: 118.

36. Ibid.: 123.

37. Césaire 2001 [1950]: 84.

38. Subcomandante Marcos 2002a: 122.

39. Ibid.: 194

40. Whereupon they exclaimed: "But we also know, as the Indigenous people that we are, that the PALESTINIAN people will resist and will rise again, that they will once again begin to walk and that they will know then that, although we are far away on the map, the Zapatista peoples embrace them today as we have before, as we always do, with our collective heart."

41. The Zapatistas' Declaration for Life is available at https://enlacezapatista .ezln.org.mx/2021/01/01/part-one-a-declaration-for-life.

42. Mignolo 2002.

43. Zapatistas' Declaration for Life, https://enlacezapatista.ezln.org.mx/2021 /01/01/part-one-a-declaration-for-life, emphasis added.

44. See Alexander 2012; Wacquant 2008.

45. See Lehman 2021.

46. Virdee 2019: 6.

47. James 2001 [1938].

48. Mignolo and Walsh 2018: 17.

References

Abdul-Mutakabbir, J. C., Casey, S., Jews, V., et al. (2021). A Three-Tiered Approach to Address Barriers to COVID-19 Vaccine Delivery in the Black Community. *Lancet Global Health, 9*(6), e749–e750. doi:10.1016/S2214-109X(21)00099-1.

Alatas, S. F., and Sinha, V. (2001). Teaching Classical Sociological Theory in Singapore: The Context of Eurocentrism. *Teaching Sociology, 29*(3), 316–331. doi:10.2307/1319190.

Alatas, S. F., and Sinha, V. (2017). *Sociological Theory beyond the Canon.* London: Palgrave. Accessed March 12, 2019. Available at https://www.palgrave.com/gb/book/9781137411334.

Alatas, S. H. (2006). The Autonomous, the Universal and the Future of Sociology. *Current Sociology, 54*(1), 7–23.

Alexander, M. (2012). *The New Jim Crow.* New York: New Press.

Almeida, A. (2021). The Government Must Not Use Pseudo-science to Dismiss COVID's Impact on BME Communities. *Runnymede Trust,* January 25. Accessed March 28, 2023. Available at https://www.runnymedetrust.org//blog/the-government-must-not-use-biology-to-dismiss-covids-impact-on-bme-communities.

Al-Ramahi, M., Elnoshokaty, A., El-Gayar, E., et al. (2021). Public Discourse against Masks in the COVID-19 Era: Infodemiology Study of Twitter Data. *JMIR Public Health and Surveillance, 7*(4), e26780. doi:10.2196/26780.

Amann, E., and Baer, W. (2002). Neoliberalism and Its Consequences in Brazil. *Journal of Latin American Studies, 34*(4), 945–959. doi:10.1017/S0022216X02006612.

Angel, A., and López-Londoño, L. M. (2018). Delinking Rhetorics of Neoliberalism: An Analysis of South American Leftist Presidents' Speeches. *Journal of International and Intercultural Communication*, 12(1), 43–62.

Anzaldúa, G. (2006 [1987]). To Live in the Borderlands Means You. In L. P. Rudnick et al. (Eds.), *American Identities: An Introductory Textbook* (316–317). Malden, MA: Blackwell.

Ashe, S. (2016). UKIP, Brexit and Postcolonial Melancholy. *Discover Society*, June 1. Accessed June 10, 2020. Available at https://discoversociety.org/2016/06/01/ukip-brexit-and-postcolonial-melancholy.

Asher, K. (2013). Latin American Decolonial Thought, or Making the Subaltern Speak. *Geography Compass*, 7(12), 832–842. doi:10.1111/gec3.12102.

Barrett, A. (2021). The K Factor: Nevermind R, Here's the Number We Need to Understand. *BBC Science Focus Magazine*. Accessed May 26, 2022. Available at https://www.sciencefocus.com/news/the-k-factor-nevermind-r-heres-the-number-we-need-to-understand.

Bateman, L. B., Schoenberger, Y.-M. M., Hansen, B., et al. (2021). Confronting COVID-19 in Under-resourced, African American Neighborhoods: A Qualitative Study Examining Community Member and Stakeholders' Perceptions. *Ethnicity and Health*, 26(1), 49–67. doi:10.1080/13557858.2021.1873250.

BBC News (2020). Coronavirus: New COVID Restrictions Could Last Six Months, Says Boris Johnson. *BBC News*, September 22. Accessed March 28, 2023. Available at https://www.bbc.com/news/uk-54250696.

Beaman, J. (2021). France's Ahmeds and Muslim Others: The Entanglement of Racism and Islamophobia. *French Cultural Studies*, 32(3), 09571558211009370. doi:10.1177/09571558211009370.

Beardall, T. R. (2021). Social-distancing the Settler-State Indigenous Peoples in the Age of COVID-19. In G. W. Muschert et al. (Eds.), *Social Problems in the Age of COVID* (39–50). Bristol, U.K.: Policy.

Beck, U. (2000). *What Is Globalization?* Oxford: Blackwell.

Bell, D. A. (1980). *Brown v. Board of Education* and the Interest-Convergence Dilemma. *Harvard Law Review*, 93(3), 518–533.

Bell, D. A. (1992). Racial Realism. *Connecticut Law Review*, 24(2), 363–379.

Bell, D. A. (1995). Serving Two Masters: Integration Ideals and Client Interests. In K. W. Crenshaw et al. (Eds.), *Critical Race Theory: The Key Writings That Formed the Movement* (5–19). New York: New Press.

Bezusko, A. (2013). Criminalizing Black Motherhood: How the War on Welfare Was Won. *Souls*, 15(1–2), 39–55. doi:10.1080/10999949.2013.803813.

Bhambra, G. K. (2007). *Rethinking Modernity: Postcolonialism and the Sociological Imagination*. London: Palgrave Macmillan.

Bhambra, G. K. (2014). *Connected Sociologies*. London: Bloomsbury.

Bhambra, G. K. (2017). Brexit, Trump, and "Methodological Whiteness": On the

Misrecognition of Race and Class. *British Journal of Sociology*, *68*(1), 214–232. doi:10.1111/1468-4446.12317.

Bhattacharyya, G. (2018). *Rethinking Racial Capitalism: Questions of Reproduction and Survival*. Lanham, MD: Rowman and Littlefield.

Black Lives Matter. (2021). Black Lives Matter Stands in Solidarity [Tweet]. Twitter, May 17. Accessed January 31, 2023. Available at https://twitter.com/Blklivesmatter/status/1394289672101064704.

Bloom, D., and Shadwell, T. (2020). Government Says "No Evidence" Wearing Face Masks Affects Coronavirus Spread. *The Mirror*, April 3. Accessed August 10, 2020. Available at https://www.mirror.co.uk/news/politics/government-says-no-evidence-wearing-21810110.

Boatcă, M. (2021). Global Inequalities *avant la Lettre*: Immanuel Wallerstein's Contribution. *Socio*, *15*, 71–91. doi:10.4000/socio.10999.

Bobo, L. D. (2000). Reclaiming a Du Boisian Perspective on Racial Attitudes. *Annals of the American Academy of Political and Social Science*, *568*(1), 186–202. doi:10.1177/000271620056800114.

Bolsonaro, J. (2017). *Bolsonaro faz discurso de ódio no Clube Hebraica* [Video]. Intercept Brasil, April 5. YouTube. Accessed June 18, 2020. Available at https://www.youtube.com/watch?v=zSTdTjsio5g.

Bolsonaro, J. (2018). *Entrevista com Jair Bolsonaro* [Video]. *Globo News*, August 4. YouTube. Accessed June 18, 2020. Available at https://www.youtube.com/watch?v=zykvBACFzGg.

Bonilla-Silva, E. (1997). Rethinking Racism: Toward a Structural Interpretation. *American Sociological Review*, *62*(3), 465–480. doi:10.2307/2657316.

Bonilla-Silva, E. (2000). "This Is a White Country": The Racial Ideology of the Western Nations of the World-System. *Sociological Inquiry*, *70*(2), 188–214. doi:10.1111/j.1475-682X.2000.tb00905.x.

Bonilla-Silva, E. (2003). Racial Attitudes or Racial Ideology? An Alternative Paradigm for Examining Actors' Racial Views. *Journal of Political Ideologies*, *8*(1), 63–82. doi:10.1080/13569310306082.

Bonilla-Silva, E. (2012). The Invisible Weight of Whiteness: The Racial Grammar of Everyday Life in Contemporary America. *Ethnic and Racial Studies*, *35*(2), 173–194. doi:10.1080/01419870.2011.613997.

Bonilla-Silva, E. (2015). More than Prejudice: Restatement, Reflections, and New Directions in Critical Race Theory. *Sociology of Race and Ethnicity*, *1*(1), 73–87. doi:10.1177/2332649214557042.

Bonilla-Silva, E. (2017a). *Racism without Racists: Color-blind Racism and the Persistence of Racial Inequality in America* (5th ed.). Lanham, MD: Rowman and Littlefield.

Bonilla-Silva, E. (2017b). What We Were, What We Are, and What We Should Be: The Racial Problem of American Sociology. *Social Problems*, *64*(2), 179–187.

Bonilla-Silva, E. (2019a). Feeling Race: Theorizing the Racial Economy of Emotions. *American Sociological Review*, *84*(1), 1–25. doi:10.1177/0003122418816958.

Bonilla-Silva, E. (2019b). Toward a New Political Praxis for Trumpamerica: New Directions in Critical Race Theory. *American Behavioral Scientist*, *63*(13), 1776–1788. doi:10.1177/0002764219842614.

Bonilla-Silva, E. (2020). Color-blind Racism in Pandemic Times. *Sociology of Race and Ethnicity*, *8*(3), 343–354. doi:10.1177/2332649220941024.

Bonilla-Silva, E. (2021). What Makes Systemic Racism Systemic? *Sociological Inquiry*, *91*(3), 513–533. doi:10.1111/soin.12420.

Bonilla-Silva, E., Goar, C., and Embrick, D. G. (2006). When Whites Flock Together: The Social Psychology of White Habitus. *Critical Sociology*, *32*(2–3), 229–253. doi:10.1163/156916306777835268.

Bonilla-Silva, E., and Ray, V. E. (2015). Getting over the Obama Hangover: The New Racism in "Post-racial" America. In K. Murji and J. Solomos (Eds.), *Theories of Race and Ethnicity: Contemporary Debates and Perspectives* (57–73). Cambridge: Cambridge University Press.

Bourdieu, P. (1990). *The Logic of Practice*. Cambridge: Polity.

Bourdieu, P., and Wacquant, L. (1992). *An Invitation to Reflexive Sociology*. Cambridge: Polity.

Briggs, C. L. (2005). Communicability, Racial Discourse, and Disease. *Annual Review of Anthropology*, *34*(1), 269–291. doi:10.1146/annurev.anthro.34.081804.120618.

Brynin, M., and Longhi, S. (2015). *The Effect of Occupation on Poverty among Ethnic Minority Groups*. York, U.K.: Joseph Rowntree Foundation. Accessed May 28, 2015. Available at http://www.jrf.org.uk/publications/effect-occupation-poverty-among-ethnic-minority-groups.

Cabral, A. (1966). *The Weapon of Theory* [Address]. Tricontinental Conference of the Peoples of Asia, Africa and Latin America, Havana, Cuba. Available at https://www.marxists.org/subject/africa/cabral/1966/weapon-theory.htm.

Cabral, A. (1969). *Selected Texts by Amílcar Cabral: Revolution in Guinea, An African People's Struggle*. London: Stage 1.

Cameron, E., Nuzzo, J., and Bell, J. (2019). *2019 Global Health Security Index: Building Collective Action and Accountability*. Baltimore: Johns Hopkins Bloomberg School of Public Health.

Carrillo, I. (2021). Racialized Organizations and Color-blind Racial Ideology in Brazil. *Sociology of Race and Ethnicity*, *7*(1), 56–70. doi:10.1177/2332649220943223.

Cassano, F. (2010). South of Every North. In M. Boatcă et al. (Eds.), *Decolonizing European Sociology: Transdisciplinary Approaches* (213–224). Surrey, U.K.: Ashgate.

Castro-Gómez, S. (2021). *Zero-Point Hubris: Science, Race, and Enlightenment in Eighteenth-Century Latin America*. Lanham, MD: Rowman and Littlefield.

Césaire, A. (2001 [1950]). *Discourse on Colonialism*. New York: New York University Press.

Césaire, A. (2010 [1956]). Letter to Maurice Thorez. *Social Text*, 28(2 [103]), 145–152. doi:10.1215/01642472-2009-072.

Chakrabarty, D. (2009). The Climate of History: Four Theses. *Critical Inquiry*, 35(2), 197–222. doi:10.1086/596640.

Chang, H.-J. (2002). *Kicking Away the Ladder: Development Strategy in Historical Perspective*. London: Anthem.

Chang, H.-J. (2008). *Bad Samaritans: The Guilty Secrets of Rich Nations and the Threat to Global Prosperity*. London: Random House.

Charron-Chénier, R., and Seamster, L. (2021). Racialized Debts: Racial Exclusion from Credit Tools and Information Networks. *Critical Sociology*, 47(6), 977–992. doi:10.1177/0896920519894635.

Christian, M. (2019). A Global Critical Race and Racism Framework: Racial Entanglements and Deep and Malleable Whiteness. *Sociology of Race and Ethnicity*, 5(2), 169–185. doi:10.1177/2332649218783220.

CNN Newsroom. (2020). Transcripts. *CNN*, April 8. Available at http://edition.cnn.com/TRANSCRIPTS/2004/08/cnr.22.html.

Cohen, J. (2020). Not Wearing Masks to Protect against Coronavirus Is a "Big Mistake," Top Chinese Scientist Says. *Science*, March 27. Accessed August 10, 2020. Available at https://www.sciencemag.org/news/2020/03/not-wearing-masks-protect-against-coronavirus-big-mistake-top-chinese-scientist-says.

Cole, L. W. (1992). Remedies for Environmental Racism: A View from the Field. *Michigan Law Review*, 90(7), 1991–1997. doi:10.2307/1289740.

Cole, M. (2009a). The Color-Line and the Class Struggle: A Marxist Response to Critical Race Theory in Education as It Arrives in the United Kingdom. *Power and Education*, 1(1), 111–124. doi:10.2304/power.2009.1.1.111.

Cole, M. (2009b). Critical Race Theory Comes to the UK: A Marxist Response. *Ethnicities*, 9(2), 246–269. doi:10.1177/1468796809103462.

Cole, M. (2017). *Critical Race Theory and Education: A Marxist Response*. London: Springer.

Cole, M., and Maisuria, A. (2007). "Shut the F*** Up," "You Have No Rights Here": Critical Race Theory and Racialisation in Post-7/7 Racist Britain. *Journal for Critical Education Policy Studies*, 5(1), 94–120.

Collins, P. H. (1986). Learning from the Outsider Within: The Sociological Significance of Black Feminist Thought. *Social Problems*, 33(6), s14–s32. doi:10.2307/800672.

Collins, P. H. (1998). *Fighting Words: Black Women and the Search for Justice*. Minneapolis: University of Minnesota Press.

Collins, P. H. (2019). *Intersectionality as Critical Social Theory*. Durham, NC: Duke University Press.

Connell, R. W. (1997). Why Is Classical Theory Classical? *American Journal of Sociology, 102*(6), 1511–1557. doi:10.1086/231125.

Connell, R. W. (2007a). The Northern Theory of Globalization. *Sociological Theory, 25*(4), 368–385. doi:10.1111/j.1467-9558.2007.00314.x.

Connell, R. W. (2007b). *Southern Theory: The Global Dynamics of Knowledge in Social Science.* Cambridge: Polity.

Connell, R. W. (2018). Decolonizing Sociology. *Contemporary Sociology, 47*(4), 399–407. doi:10.1177/0094306118779811.

Coulthard, G. S. (2014). *Red Skin, White Masks: Rejecting the Colonial Politics of Recognition.* Minneapolis: University of Minnesota Press.

Cox, Oliver C. (1944). The Racial Theories of Robert E. Park and Ruth Benedict. *Journal of Negro Education, 13*(4), 452–463.

Crenshaw, K. W. (1988). Race, Reform, and Retrenchment: Transformation and Legitimation in Antidiscrimination Law. *Harvard Law Review, 101*(7), 1331–1387.

Crenshaw, K. W. (2011). Twenty Years of Critical Race Theory: Looking back to Move Forward. *Connecticut Law Review, 43*(5), 1253–1354.

Crenshaw, K. W., Gotanda, N., Peller, G., et al. (1995a). *Critical Race Theory: The Key Writings That Formed the Movement.* New York: New Press.

Crenshaw, K. W., Gotanda, N., Peller, G., et al. (1995b). Introduction. In K. W. Crenshaw et al. (Eds.), *Critical Race Theory: The Key Writings That Formed the Movement* (xiii–xxxii). New York: New Press.

Darrah-Okike, J. (2020). Theorizing Race in Hawai'i: Centering Place, Indigeneity, and Settler Colonialism. *Sociology Compass, 14*(7), e12791. doi:10.1111/soc4.12791.

Davey, J., and Ebner, J. (2019). *The "Great Replacement": The Violent Consequences of Mainstreamed Extremism.* London: Institute for Strategic Dialogue.

Davis, A. Y. (1984). *Women, Culture, and Politics.* New York: Vintage.

Davis, A. Y. (1998). *The Angela Y. Davis Reader.* Malden, MA: Blackwell.

Davis, A. Y. (2006 [1987]). Racialized Punishment and Prison Abolition. In T. L. Lott and J. P. Pittman (Eds.), *A Companion to African-American Philosophy* (360–369). Malden, MA: Blackwell. doi:10.1002/9780470751640.ch23.

Davis, A. Y. (2016). *Freedom Is a Constant Struggle: Ferguson, Palestine, and the Foundations of a Movement.* Chicago: Haymarket.

Delgado, R., and Stefancic, J. (Eds.). (2000 [1995]). *Critical Race Theory: The Cutting Edge* (2d ed.). Philadelphia: Temple University Press.

Delgado, R., and Stefancic, J. (2001). *Critical Race Theory: An Introduction.* New York: New York University Press.

Desai, M. (2020). *The United States of India: Anticolonial Literature and Transnational Refraction.* Philadelphia: Temple University Press.

Dixon, C. (2017). Brexit Demands for Migration Control Do Not Make People Racist, Says Report. *The Express*, December 21. Accessed June 11, 2020. Available at https://www.express.co.uk/news/uk/895400/brexit-immigration-con trol-racism-intolerance-EU-report.

Doane, A. (2017). Beyond Color-blindness: (Re)Theorizing Racial Ideology. *Sociological Perspectives*, *60*(5), 975–991. doi:10.1177/0731121417719697.

Doward, J. (2020). Children as Young as Eight Picked Coffee Beans on Farms Supplying Starbucks. *The Observer*, March 1. Accessed August 31, 2022. Available at https://www.theguardian.com/business/2020/mar/01/children -work-for-pittance-to-pick-coffee-beans-used-by-starbucks-and-nespresso.

Drake, S. C., and Cayton, H. R. (1962). *Black Metropolis: A Study of Negro Life in a Northern City*. New York: Harper and Row.

Du Bois, W.E.B. (1898). The Study of the Negro Problems. *Annals of the American Academy of Political and Social Science*, *11*, 1–23.

Du Bois, W.E.B. (1954). The Status of Colonialism, June 18, 1954. *W.E.B. Du Bois Papers, 1803–1999*. Special Collections and University Archives, University of Massachusetts Amherst Libraries. Accessed July 11, 2019. Available at https://credo.library.umass.edu/view/full/mums312-b204-i042.

Du Bois, W.E.B. (1967 [1899]). *The Philadelphia Negro: A Social Study*. New York: Schocken.

Du Bois, W.E.B. (1968). *The Autobiography of W.E.B. Du Bois: A Soliloquy on Viewing My Life from the Final Decade of Its First Century* (H. Aptheker, Ed.). New York: International.

Du Bois, W.E.B. (2007 [1903]). *The Souls of Black Folk*. Oxford: Oxford University Press.

Du Bois, W.E.B. (2007 [1940]). *Dusk of Dawn: An Essay Toward an Autobiography of a Race Concept*. Oxford: Oxford University Press.

Du Bois, W.E.B. (2007 [1947]). *The World and Africa: An Inquiry into the Part Which Africa Has Played in World History and Color and Democracy*. Oxford: Oxford University Press.

Du Bois, W.E.B. (2008 [1920]). The Souls of White Folk. In S. Appelrouth and L. D. Edles (Eds.), *Classical and Contemporary Sociological Theory: Text and Readings* (305–309). Los Angeles: Pine Forge.

Du Bois, W.E.B. (2014 [1935]). *Black Reconstruction in America: An Essay Toward a History of the Part Which Black Folk Played in the Attempt to Reconstruct Democracy in America, 1860–1880*. Oxford: Oxford University Press.

Dussel, E. D. (1999). Beyond Eurocentrism: The World-System and the Limits of Modernity. In F. Jameson and M. Miyoshi (Eds.), *The Cultures of Globalization* (3–31). Durham, NC: Duke University Press.

Dussel, E. D. (2002). World-System and "Trans"-Modernity (A. Fornazzari, Trans.). *Nepantla: Views from South*, *3*(2), 221–244.

Egbert, A., and Liao, K. (2020). *Color of Coronavirus, 2020 in Review*. APM Research Lab, December 21. Accessed August 31, 2022. Available at https://www .apmresearchlab.org/covid/deaths-2020-review.

Emirbayer, M., and Desmond, M. (2015). *The Racial Order*. Chicago: University of Chicago Press.

Fallows, J. (2016). The Revolt of the Masses: Confusing Taste and Fact. *The Atlantic*, April 14. Accessed June 11, 2020. Available at https://www.theatlantic.com/notes/2016/04/the-revolt-of-the-masses-confusing-taste-and-fact/478212.

Fanon, F. (1963 [1961]). *The Wretched of the Earth*. New York: Grove Weidenfeld.

Feagin, J. R. (2006). *Systemic Racism: A Theory of Oppression*. New York: Routledge.

Fecht, D., Fischer P., Fortunato, L., et al. (2015). Associations between Air Pollution and Socioeconomic Characteristics, Ethnicity and Age Profile of Neighbourhoods in England and the Netherlands. *Environmental Pollution, 198*, 201–210. doi:10.1016/j.envpol.2014.12.014.

Figueroa Helland, L. E., and Lindgren, T. (2016). What Goes around Comes around: From the Coloniality of Power to the Crisis of Civilization. *Journal of World-Systems Research, 22*(2), 430–462.

Fitzhugh, G. (1854). *Sociology for the South, or the Failure of Free Society*. Richmond, VA: A. Morris.

Frakt, A. (2020). *Social Determinants, Racism, and COVID-19*. Cambridge, MA: Harvard Global Health Institute. Accessed August 31, 2022. Available at https://globalhealth.harvard.edu/social-determinants-racism-and-covid-19.

Frazier, E. F. (1947). Sociological Theory and Race Relations. *American Sociological Review, 12*(3), 265. doi:10.2307/2086515.

Frazier, E. F. (1957 [1955]). *Black Bourgeoisie*. New York: Free Press.

Freeman, A. D. (1995). Legitimizing Racial Discrimination through Antidiscrimination Law: A Critical Review of Supreme Court Doctrine. In K. W. Crenshaw et al. (Eds.), *Critical Race Theory: The Key Writings That Formed the Movement* (29–45). New York: New Press.

Friedman, L. (2022). White House Takes Aim at Environmental Racism, but Won't Mention Race. *New York Times*, February 15. Accessed August 31, 2022. Available at https://www.nytimes.com/2022/02/15/climate/biden-environment-race-pollution.html.

Fuentes, F. (2014). Bolivian Reality versus the "Extractivism" Debate. *Climate and Capitalism*, August 10. Accessed May 11, 2020. Available at https://climateandcapitalism.com/2014/08/10/bolivian-reality-versus-the-extractivism-debate.

Fúnez-Flores, J. I. (2022). Decolonial and Ontological Challenges in Social and Anthropological Theory. *Theory, Culture and Society, 58*(5–6), 596–619. doi:10.1177/02632764211073011.

Gao, G., and Sai, L. (2020). Opposing the Toxic Apartheid: The Painted Veil of the COVID-19 Pandemic, Race and Racism. *Gender, Work and Organization, 28*(S1), 183–189. doi:10.1111/gwao.12523.

García Álvarez, S. (2013). Sumak kawsay *o buen vivir como alternativa al desarrollo en Ecuador: Aplicación y resultados en el gobierno de Rafael Correa*

(2007-2011) (Doctoral thesis, Universidad Complutense de Madrid). Available at https://eprints.ucm.es/id/eprint/24571/1/T35153.pdf.

Getachew, A. (2019). *Worldmaking after Empire: The Rise and Fall of Self-Determination*. Princeton, NJ: Princeton University Press.

Giddens, A. (1984). *The Constitution of Society: Outline of the Theory of Structuration*. Cambridge: Polity.

Giddens, A. (2002). *Runaway World: How Globalisation Is Reshaping Our Lives* (2d ed.). London: Profile.

Gillborn, D. (2005). Education Policy as an Act of White Supremacy: Whiteness, Critical Race Theory and Education Reform. *Journal of Education Policy*, 20(4), 485–505. doi:10.1080/02680930500132346.

Gillborn, D. (2006). Rethinking White Supremacy: Who Counts in "White-World." *Ethnicities*, 6(3), 318–340. doi:10.1177/1468796806068323.

Gilmore, R. W. (2007). *Golden Gulag: Prisons, Surplus, Crisis, and Opposition in Globalizing California*. Berkeley: University of California Press.

Gilroy, P. (1993). *Small Acts: Thoughts on the Politics of Black Cultures*. London: Serpent's Tail.

Gilroy, P. (2001). Joined-up Politics and Postcolonial Melancholia. *Theory, Culture and Society*, 18(2–3), 151–167. doi:10.1177/02632760122051832.

Gilroy, P. (2004). *After Empire: Melancholia or Convivial Culture?* London: Routledge.

Giroux, H. A. (2006). Reading Hurricane Katrina: Race, Class, and the Biopolitics of Disposability. *College Literature*, 33(3), 171–196.

Go, J. (2009). The "New" Sociology of Empire and Colonialism. *Sociology Compass*, 3(5), 775–788. doi:10.1111/j.1751-9020.2009.00232.x.

Go, J. (2011). *Patterns of Empire: The British and American Empires, 1688 to the Present*. Cambridge: Cambridge University Press.

Go, J. (2014). Beyond Metrocentrism: From Empire to Globalism in Early U.S. Sociology. *Journal of Classical Sociology*, 14(2), 178–202. doi:10.1177/1468795 X13491647.

Go, J. (2016a). Globalizing Sociology, Turning South: Perspectival Realism and the Southern Standpoint. *Sociologica*, 2, 1–42. doi:10.2383/85279.

Go, J. (2016b). *Postcolonial Thought and Social Theory*. New York: Oxford University Press.

Go, J. (2018). Postcolonial Possibilities for the Sociology of Race. *Sociology of Race and Ethnicity*, 4(4), 439–451. doi:10.1177/2332649218793982.

Go, J. (2020a). The Imperial Origins of American Policing: Militarization and Imperial Feedback in the Early 20th Century. *American Journal of Sociology*, 125(5), 1193–1254. doi:10.1086/708464.

Go, J. (2020b). Race, Empire, and Epistemic Exclusion: Or the Structures of Sociological Thought. *Sociological Theory*, 38(2), 79–100. doi:10.1177/0735275 120926213.

Go, J. (2021). Three Tensions in the Theory of Racial Capitalism. *Sociological Theory, 39*(1), 38–47. doi:10.1177/0735275120979822.

Golash-Boza, T. (2016). A Critical and Comprehensive Sociological Theory of Race and Racism. *Sociology of Race and Ethnicity, 2*(2), 129–141. doi:10.1177/2332649216632242.

Goldberg, D. T. (2009). *The Threat of Race: Reflections on Racial Neoliberalism.* Malden, MA: Wiley-Blackwell.

Goldberg, D. T. (2015). Racial Comparisons, Relational Racisms: Some Thoughts on Method. In K. Murji and J. Solomos (Eds.), *Theories of Race and Ethnicity: Contemporary Debates and Perspectives* (251–262). Cambridge: Cambridge University Press.

Goldberg, D. T., and Essed, P. (2002). Introduction: From Racial Demarcations to Multiple Identifications. In P. Essed and D. T. Goldberg (Eds.), *Race Critical Theories: Text and Context* (1–11). Oxford: Blackwell. Accessed August 11, 2020. Available at https://dare.uva.nl/search?identifier=1e388004-7fa2-4adc-9a12-876df5fd66a3.

Goldhill, O. (2019). Brazil's Nominated U.S. Ambassador Spends His Days with a Gun-Toting Trump Figurine. *Quartz*, July 13. Accessed August 12, 2020. Available at https://qz.com/1665165/eduardo-bolsonaros-vision-for-brazil-and-the-us.

Gopal, P. (2019). *Insurgent Empire: Anticolonialism and the Making of British Dissent.* London: Verso.

Goswami, N. (2013). The (M)other of All Posts: Postcolonial Melancholia in the Age of Global Warming. *Critical Philosophy of Race, 1*(1), 104–120.

Greenhalgh, T., Schmid, M. B., Czypionka, T., et al. (2020). Face Masks for the Public during the COVID-19 Crisis. *British Medical Journal, 369.* doi:10.1136/bmj.m1435.

Grosfoguel, R. (2007). The Epistemic Decolonial Turn: Beyond Political-Economy Paradigms. *Cultural Studies, 21*(2–3), 211–223. doi:10.1080/09502380601162514.

Grosfoguel, R. (2008). Para descolonizar os estudos de economia política e os estudos pós-coloniais: Transmodernidade, pensamento de fronteira e colonialidade global (I. M. Ferreira, Trans.). *Revista Crítica de Ciências Sociais, 80*, 115–147. doi:10.4000/rccs.697.

Grosfoguel, R. (2013). The Structure of Knowledge in Westernized Universities: Epistemic Racism/Sexism, Westernized Universities and the Four Genocides/Epistemicides of the Long 16th Century. *Tabula Rasa, 19*, 31–58.

Grosfoguel, R. (2017). Decolonizing Western Universalisms: Decolonial Pluriversalism from Aime Césaire to the Zapatistas. In J. M. Paraskeva (Ed.), *Towards a Just Curriculum Theory: The Epistemicide* (147–164). New York: Routledge.

Gross, E., and Stretesky, P. (2015). Environmental Justice in the Courts. In D. M.

Konisky (Ed.), *Failed Promises: Evaluating the Federal Government's Response to Environmental Justice* (205–232). Cambridge, MA: MIT Press.

Guaman Poma de Ayala, F. (2009 [1615]). *The First New Chronicle and Good Government: On the History of the World and the Incas up to 1615.* Austin: University of Texas Press.

Hall, S. (1991). Old and New Identities, Old and New Ethnicities. In A. King (Ed.), *Culture, Globalization and the World System: Contemporary Conditions for the Representation of Identity* (41–68). Minneapolis: University of Minnesota Press.

Hall, S. (1992). The West and the Rest. In S. Hall and B. Gieben (Eds.), *Formations of Modernity* (275–332). Cambridge: Polity.

Hall, S. (2017). *Selected Political Writings: The Great Moving Right Show and Other Essays* (S. Davidson et al., Eds.). London: Lawrence and Wishart.

Hancock, M. (2020). Downing Street Briefing [BBC broadcast], February 6. London.

Haque, Z., Becares, L., and Treloar, N. (2020). *Over-exposed and Under-protected: The Devastating Impact of COVID-19 on Black and Minority Ethnic Communities in Great Britain.* London: Runnymede Trust.

Harding, S. G. (2004). *The Feminist Standpoint Theory Reader: Intellectual and Political Controversies.* London: Routledge.

Hochschild, A. R. (2016). *Strangers in Their Own Land: Anger and Mourning on the American Right.* New York: New Press.

Hong, J. Y. (2021). "Can You Hear my Fear?" A Korean Immigrant with Hearing Loss Reflects on Surviving the COVID-19 Pandemic in the United States. *Disability Studies Quarterly, 41*(3). doi:10.18061/dsq.v41i3.8354.

Hopewell, K. (2013). New Protagonists in Global Economic Governance: Brazilian Agribusiness at the WTO. *New Political Economy, 18*(4), 603–623. Accessed April 15, 2022. Available at https://www.tandfonline.com/doi/full/10.1080/13563467.2013.736957.

Horkheimer, M., and Adorno, T. W. (2002 [1944]). *Dialectic of Enlightenment: Philosophical Fragments* (G. S. Noerr, Ed.). Stanford, CA: Stanford University Press.

Howard, J. (2020). Face Masks: WHO Stands by Recommendation to Not Wear Them if You Are Not Sick or Not Caring for Someone Who Is Sick. *CNN*, March 31. Accessed August 10, 2020. Available at https://edition.cnn.com/2020/03/30/world/coronavirus-who-masks-recommendation-trnd/index.html.

Hu, Y. (2020). Intersecting Ethnic and Native-Migrant Inequalities in the Economic Impact of the COVID-19 Pandemic in the UK. *Research in Social Stratification and Mobility, 68*, art. 100528. doi:10.1016/j.rssm.2020.100528.

Hund, W. D. (2015). Racist King Kong Fantasies: From Shakespeare's Monster to Stalin's Ape-Man. In W. D. Hund et al. (Eds.), *Simianization: Apes, Gender, Class, and Race* (43–73). Berlin: Lit.

ITV News. (2020). Coronavirus Restrictions for the North West: What you Can and Can't Do. *ITV News*, July 31. Accessed August 10, 2020. Available at https://www.itv.com/news/2020-07-31/coronavirus-restrictions-for-the-north-west-what-you-can-and-cant-do.

Itzigsohn, J., and Brown, K. L. (2020). *The Sociology of W.E.B. Du Bois: Racialized Modernity and the Global Color Line*. New York: New York University Press.

Jackson, P. B., and Stewart, Q. T. (2003). A Research Agenda for the Black Middle Class: Work Stress, Survival Strategies, and Mental Health. *Journal of Health and Social Behavior*, 44(3), 442–455. doi:10.2307/1519789.

James, C.L.R. (2001 [1938]). *The Black Jacobins: Toussaint L'Ouverture and the San Domingo Revolution*. London: Penguin U.K.

Jardina, A. (2019). *White Identity Politics*. Cambridge: Cambridge University Press.

Johnson, B. (2016). Boris Johnson's Speech on the EU Referendum. *Conservative Home*, May 9. Accessed June 11, 2020. Available at https://www.conservativehome.com/parliament/2016/05/boris-johnsons-speech-on-the-eu-referendum-full-text.html.

Kapoor, N. (2011). The Advancement of Racial Neoliberalism in Britain. *Ethnic and Racial Studies*, 36(6), 1028–1046. doi:10.1080/01419870.2011.629002.

Kauanui, J. K. (2016). "A Structure, Not an Event": Settler Colonialism and Enduring Indigeneity. *Lateral*, 5(1), 1–8. Accessed May 22, 2019. Available at http://csalateral.org/issue/5-1/forum-alt-humanities-settler-colonialism-enduring-indigeneity-kauanui.

Kaufmann, E. (2017). *"Racial Self-Interest" Is Not Racism*. London: Policy Exchange. Accessed June 11, 2020. Available at https://policyexchange.org.uk/publication/racial-self-interest-is-not-racism.

Kenyatta, J. (1979 [1938]). *Facing Mount Kenya*. London: Heinemann.

Kliff, S. (2020). Most Coronavirus Tests Cost about $100. Why Did One Cost $2,315? *New York Times*, June 16. Accessed May 5, 2022. Available at https://www.nytimes.com/2020/06/16/upshot/coronavirus-test-cost-varies-widely.html.

Kukutai, T., and Didham, R. (2012). Re-making the Majority? Ethnic New Zealanders in the 2006 Census. *Ethnic and Racial Studies*, 35(8), 1427–1446. doi:10.1080/01419870.2011.607508.

Ladner, J. A. (Ed.). (1973). *The Death of White Sociology: Essays on Race and Culture*. Baltimore: Black Classic.

Ladson-Billings, G. (1999). Just What Is Critical Race Theory, and What's It Doing in a Nice Field like Education? In L. Parker et al. (Eds.), *Race Is . . . Race Isn't: Critical Race Theory and Qualitative Studies in Education* (7–30). Boulder, CO: Westview.

Ladson-Billings, G. (2011). Race to the Top, Again: Comments on the Genealogy of Critical Race Theory Commentary. *Connecticut Law Review*, 43(5), 1439–1457.

Ladson-Billings, G. (2013). Critical Race Theory—What It Is Not! In M. Lynn and A. D. Dixson (Eds.), *The Handbook of Critical Race Theory in Education* (34–47). London: Routledge.

Lalander, R. (2016). The Ecuadorian Resource Dilemma: *Sumak Kawsay* or Development? *Critical Sociology, 42*(4–5), 623–642. doi:10.1177/0896920514557959.

Lamont, M., Moraes Silva, G., Welburn, J. S., et al. (2016). *Getting Respect: Responding to Stigma and Discrimination in the United States, Brazil, and Israel.* Princeton, NJ: Princeton University Press.

Lamont, M., Park, B. Y., and Ayala-Hurtado, E. (2017). Trump's Electoral Speeches and His Appeal to the American White Working Class. *British Journal of Sociology, 68*(S1), S153–S180. doi:10.1111/1468-4446.12315.

Laster Pirtle, W. N. (2020). Racial Capitalism: A Fundamental Cause of Novel Coronavirus (COVID-19) Pandemic Inequities in the United States. *Health Education and Behavior, 47*(4), 504–508. doi:10.1177/1090198120922942.

Leal, P. H. (2017). Bolsonaro and the Brazilian Far Right. *OpenDemocracy*, April 24. Accessed June 18, 2020. Available at https://www.opendemocracy.net/en/democraciaabierta/bolsonaro-and-brazilian-far-right.

Lehmann, D. (2021). *After the Decolonial: Ethnicity, Gender and Social Justice in Latin America.* Cambridge: Polity.

Lemon, D. (Prod.). (2020). "The Color of COVID" [Broadcast]. *CNN Tonight*, May 15.

Lentin, A. (2020). *Why Race Still Matters.* Cambridge: Polity.

Lewis, A. E. (2004). "What Group?" Studying Whites and Whiteness in the Era of "Color-blindness." *Sociological Theory, 22*(4), 623–646. doi:10.1111/j.0735-2751.2004.00237.x.

Lewis, D. (2020). Why Many Countries Failed at COVID Contact-Tracing—but Some Got It Right. *Nature, 588*(7838), 384–387. doi:10.1038/d41586-020-03518-4.

Li, Y., and Heath, A. (2020). Persisting Disadvantages: A Study of Labour Market Dynamics of Ethnic Unemployment and Earnings in the UK (2009–2015). *Journal of Ethnic and Migration Studies, 46*(5), 857–878. doi:10.1080/1369183X.2018.1539241.

Liévanos, R. S. (2012). Certainty, Fairness, and Balance: State Resonance and Environmental Justice Policy Implementation. *Sociological Forum, 27*(2), 481–503. doi:10.1111/j.1573-7861.2012.01327.x.

Link, B. G., and Phelan, J. (1995). Social Conditions as Fundamental Causes of Disease. *Journal of Health and Social Behavior* (special issue), (80–94). doi:10.2307/2626958.

Lipsitz, G. (1998). *The Possessive Investment in Whiteness: How White People Profit from Identity Politics.* Philadelphia: Temple University Press.

Long, L. J. (2018). *Perpetual Suspects: A Critical Race Theory of Black and Mixed-Race Experiences of Policing.* London: Palgrave.

Malcolm X. (2013 [1963]). Racial Separation. *Black Past*, January 22. Accessed August 31, 2022. Available at https://www.blackpast.org/african-american -history/speeches-african-american-history/1963-malcolm-x-racial-sep aration.

Maldonado-Torres, N. (2007). On the Coloniality of Being. *Cultural Studies*, *21*(2–3), 240–270. doi:10.1080/09502380601162548.

Mann, M. (2012). *The Sources of Social Power, Volume 1: A History of Power from the Beginning to AD 1760*. Cambridge: Cambridge University Press.

Mariátegui, J. C. (2014). *Seven Interpretive Essays on Peruvian Reality*. Austin: University of Texas Press.

Marques, A., and Rocha, L. (2015). Bolsonaro diz que OAB só defende bandido e reserva indígena é um crime. *Campo Grande News*, April 22. Accessed June 18, 2020. Available at https://www.campograndenews.com.br/politica/bolso naro-diz-que-oab-so-defende-bandido-e-reserva-indigena-e-um-crime.

Marx, K. (1853). The British Rule in India. *New-York Daily Tribune*, June 25. Accessed July 16, 2019. Available at https://www.marxists.org/archive/marx /works/1853/06/25.htm.

Marx, K. (1973 [1939]). *Grundrisse: Foundations of the Critique of Political Economy*. London: Penguin.

Marx, K. (2007 [1932]). *Economic and Philosophic Manuscripts of 1844*. Chelmsford, MA: Courier.

May, T. (2017). I'm Determined to Build the Shared Society for Everyone. *The Telegraph*, January 7. Accessed October 15, 2021. Available at https://www .telegraph.co.uk/news/2017/01/07/determined-build-shared-society-every one.

Mbembe, A. (2000). Necropolitics. *Raisons Politiques*, *21*(1), 29–60.

McGuinness, A. (2020). Coronavirus: UK Minister Suggests Other Countries' Strategies Are Based on "Populism" Not Science. *Sky News*, March 16. Accessed August 10, 2020. Available at https://news.sky.com/story/corona virus-uk-response-driven-by-the-evidence-not-populism-says-minister -11958203.

Meghji, A. (2020). *Decolonizing Sociology: An Introduction*. Cambridge: Polity.

Meghji, A. (2021). Just What Is Critical Race Theory, and What Is It Doing in British Sociology? From "BritCrit" to the Racialized Social System Approach. *British Journal of Sociology*, *72*(2), 347–359. doi:10.1111/1468-4446.12801.

Meghji, A. (2022a). *The Racialized Social System: Critical Race Theory as Social Theory*. Cambridge: Polity.

Meghji, A. (2022b). Towards a Theoretical Synergy: Critical Race Theory and Decolonial Thought in Trumpamerica and Brexit Britain. *Current Sociology*, *70*(5), 647–664. doi:10.1177/0011392120969764.

Meghji, A., and Niang, S. M. (2021). Between Post-racial Ideology and Provincial Universalisms: Critical Race Theory, Decolonial Thought and COVID-19

in Britain. *Sociology*, *56*(1), 00380385211011575. doi:10.1177/003803852110
11575.

Meghji, A., and Saini, R. (2018). Rationalising Racial Inequality: Ideology, Hegemony and Post-racialism among the Black and South Asian Middle-Classes. *Sociology*, *52*(4), 671–687. doi:10.1177/0038038517726645.

Meyer, M. A. (2008). Indigenous and Authentic: Hawaiian Epistemology and the Triangulation of Meaning. In N. Denzin et al. (Eds.), *Handbook of Critical and Indigenous Methodologies* (217–232). Thousand Oaks, CA: Sage. doi:10.4135/9781483385686.n11.

Mignolo, W. D. (2002). The Zapatistas' Theoretical Revolution: Its Historical, Ethical, and Political Consequences. *Review*, *25*(3), 245–275.

Mignolo, W. D. (2005). *The Idea of Latin America*. Cambridge: Wiley.

Mignolo, W. D. (2007). Delinking: The Rhetoric of Modernity, the Logic of Coloniality and the Grammar of De-coloniality. *Cultural Studies*, *21*(2–3), 449–514.

Mignolo, W. D. (2011a). *The Darker Side of Western Modernity: Global Futures, Decolonial Options*. Durham, NC: Duke University Press.

Mignolo, W. D. (2011b). Epistemic Disobedience and the Decolonial Option: A Manifesto. *Transmodernity*, *1*(2), 44–66.

Mignolo, W. D. (2011c). Geopolitics of Sensing and Knowing: On (De)coloniality, Border Thinking and Epistemic Disobedience. *Postcolonial Studies*, *14*(3), 273–283. doi:10.1080/13688790.2011.613105.

Mignolo, W. D., and Walsh, C. (2018). *On Decoloniality: Concepts, Analytics, Praxis*. Durham, NC: Duke University Press.

Mills, C. W. (1997). *The Racial Contract*. Ithaca, NY: Cornell University Press.

Mills, C. W. (2009). Critical Race Theory: A Reply to Mike Cole. *Ethnicities*, *9*(2), 270–281.

Mintz, O., Currim, I., and Deshpande, R. (2021). Overcoming COVID-19 Vaccine Hesitancy: The Greatest Marketing Communication Challenge of Our Lives. Accessed March 28, 2023. Available at https://opus.lib.uts.edu.au/rest/bitstreams/699e7a51-1403-471e-a7b7-6fef64a48656/retrieve.

Mondon, A., and Winter, A. (2020). *Reactionary Democracy: How Racism and the Populist Far Right Became Mainstream*. London: Verso.

Moore, M. (2021). Don't Airbrush British History, Government Tells Heritage Groups. *The Times*, February 15. Accessed March 28, 2023. Available at https://www.thetimes.co.uk/article/dont-airbrush-british-history-government-tells-heritage-groups-krpn5cztf.

Mora, M. (2017). *Kuxlejal Politics: Indigenous Autonomy, Race, and Decolonizing Research in Zapatista Communities*. Austin: University of Texas Press.

Naber, N. (2017). "The U.S. and Israel Make the Connections for Us": Anti-Imperialism and Black-Palestinian Solidarity. *Critical Ethnic Studies*, *3*(2), 15–30. doi:10.5749/jcritethnstud.3.2.0015.

Narayan, J. (2019). Huey P. Newton's Intercommunalism: An Unacknowledged Theory of Empire. *Theory, Culture and Society*, *36*(3), 57–85. doi:10.1177/0263276417741348.

Nelson, S. (2020). Anthony Fauci Compares Race Disparities of Coronavirus to AIDS Epidemic. *New York Post*, April 8. Accessed August 31, 2022. Available at https://nypost.com/2020/04/07/anthony-fauci-compares-race-disparities-of-coronavirus-to-aids-epidemic.

Newton, H. P. (2002). *The Huey P. Newton Reader*. Newcastle, U.K.: Seven Stories.

Nkrumah, K. (1970). *Class Struggle in Africa*. Bedford, U.K.: Panaf.

Nkrumah, K. (1971). *Neo-colonialism: The Last Stage of Imperialism*. Bedford, U.K.: Panaf.

O'Donoghue, D. (2020). Coronavirus: Boris Johnson Refuses to Rule Out Lockdown to Stop Spread of Outbreak. *Press and Journal*, March 18. Accessed August 10, 2020. Available at https://www.pressandjournal.co.uk/fp/news/politics/uk-politics/2084563/coronavirus-boris-johnson-refuses-to-rule-out-lock-down-to-stop-spread-of-outbreak.

Odum, H. (2010 [1910]). *Social and Mental Traits of the Negro*. Whitefish, MT: Kessinger.

Olutayo, A. O. (2014). "Verstehen," Everyday Sociology and Development: Incorporating African Indigenous Knowledge. *Critical Sociology*, *40*(2), 229–238. doi:10.1177/0896920512446094.

Omi, M., and Winant, H. (2015). *Racial Formation in the United States* (3rd ed.). New York: Routledge.

O'Neill, B. (2016). Not Thick or Racist: Just Poor. *The Spectator*, July 2. Accessed June 11, 2020. Available at https://www.spectator.co.uk/article/not-thick-or-racist-just-poor.

Oppenheim, B., Gallivan, M., Madhav, N. K., et al. (2019). Assessing Global Preparedness for the Next Pandemic: Development and Application of an Epidemic Preparedness Index. *BMJ Global Health*, *4*(1), e001157. doi:10.1136/bmjgh-2018-001157.

Outten, H. R., Schmitt, M. T., Miller, D. A., and Garcia, A. L. (2012). Feeling Threatened about the Future: Whites' Emotional Reactions to Anticipated Ethnic Demographic Changes. *Personality and Social Psychology Bulletin*, *38*(1), 14–25. doi:10.1177/0146167211418531.

Pachá, P. (2019). Why the Brazilian Far Right Loves the European Middle Ages. *Pacific Standard*, March 12. Accessed June 11, 2020. Available at https://psmag.com/ideas/why-the-brazilian-far-right-is-obsessed-with-the-crusades.

Park, R. E. (1914). Racial Assimilation in Secondary Groups with Particular Reference to the Negro. *American Journal of Sociology*, *19*(5), 606–623.

Park, R. E. (1928a). The Bases of Race Prejudice. *Annals of the American Academy of Political and Social Science*, *140*(1), 11–20. doi:10.1177/000271622814000104.

Park, R. E. (1928b). Human Migration and the Marginal Man. *American Journal of Sociology*, *33*(6), 881–893.

Park, R. E. (1950). *Race and Culture*. New York: Free Press.

Park, R. E., and Burgess, E. W. (1921). *Introduction to the Science of Sociology*. Chicago: University of Chicago Press.

Parker, L., Deyhle, D., and Villenas, S. (Eds.). (1999). *Race Is . . . Race Isn't: Critical Race Theory and Qualitative Studies in Education*. Boulder, CO: Westview.

Parks, G., and Rachlinski, J. (2013). Implicit Bias, Election 2008, and the Myth of a Postracial America. In R. Delgado and J. Stefancic (Eds.), *Critical Race Theory: The Cutting Edge* (3d ed.) (197–210). Philadelphia: Temple University Press.

Patnaik, U. (2017). Revisiting the "Drain," or Transfer from India to Britain in the Context of Global Diffusion of Capitalism. In S. Chakrabarti and U. Patnaik (Eds.), *Agrarian and Other Histories: Essays for Binay Bhushan Chaudhuri* (278–317). New Delhi: Tulika.

Patnaik, U., and Patnaik, P. (2021). *Capital and Imperialism: Theory, History, and the Present*. New York: New York University Press.

Pattillo, M. (2013). *Black Picket Fences: Privilege and Peril among the Black Middle Class* (2d ed.). Chicago: University of Chicago Press.

Pattisson, P. (2021). "Like Slave and Master": DRC Miners Toil for 30p an Hour to Fuel Electric Cars. *The Guardian*, November 8. Accessed August 31, 2022. Available at https://www.theguardian.com/global-development/2021/nov/08/cobalt-drc-miners-toil-for-30p-an-hour-to-fuel-electric-cars.

Phelan, J. C., and Link, B. G. (2015). Is Racism a Fundamental Cause of Inequalities in Health? *Annual Review of Sociology*, *41*(1), 311–330. doi:10.1146/annurev-soc-073014-112305.

Phillips, D. (2019). Bolsonaro Declares Brazil's "Liberation from Socialism" as He Is Sworn In. *The Guardian*, January 1. Accessed June 18, 2020. Available at https://www.theguardian.com/world/2019/jan/01/jair-bolsonaro-inauguration-brazil-president.

Platt, L., and Warwick, R. (2020). *Are Some Ethnic Groups More Vulnerable to COVID-19 than Others?* London: Institute for Fiscal Studies.

Prause, L. (2020). Conflicts Related to Resources: The Case of Cobalt Mining in the Democratic Republic of Congo. In A. Bleicher and A. Pehlken (Eds.), *The Material Basis of Energy Transitions* (153–167). Amsterdam: Elsevier Science. doi:10.1016/B978-0-12-819534-5.00010-6.

Public Health England. (2020). *Beyond the Data: Understanding the Impact of COVID-19 on BAME Communities*. London: Public Health England. Available at https://assets.publishing.service.gov.uk/government/uploads/system/uploads/attachment_data/file/892376/COVID_stakeholder_engagement_synthesis_beyond_the_data.pdf.

Pulido, L. (2017). Geographies of Race and Ethnicity II: Environmental Racism, Racial Capitalism and State-sanctioned Violence. *Progress in Human Geography*, *41*(4), 524–533. doi:10.1177/0309132516646495.

Quijano, A. (2007). Coloniality and Modernity/Rationality. *Cultural Studies*, *21*(2–3), 168–178. doi:10.1080/09502380601164353.

Radcliffe, S. A. (2012). Development for a Postneoliberal Era? *Sumak Kawsay*, Living Well and the Limits to Decolonisation in Ecuador. *Geoforum*, *43*(2), 240–249. doi:10.1016/j.geoforum.2011.09.003.

Ray, V. (2022). *On Critical Race Theory: Why It Matters and Why You Should Care*. New York: Random House.

Roberts, J. T., and Parks, B. (2006). *A Climate of Injustice: Global Inequality, North-South Politics, and Climate Policy*. Cambridge, MA: MIT Press.

Robertson, N. (2020). Trump Doesn't Think We Need a National Mask Mandate. *CNN*, July 18. Accessed August 31, 2022. Available at https://edition.cnn.com/2020/07/18/politics/trump-us-mask-mandate-coronavirus/index.html.

Robinson, C. J. (1983). *Black Marxism: The Making of the Black Radical Tradition*. London: Zed.

Rodger, J. (2020). Matt Hancock and Chris Whitty Give Advice to Muslims Celebrating Eid [Video]. *Birmingham Live*, May 22. Accessed March 28, 2023. Available at https://www.birminghammail.co.uk/news/midlands-news/matt-hancock-chris-whitty-give-18294312.

Rodney, W. (2018 [1972]). *How Europe Underdeveloped Africa*. London: Verso.

Rodriguez, B. (2006). "Long Live Third World Unity! Long Live Internationalism": Huey P. Newton's Revolutionary Intercommunalism. *Souls*, *8*(3), 119–141.

Rodriguez Fernandez, G. V. (2020). Neo-extractivism, the Bolivian State, and Indigenous Peasant Women's Struggles for Water in the Altiplano. *Human Geography*, *13*(1), 27–39. doi:10.1177/1942778620910896.

Roediger, D. (2007 [1991]). *The Wages of Whiteness: Race and the Making of the American Working Class* (Rev. ed.). London: Verso.

Roser, M., and Ortiz-Ospina, E. (2013). Global Extreme Poverty [Report]. *Our World in Data* [Preprint]. Available at https://ourworldindata.org/poverty.

Said, E. W. (1978). *Orientalism*. London: Penguin.

Said, E. W. (1989). Representing the Colonized: Anthropology's Interlocutors. *Critical Inquiry*, *15*, 205–225.

Saldanha, A. (2020). A Date with Destiny: Racial Capitalism and the Beginnings of the Anthropocene. *Environment and Planning D: Society and Space*, *38*(1), 12–34. doi:10.1177/0263775819871964.

Santos, B. de S. (2014). *Epistemologies of the South: Justice against Epistemicide*. New York: Routledge.

Schaefer, D. O. (2019). Whiteness and Civilization: Shame, Race, and the Rhetoric of Donald Trump. *Communication and Critical/Cultural Studies*, *17*(1), 1–18. doi:10.1080/14791420.2019.1667503.

Sealey-Huggins, L. (2017). "1.5°C to Stay Alive": Climate Change, Imperialism and Justice for the Caribbean. *Third World Quarterly*, *38*(11), 2444–2463. doi: 10.1080/01436597.2017.1368013.

Seamster, L., and Ray, V. (2018). Against Teleology in the Study of Race: Toward the Abolition of the Progress Paradigm. *Sociological Theory*, *36*(4), 315–342. doi:10.1177/0735275118813614.

Sengul, K. (2021). "It's OK to Be White": The Discursive Construction of Victimhood, "Anti-White Racism" and Calculated Ambivalence in Australia. *Critical Discourse Studies*, *19*(6), 593–609. doi:10.1080/17405904.2021.1921818.

Sennett, R. (2002). *Flesh and Stone: The Body and the City in Western Civilization*. London: Penguin.

Shilliam, R. (2020). Redeeming the "Ordinary Working Class." *Current Sociology*, *68*(2), 223–240. doi:10.1177/0011392119886862.

Silva, G. M. (2016). After Racial Democracy: Contemporary Puzzles in Race Relations in Brazil, Latin America and beyond from a Boundaries Perspective. *Current Sociology*, *64*(5), 794–812. doi:10.1177/0011392115590488.

Simi, P., Blee, K., DeMichele, M., and Windisch, S. (2017). Addicted to Hate: Identity Residual among Former White Supremacists. *American Sociological Review*, *82*(6), 1167–1187. doi:10.1177/0003122417728719.

Simpson, A. (2017). The Ruse of Consent and the Anatomy of "Refusal": Cases from Indigenous North America and Australia. *Postcolonial Studies*, *20*(1), 18–33. doi:10.1080/13688790.2017.1334283.

Skelton, D. (2019). *Little Platoons: How a Revived One Nation Can Empower England's Forgotten Towns and Redraw the Political Map*. London: Biteback.

Solorzano, D. G., and Yosso, T. J. (2001). Critical Race and LatCrit Theory and Method: Counter-storytelling. *International Journal of Qualitative Studies in Education*, *14*(4), 471–495. doi:10.1080/09518390110063365.

Song, M. (2014). Challenging a Culture of Racial Equivalence. *British Journal of Sociology*, *65*(1), 107–129. doi:10.1111/1468-4446.12054.

Sowell, T. (2009 [1984]). *Civil Rights: Rhetoric or Reality*. New York: HarperCollins.

Stalin, J. (1938). Dialectical and Historical Materialism. *Marxists Internet Archive*, n.d. Accessed August 31, 2022. Available at https://www.marxists.org/reference/archive/stalin/works/1938/09.htm.

Stanfield, J. H., II. (2011). *Black Reflective Sociology: Epistemology, Theory, and Methodology*. Walnut Creek, CA: Left Coast.

Statista. (2022). Coronavirus (COVID-19) Deaths Worldwide per One Million Population as of July 13, 2022, by Country. *Statista*, July 27. Accessed January 31, 2023. Available at https://www.statista.com/statistics/1104709/coronavirus-deaths-worldwide-per-million-inhabitants.

Staunton, D. (2020). Unflappable Confidence of UK's Health Establishment about to Be Tested. *Irish Times*, March 27. Accessed August 10, 2020. Available at

https://www.irishtimes.com/news/world/uk/unflappable-confidence-of-uk
-s-health-establishment-about-to-be-tested-1.4214245.

Steinmetz, G. (2014). The Sociology of Empires, Colonies, and Postcolonialism. *Annual Review of Sociology*, *40*(1), 77–103. doi:10.1146/annurev-soc-071913 -043131.

Stewart-Harawira, M. (2005). *The New Imperial Order: Indigenous Responses to Globalization*. London: Zed.

Stubley, P. (2021) Universities Minister Compares "Decolonisation" of History to "Soviet Union–style" Censorship. *The Independent*, February 28. Accessed March 28, 2023. Available at https://www.independent.co.uk/news/educa tion/education-news/history-curriculum-university-michelle-donelan-cul ture-war-b1808601.html.

Subcomandante Marcos. (1997). The Fourth World War Has Begun. *Le Monde Diplomatique*, September. Accessed August 31, 2022. Available at https:// mondediplo.com/1997/09/marcos.

Subcomandante Marcos. (2002a). *Our Word Is Our Weapon: Selected Writings*. Newcastle, U.K.: Seven Stories

Subcomandante Marcos. (2002b). Tomorrow Begins Today. In *Our Word Is Our Weapon: Selected Writings* (115–123). Newcastle, U.K.: Seven Stories.

Sultana, F. (2022). The Unbearable Heaviness of Climate Coloniality. *Political Geography*, *99*, art. 102638. doi:10.1016/j.polgeo.2022.102638.

Thomas, J. M. (2020). Du Bois, Double Consciousness, and the "Jewish Question." *Ethnic and Racial Studies*, *43*(8), 1333–1356. doi:10.1080/01419870.2 020.1705366.

Ting, V. (2020). Debate over Face Masks Ends: Hong Kong Was Right All Along. *South China Morning Post*, April 4. Accessed August 10, 2020. Available at https://www.scmp.com/news/hong-kong/health-environment/article/3078 437/mask-or-not-mask-who-makes-u-turn-while-us.

Tinsley, M. (2020). Revisiting Nostalgia: Imperialism, Anticolonialism, and Imagining Home. *Ethnic and Racial Studies*, *43*(13), 2327–2355. doi:10.1080/0141 9870.2020.1727935.

Topolski, A. (2020). The Dangerous Discourse of the "Judaeo-Christian" Myth: Masking the Race-Religion Constellation in Europe. *Patterns of Prejudice*, *54*(1–2), 71–90. doi:10.1080/0031322X.2019.1696049.

Treviño, A. J., Harris, M. A., and Wallace, D. (2008). What's So Critical about Critical Race Theory? *Contemporary Justice Review*, *11*(1), 7–10. doi:10.1080 /10282580701850330.

TRTWorld. (2020). Top 1 Percent of Households Own 43 Percent of Global Wealth. *TRTWorld*, December 7. Accessed August 31, 2022. Available at https://www .trtworld.com/magazine/top-1-percent-of-households-own-43-percent-of -global-wealth-42134.

Ungoed-Thomas, J. (2022). Cadbury Faces Fresh Accusations of Child Labour on Cocoa Farms in Ghana. *The Observer*, April 3. Accessed August 31, 2022. Available at https://www.theguardian.com/law/2022/apr/03/cadbury-faces -fresh-accusations-of-child-labour-on-cocoa-farms-in-ghana.

Unicef. (2022). Child Labour Rises to 160 million—First Increase in Two Decades [Press release]. *Unicef*, June 10. Accessed August 31, 2022. Available at https://www.unicef.org/press-releases/child-labour-rises-160-million-first -increase-two-decades.

Villalba, U. (2013). *Buen Vivir* vs. Development: A Paradigm Shift in the Andes? *Third World Quarterly*, *34*(8), 1427–1442. Accessed May 11, 2022. Available at https://www.tandfonline.com/doi/full/10.1080/01436597.2013.831594.

Villavicencio Calzadilla, P., and Kotzé, L. J. (2018). Living in Harmony with Nature? A Critical Appraisal of the Rights of Mother Earth in Bolivia. *Transnational Environmental Law*, *7*(3), 397–424. doi:10.1017/S2047102518000201.

Virdee, S. (2015). Opening a Dialogue on Race, Class and National Belonging. *Ethnic and Racial Studies*, *38*(13), 2259–2266. doi:10.1080/01419870.2015.1 058508.

Virdee, S. (2019). Racialized Capitalism: An Account of Its contested Origins and Consolidation. *Sociological Review*, *67*(1), 3–27. doi:10.1177/0038026 118820293.

Virdee, S., and McGeever, B. (2018). Racism, Crisis, Brexit. *Ethnic and Racial Studies*, *41*(10), 1802–1819. doi:10.1080/01419870.2017.1361544.

Wacquant, L. (2008). *Urban Outcasts: A Comparative Study of Advanced Marginality*. Cambridge: Polity.

Wacquant, L. (2010). Crafting the Neoliberal State: Workfare, Prisonfare, and Social Insecurity. *Sociological Forum*, *25*(2), 197–220.

Wallerstein, I. M. (2000). *The Essential Wallerstein*. New York: New Press.

Warmington, P. (2020). Critical Race Theory in England: Impact and Opposition. *Identities*, *27*(1), 20–37. doi:10.1080/1070289X.2019.1587907.

Waterson, J. (2020). Proms Row: Johnson Calls for End to "Cringing Embarrassment" over UK History. *The Guardian*, August 25. Accessed March 28, 2023. Available at https://www.theguardian.com/music/2020/aug/25/boris-john son-scolds-bbc-over-suggestion-proms-would-drop-rule-britannia.

Watson, K. (2020). Racism Denier to Defend Black Rights in Brazil. *BBC News*, February 15. Accessed June 18, 2020. Available at https://www.bbc.com/news /world-latin-america-51501111.

Weber, M. (1959). *The Religion of China*. Glencoe, IL: Free Press.

Weber, M. (2000 [1958]). *The Religion of India*. Glencoe, IL: Free Press.

Weber, M. (2002 [1905]). *The Protestant Ethic and the Spirit of Capitalism, and Other Writings*. London: Penguin.

Weiner, M. F. (2018). Decolonial Sociology: W.E.B. Du Bois's Foundational Theoretical and Methodological Contributions. *Sociology Compass*, *12*(8), e12601. doi:10.1111/soc4.12601.

Whyte, K. P. (2017). Indigenous Climate Change Studies: Indigenizing Futures, Decolonizing the Anthropocene. *English Language Notes*, 55(1), 153–162.

Whyte, K. P. (2018). Indigenous Science (Fiction) for the Anthropocene: Ancestral Dystopias and Fantasies of Climate Change Crises. *Environment and Planning E: Nature and Space*, 1(1–2), 224–242. doi:10.1177/2514848618777621.

Whyte, K. P. (2020). Too Late for Indigenous Climate Justice: Ecological and Relational Tipping Points. *WIREs Climate Change*, 11(1), e603.

Williams, E. (1944). *Capitalism and Slavery*. Chapel Hill: University of North Carolina Press.

Williams, R. (1977). *Marxism and Literature*. Oxford: Oxford University Press.

World Bank. (2020). Debt Burden of Least Developed Countries Continues to Climb to a Record $744 Billion in 2019 [Press release]. *World Bank*, October 12. Accessed September 1, 2022. Available at https://www.worldbank.org/en news/press-release/2020/10/12/debt-burden-of-least-developed-countries -continues-to-climb-to-a-record-744-billion-in-2019.

World Vision. (2021). Global Poverty: Facts, FAQs, and How to Help. *World Vision*, August 23. Accessed August 31, 2022. Available at https://www.world vision.org/sponsorship-news-stories/global-poverty-facts.

Wright, E., II. (2002). The Atlanta Sociological Laboratory 1896–1924: A Historical Account of the First American School of Sociology. *Western Journal of Black Studies*, 26(3), 165–174.

Yam, K. (2022). Anti-Asian Hate Crimes Increased 339 Percent Nationwide Last Year, Report Says. *NBC News*, January 31. Accessed August 31, 2022. Available at https://www.nbcnews.com/news/asian-america/anti-asian-hate -crimes-increased-339-percent-nationwide-last-year-repo-rcna14282.

Zuberi, T. (2001). *Thicker than Blood: How Racial Statistics Lie*. Minneapolis: University of Minnesota Press.

Zuberi, T., and Bonilla-Silva, E. (Eds.). (2008). *White Logic, White Methods: Racism and Methodology*. Lanham, MD: Rowman and Littlefield.

Index

Ali Meghji is Associate Professor in Social Inequalities in the Department of Sociology at the University of Cambridge. He is the author of *The Racialized Social System: Critical Race Theory as Social Theory*, *Decolonizing Sociology: An Introduction*, and *Black Middle-Class Britannia: Identities, Repertoires, Cultural Consumption*.

www.ingramcontent.com/pod-product-compliance
Lightning Source LLC
Chambersburg PA
CBHW020703270326
41928CB00005B/251